Mario L. D'Avanzo is associate professor of English at Providence College in Providence, Rhode Island. He has published essays on Melville, and a number of articles in scholarly literary journals.

For Sylvia, Michael, and Sue

Mario L. D'Avanzo

Keats's metaphors for the poetic imagination

Duke University Press
Durham, N. C. 1967

© 1967, Duke University Press

L.C.C. number 67–17149

Printed in the United States of
America by Kingsport Press, Inc.

Acknowledgments

I should like to acknowledge my indebtedness to Professor I. J. Kapstein, of Brown University, whose teaching of English Romantic poetry has been the primal influence on my understanding of Keats. This book is the issue of his teaching, advice, and encouragement.

I wish to thank Rodney K. Delasanta and René E. Fortin, friends and colleagues, for reading my manuscript and offering suggestions for improvement. More generally, I should mention how highly I value their discussions of literature with me, and how influential they have been, over the last few years, as regards my critical understanding of literature.

My thanks are also due to Professors Charles H. Philbrick and C. A. Hackett for reading my manuscript and offering useful commentary and advice. My gratitude also goes to David Jonah and his staff at the libraries of Brown University for their help and innumerable favors extended to me throughout the preparation of this book. Finally, I owe my thanks to the readers and editors of Duke University Press, who offered valuable advice for improving and refining my text.

M. L. D.

Contents

Introduction

The central idea developed in this study is that Keats makes repeated use of certain organizing metaphors and images to describe poetic inspiration, the poetry-making process, and the structure of poetry itself. Important to note is Keats's sustained interest in all forms of art as subject matter for his poems: poetry, painting, sculpture, and architecture are celebrated as triumphs of imagination in such poems as "If by dull rhymes," "On First Looking into Chapman's Homer," "On a Leander Gem," "Ode on a Grecian Urn," the sonnets on the Elgin marbles, and "Ode to Apollo." In writing about poetry and the imaginative process, Keats turns again and again to a theme that fascinated him from the very start of his poetic career to its very end. Therefore, he uses the same basic metaphors, slightly altered or refined or elaborated as he progresses in his work. I have attempted to trace these figures in detail, proceeding from the early poems, where they are fairly apparent and explicit, to the later poems, which are more indirect, allusive, and sometimes private. Once we understand Keats's metaphorical and imagistic schemata, many poems including "Ode to Psyche" and "La Belle Dame sans Merci" may be interpreted beyond their literal meaning as figurative statements of the activity of the imagination wherein poetic vision is attained and poetry is born. When read with a full understanding of Keats's metaphors, the poetry reveals depths of meaning hitherto unexplored. Through its figures the poetry also reveals Keats as a cartographer of the mind, investigating and mapping its mysterious processes.

Since Keats wrote his best and most significant poetry in a short span of five years, one notes no radical departure from the metaphors which he employed in his earlier work, such as "Sleep and Poetry," and his later work, such as "Ode to Psyche." What we do note, however, is an increasing tendency of the poet to use his metaphors in so subtle a fashion that, like the half-invisible and tenuous filaments of the spider's web, their presence, their design, and their meaning are not readily apparent. As a result, scholars have failed to note the highly functional nature of the figurative language. For example, E. C. Pettet's chapter on "characteristic" imagery, in *On the Poetry of Keats*, seems to be fairly typical of critical analysis which fails to read perceptively. Keats's caves and grottos, Pettet states, "often suggest curved, flowing lines," [1] a comment that leaves the significance of such imagery unresolved. Equally unprofitable, I feel, is R. H. Fogle's quantitative analysis of imagery in *The Imagery of Keats and Shelley*.[2] As I shall have occasion to demonstrate, the figures and images are more than textural ornaments; they are at the center of meaning rather than at the circumference. They are vehicles that carry Keats's special theme.

The recurrence of the basic metaphors that depict the imagination at work links the poems together and makes each an organic part of the whole body of his work—letters as well as poems. This relationship may be described, in an analogy expressed by Wordsworth and later exploited by Keats in his poetry, as the same that an "ante-chapel has to the body of a gothic church.... [The poet's] minor Pieces ... have such connection with the main Work as may give them claim to be likened to the little cells, oratories, and sepulchral recesses, ordinarily included in those edifices."[3] I should consider *Poems* (1817), especially "Sleep and Poetry," as the ante-chapel to Keats's church. In the center stands *Endymion*, the repository of special metaphors, and hence a pivotal poem around which the majority of the other poems turn. The figures in *Endymion* must be fathomed if one is to understand the full significance of the Hyperion fragments, *Lamia*, the odes—especially "Ode to Psyche" —and "La Belle Dame sans Merci." The relationship between *Endymion* and the rest of the corpus reveals the "treasures" of figures which Shelley admired and which Keats, significantly, described as "food for a Week's stroll."

Because Keats's poetry is all of a piece, it is not only advisable but necessary, if one is to discover the full meaning of his work in all its

1. E. C. Pettet, *On the Poetry of Keats* (Cambridge, 1957), p. 65.
2. Richard Harter Fogle, *The Imagery of Keats and Shelley: A Comparative Study* (Chapel Hill, 1949).
3. "Preface to the Edition of 1814 of *The Excursion*," *The Poetical Works of William Wordsworth*, ed. E. de Selincourt, V (Oxford, 1949), 2.

allusiveness and subtlety, to go beyond the confines of the individual poem and trace the development and refinement of his special metaphors and images. As Earl R. Wasserman in *The Finer Tone* has rightly remarked: "The poem ... cannot be fully defined from the inside alone." [4] Hence the method of this study is collation: that is, all uses of a particular metaphor or image are noted from poem to poem, or from letter to poem. Very frequently the meaning of a recondite metaphor can be ascertained by noting its repeated appearance in clusters of other metaphors whose values are already known. At the same time close contextual reading will explain how the meaning of a figure or image is supported in its own local context. Thus, the labyrinth, one of Keats's most private metaphors, is throughout the letters and in "Sleep and Poetry" associated with the imagination. In later poems, however, it is more subtly employed, as in "Ode to Psyche." Only the most careful collation of all uses of this metaphor as well as a textual explication of the ode will reveal the meaning of such phrases as "branched thoughts" and "In some untrodden region of my mind."

While the method of probing the meaning of the figures will necessarily be exercised upon the poetry, the letters are an important extratextual reservoir that often points up the meaning of the recurrent metaphors and images in the poems. The offhand remarks on poetry in the letters have a highly functional relationship to the poetry itself. For example, the repeated reference in different letters to Pegasus, the pacing steed, and the Apollonian chariot illuminates the intrepid soaring of Endymion in Book IV of *Endymion* and, as well, the regularity of the knight-at-arms' pacing steed on which La Belle Dame sans Merci sits. Since the letters are literally more prosy, they often provide the key to the meaning of metaphors whose significance would otherwise be uncertain.

In addition to the letters, Keats's adaptation of source materials provides us with added insight into the meaning of several figures. These adaptations from literary works show the subtlety and inventiveness of a highly sensitive imagination. As an apprentice poet who immersed himself in Shakespeare, Sandys, Virgil, and others, he very often interpreted them in his own private manner and culled useful images and figures for his own poetry. His use of such figures as flower-dew and the muses at their weaving provides two striking examples of an imaginative

4. Earl R. Wasserman, *The Finer Tone* (Baltimore, 1953), p. 6.

working of source material and shows the highly subjective and private meanings he assigned to many of his metaphors. But his appropriations, it will be seen, were never obvious and never peripheral: they were always central, woven with care and meaningful design into the fabric of the poems.

Keats's reading of such works as Lemprière's classical dictionary and Plato's dialogues has also proved useful in tracing his poetic labyrinth. Some of the special metaphors are derived from his extensive knowledge of the Delphic world of the classical poets, a world into which he repeatedly tended to thrust himself. His awareness of the poet as priest and prophet, his acceptance of the Platonic idea of the poet in a fine frenzy, voicing truths in hexameters, account for the significance of certain metaphors, such as the laurel and manna-dew, in his work. Not only did he want to be a Romantic hierophant; his broad knowledge of the lore of the classical poetic past and of its belief in the holy nature of the poetic imagination assuredly explains his fascination with Delphic exuberance. It also enables us to understand why he would assume the oracular throne of Apollo, a throne which he, as a poet, thought rightfully his.

Certain biographical facts are also sometimes relevant to our understanding of the metaphors. For example, Keats's own admission of an enthralment to poetry may be taken as a clue to the significance behind all of the demon-women in his poems. In his biography we note an attraction to both women and poetry; it was quite natural, therefore, that he would make one the symbol for the other. Yet another biographical fact—that Keats was tubercular—may well account for the vivid, metaphorical descriptions of the poet who experiences all the giddiness and elevation of a frenzied priest of Delphi. The intense sensation undergone in moments of imaginative vision when his poetry was being formed may have had an actual physiological basis. His Delphic life may be factual and literal as well as imaginative and metaphorical.

It will be seen that Keats, according to this study of metaphors, lived up to his dictum that "poetry should surprise by a fine excess." In one particular sense, that "excess" refers to the metaphorical richness of poems which speak on one level of meaning of the subject of poetry and imagination. That richness has been insufficiently perceived because his metaphors have not been seen in the full context of his work. Once seen and understood, they can lead to greater appreciation of the poetry.

Keats's metaphors for the poetic imagination

Chapter one

Keats's poetic theory

I

"I long to be talking about the imagination," said Keats to Benjamin Bailey. This statement summarizes an abiding aim and interest common to all the Romantic poets in both their criticism and their poetry. For Romanticism evinces a noticeable turning inward on the part of the poet to explore the unique power which sets him off from other men. The poet, as a kind of bemused Narcissus, becomes enamored of his own artistic problems and the inner life of the imagination. Indeed, the entire first book of *The Prelude* poses one question whose answer is developed in epic proportions: What shall the poet talk about? Wordsworth proceeds to talk about himself,[1] or to put it more precisely, about his poetic imagination. The poet as hero on an epic quest for a voice and an aesthetic is common to the rest of the Romantic poets. Blake's Los, Keats's Endymion, Shelley's youthful poet in *Alastor* and even Coleridge's Ancient Mariner are personae dramatizing their creators' journeys of imagination.

Although introspection is a primary characteristic of Romanticism, the poet's concern for the problems of his craft and his compulsion to write about it are not peculiar to Romantic poetry alone. Such concern had occurred long before Blake and Wordsworth. Shakespeare himself

---

1. "A thing unprecedented in literary history that a man should talk so much about himself," said Wordsworth in a letter to Sir George Beaumont, May 1, 1805. *Letters of William Wordsworth*, ed. Philip Wayne (London, 1954), p. 72.

(whom the Romantics significantly claim as one of their own) wrote about his craft in Hamlet's conversation with the players. One notices Shakespeare's sentiments about his art also in the highly fictive romantic comedies where the poet, in the guise of a Prospero or a sprite, steps forward and speaks of the imagination and its strange powers. Spenser is similarly fascinated. Only recently the Garden of Adonis episode in Book III of *The Faerie Queene* has been read as Spenser's ideas on creation, including poetic creation.[2] English poets have been fascinated not only by aesthetic considerations (the formal cause of poetry), but also by function (the final cause). The Elizabethan sonnet sequences often pose the question of the role which poetry plays in the poets' lives; and in the eighteenth century it seemed necessary for the pre-Romantics to define anew the poetical character, as for example in Akenside's *Pleasures of Imagination*. These peripheral concerns, ordinarily amplified in prose literary criticism, become a central subject for Romantic poetry, for the poet in this period is essentially a maker rather than a critic. Poems about poetry, then, have an established tradition in English literature, which the Romantics carry on with added vigor.

It would be easy to cite the decline of the patron system of private support for the poet as a reason for the Romantics' turning inward to write poems about poetry and imagination. A more important consideration in accounting for this new introspection in poetry is the poet's relationship with his audience. It is evident that the Romantics bore the confusion of not knowing who their audience was, as F. W. Bateson has observed.[3] Up until about the time of Dr. Johnson's short but devastating letter to the Earl of Chesterfield—marking the decline of the patron's influence in literature—an existing standard of poetic taste, which was still determined and dictated by a public, required the poet to reflect manners based on general nature and a morality grounded on reason. Income and approbation often depended upon the poet's willingness to write to these requirements. But by the advent of the Romantic age, this accord between public and poet was already well on the wane. In the midst of the pedestrian Augustan poetry still being written after 1784, the Romantics were attempting to subvert the commonly

2. Harry Berger, Jr., "Spenser's Gardens of Adonis: Force and Form in the Renaissance Imagination," *University of Toronto Quarterly*, XXX (1960), 128–149.
3. F. W. Bateson, *English Poetry: A Critical Introduction* (London, 1950), pp. 68–69.

accepted form and subject matter of poetry. The poet felt more of a responsibility to his imagination and its visions than to an audience. The tendency was to turn his back to an often unsympathetic and even apathetic audience and sing to himself, like the elevated nightingale of his poetry. One thinks immediately of Blake and Shelley in this regard, but Keats, too, in one of his unusually strident moments, voices a romantic independence of the audience:

I have not the slightest feel of humility towards the Public—or to any thing in existence,—but the eternal Being, the Principle of Beauty,—and the Memory of great Men—When I am writing for myself for the mere sake of the Moment's enjoyment, perhaps nature has its course with me —but a Preface is written to the Public; a thing I cannot help looking upon as an Enemy, and which I cannot address without feelings of Hostility. . . .[4]

And with equal contempt a year later at the printing of *Lamia* in *The Indicator* he signs not his name but merely "Caviare," having in mind Hamlet's comment " 'Twas caviare to the general," meaning that *Lamia* was above the taste of the common people. Keats's manifest aggressiveness here is uncommon in his letters, which show, generally, an indifference toward his audience, but in a rare instance or two, a jealous watchfulness for poetic fame. His attitude stands in sharp contrast to Pope's keen awareness of his audience, both enemies and friends, and perhaps most important, of his paying readers also.

Undoubtedly the similar frustration that Shelley and Blake [5] felt at their inability to find audiences led them to write for themselves. Notwithstanding those few moments in which Shelley wants all mankind to be his audience, for example, in the last stanza of "Ode to the West Wind," he shows himself rather unwilling to court the reading public; and yet he is certainly not indifferent to it, for the apocalyptic nature of his poetry presumes a wide audience. Perhaps he felt like a hierophant in an almost empty oracle. Except for Byron's commercial success, this general lack of rapport between poet and reader persisted through the Romantic period. In such literary circumstance it seems that the alienated poet is thrown back to the problems of self and is forced to justify

4. *The Letters of John Keats*, ed. Hyder E. Rollins (Cambridge, Mass., 1958), I, 266–267. Hereinafter cited as *Letters*.
5. Mark Schorer, *William Blake: The Politics of Vision* (New York, 1959), p. 77.

his existence as a poet. He defends himself by speaking of the worth, power, and sanctity of the poetic imagination, whose truths he considers important enough to trumpet to an audience of men. Sadly, his poetry generally falls on dumb ears.

The altered literary state alone does not account for the Romantic poet's alienation and for his interest in his imagination. The Romantic revolt repudiates two major philosophic heresies: the mechanistic world view of the rationalists; and eighteenth-century epistemology. The sense of futility engendered by mechanistic philosophy, with its endless cycle of death and decay within fixed laws, beset the Romantics. Finding himself in a cold and alien universe, man possessed no innate ideas which could help him make his existence meaningful; he saw only chaos, as did Wordsworth, who painfully felt "the weight / Of all this unintelligible world." [6]

The problem of how one knows was of far-reaching importance to Romantic poetic theory and a concept of the imagination. The poetry is wholly at odds with the prevailing mechanistic epistemology of Locke. If, according to Locke, knowledge comes only from sense experience, the mind is a passive agent, a mere receptacle receiving and recording impressions. By association it forms ideas and is able to reason, but its capabilities to create knowledge are severely limited. By this epistemology—underscored by Locke and Samuel Johnson—poetry becomes merely wit, a display of talent for combining ideas by association. Hartley himself allows no grandly generative force to the imagination. He defines poetry as "The Recurrence of Ideas, especially visible and audible ones, in a vivid manner, but without any regard to the Order observed in past Facts." [7] Johnson, similarly, denies any special transcendental power to the imagination and warns of its "dangerous prevalence." [8] He regards imagination in its literal sense, "image maker," and the poet as a plumber who joins words together through acquired skill. Indeed, any man can be a poet if he has "a mind of large general powers" [9] capable of imitation of nature. His statement that Newton could as

6. "Tintern Abbey," *Poetical Works*, II (Oxford, 1944), 260, ll. 39–40.
7. David Hartley, *Observations on Man* (London, 1749), I, 383.
8. Samuel Johnson, *The History of Rasselas*, ed. R. W. Chapman (Oxford, 1927), p. 189.
9. "Lives of the Poets: Cowley," *The Works of Samuel Johnson* (London, 1818), VI, 1.

easily have been a poet and his offhand dismissal of poetic genius—"Sir, the man who has vigour, may walk to the east, just as well as to the west, if he happens to turn his head that way" [10]—dramatizes his mechanistic attitude toward poetic genius. The practice of poetry is therefore no different from the practice of law or mathematics.

Perhaps the best example of hand-to-hand combat between neoclassical and Romantic ideas on the imagination is to be found in Keats's annotations to critical commentary by Johnson in a copy of Shakespeare. Johnson wrote of A Midsummer Night's Dream:

Wild and fantastical as this play is, all the parts in their various modes are well written, and give the kind of pleasure which the author designed. Fairies in his time were much in fashion; common tradition had made them familiar, and Spencer's poem made them great.

Keats scribbles out the paragraph, writes "Fie" before "Johnson," and assaults him with lines from the play altered to his purpose:

Such tricks hath *weak* imagination.
To kill cankers in the Musk rose buds.
The clamorous Owl that hoots at our quaint Spirits.
Newts and blind worms do no wrong
Come not near our faery queen.

Johnson is annihilated in this and other broadsides in which he is called "fool," "proud man," and "calumnising knave." [11]

With much the same resentment, Blake, commenting on Reynolds' assertion that "The mind is but a barren soil; a soil which is soon exhausted, and will produce no crop," said, "The mind that could have produced this Sentence must have been a Pitiful, a Pitiable Imbecility. I always thought that the Human Mind was the most Prolific of All Things & Inexhaustible. I certainly do Thank God that I am not like Reynolds." [12]

The need to control the Urizenic impulse in man extends throughout the work of the Romantics and posits as the necessary condition of creativity the vital integration of spirit, body, and mind. Without this

10. James Boswell, *Journal of a Tour to the Hebrides*, ed. H. B. Cotterill (London, 1926), p. 18.
11. Caroline Spurgeon, *Keats's Shakespeare* (London, 1928), pp. 29–32.
12. "Annotations to Sir Joshua Reynolds's Discourses," *Poetry and Prose of William Blake*, ed. Geoffrey Keynes (New York, 1956), p. 802.

equilibrium the poet knows the dejection of refracted vision. Philosophy (i.e., scientific rationalism or any mechanical and lifeless systems of thought) will indeed "clip an Angel's wings," as Keats said in *Lamia*. Blake's meddling Urizen becomes the devil that enslaves man, causing him to worship what Wordsworth calls "that false secondary power / By which we multiply distinctions." [13] Keats castigates his close friend, Dilke, for relying too much on precept and methodology; for doing so he "will never come at a truth as long as he lives; because he is always trying at it." [14] And one is reminded of the despair with which the skeptical Ancient Mariner sees a slimy materialistic universe ruled by Life-in-Death.

Wherein lay salvation for the Romantic poet? First, the imagination is conceived of as intensely active. No longer considered passive, no longer considered a mere combiner and assorter of images and ideas, no longer considered a mirror of nature, the imagination is conceived as ordering and shaping the apparently chaotic world and giving it meaning. The theory of the imagination is central to the Romantic conception of life and literature. All of the Romantics, when speaking of the imagination, are talking epistemologically, in large measure, and so sustained are their inquiries that the imagination and its attendant suzerainty over poetry are carried as subject matter into their poems. Poems "about" poetry are frequently attempts to divine the nature and domain of the imagination. Poetry becomes an experience of discovery, an inward-turning awareness of the power which is vastly creative. Poems about poetry, then, are a kind of obeisance of the poet to the most sublime power within him.

Second, the Romantic poet regards the universe not as static or mechanical but as organic. Organicism [15] provides the necessary metaphysics for a Romantic theory of the imagination. If indeed the universe

13. *The Prelude*, ed. Carlos Baker (New York, 1948), Bk. II, p. 156, ll. 216–217. Douglas Bush's *Science and English Poetry* (New York, 1950) discusses this subject with acumen.

14. *Letters*, II, 213.

15. See Morse Peckham, "Toward a Theory of Romanticism," *PMLA*, LXVI (1951), 5–23. Peckham's identification of "dynamic organicism" with the creative process of the imagination is carefully argued. He concludes, "What then is Romanticism? Whether philosophic, theologic, or aesthetic, it is the revolution in the European mind against thinking in terms of static mechanism and the redirection of the mind to thinking in terms of dynamic organicism. Its values are change, imperfection, growth, diversity, the creative imagination, the unconscious" (p. 14).

is conceived as growing like a plant, organically connected and interdependent in its parts, then any change in the stem has an effect on the roots and leaves. Change, inherent in the nature of things, assumes positive value. If the force behind the universe is self-creative and still growing toward self-realization, and Promethean man is a part of this universe, then he, too, contributes to its change through his power of imagination. The poet's creating of new forms of beauty is comparable to the creative act unfolding in the organic universe. The poet while embodying beauty is at the same time creating new and higher truths, kindling new ideas in man.

The oneness of all existence is predicated on dynamic organicism. When Wordsworth calls nature "the guide...and soul / Of all my moral being," [16] we understand, therefore, his assumption of God's immanence. At rare moments of intense stimulation, the imagination senses the indwelling divinity in all nature. In such moments the Romantic poet believed himself to be united with the Divine. Keats attests to the "authenticity of imagination" in its power to perceive "truth." Similarly, Blake considered the imagination as the informing God speaking from within himself,[17] and Shelley, in "A Defence of Poetry," exclaimed (as Plato did in the *Ion*), "A poet participates in the eternal, the infinite and the one." Moreover, poetry "creates anew the universe" because "it subdues to union under its light yoke all irreconcilable things." [18] Imagination, that "imperial faculty," reveals the oneness of all things, whereas the reason merely divides: "Reason is the enumeration of quantities already known; imagination is the perception of the value of those quantities, both separately and as a whole." [19] The poets regard the imagination, then, as the unifying power at the center and circumference of all artistic creation and metaphysical perception.

II

The intensely creative imagination is best celebrated in Keats's letter to Benjamin Bailey, November 22, 1817. The most startling claim for

16. "Tintern Abbey," *Poetical Works*, II, 262, ll. 110–111.
17. Shorer, pp. 19, 96.
18. "A Defence of Poetry," *The Complete Works of Percy Bysshe Shelley*, ed. Roger Ingpen and Walter E. Peck (London, 1930), VII, 137.
19. *Ibid.*, p. 109.

the imagination in this letter is its prefigurative capacity. The imagination is no mirror of the empyrean realm but rather envisions, indeed creates, beauty that is truth, "whether it existed before or not." As Adam's dream revealed a heretofore non-existent Eve, whom he found real on awakening, so the active imagination adumbrates that which will be a reality hereafter. The power of imagination, to Keats, seems auto-apocalyptic indeed.

Before the imagination can envision truth and figure it in poetic form, it must first be stirred to life. The letter suggests that the passions induce imaginative activity. For this reason the emotions or "Hearts' affections" are "holy." Rational conclusions are suspect; truth is arrived at without the tortuous route taken (with frequent dead-ends) by "consequitive" reason. Moreover, the affections take on the role of arbiter, according to Keats: "axioms in philosophy are not axioms until they are proved upon our pulses." [20] That is to say, one judges the validity of an idea not merely by testing it on the intellect, but by testing it on the feelings. We are now able to find meaning in his often misunderstood ejaculation, "O for a Life of Sensations rather than of Thoughts!" By "sensations" it would seem Keats means both the emotional experience and intense sensory experience; the second predicates the first. Accordingly, we may rephrase the statement to read, "O for a life of immediate experience rather than *a priori* ideas." Keats is attempting, I think, to describe throughout this germinal letter the proper sequence of events which lead to an intuitive perception of beauty that is truth.[21] The letter suggests the poetic process to be a chain reaction in which sensory experience kindles the emotions. The emotions in turn provide for an imaginative release, culminating in a vision of truth-beauty. The path to truth, then, is through "consequitive" emotional intensities.

To tease out his imagination Keats actively seeks a life of direct sensation; he even categorizes the different intensities of sensation and emotion according to a "pleasure thermometer" [22] where natural beauty is placed at the lowest point, and love at the highest.

20. *Letters,* I, 279.
21. As Earl R. Wasserman points out in "Keats and Benjamin Bailey on the Imagination," *Modern Language Notes,* LXVIII (1953), 361–365, the imagination discovers "authentic truth, not analogous truth."
22. See *Endymion,* Bk. I, ll. 777–801; *Letters,* I, 218; and Wasserman, *The Finer Tone,* pp. 69–70.

We can further understand how a poetry of extreme luxuriance log-ically derives from such an aesthetic. But in addition, the aesthetic be-comes a religion, for Keats believes that his imagination can create his forthcoming existence in heaven:

O for a Life of Sensations rather than of Thoughts! It is 'a Vision in the form of Youth' a Shadow of reality to come—and this consideration has further conv[i]nced me for it has come as auxiliary to another favorite Speculation of mine, that we shall enjoy ourselves here after by having what we called happiness on Earth repeated in a finer tone and so re-peated—And yet such a fate can only befall those who delight in sensa-tion rather than hunger as you do after Truth—Adam's dream will do here and seems to be a conviction that Imagination and its empyreal reflection is the same as human Life and its spiritual repetition.[23]

Intense sensory experience on earth, then, promises unmitigated ecstasies in the afterworld, but in a finer tone compared to the imperfect and transitory quality of sublunary sensations. This aesthetic makes the imag-ination the First Cause, being determinant of one's fate hereafter; through imagination the poet prefigures his forthcoming existence in heaven by living the appropriate and intense life of sensory experience here on earth. Furthermore, Keats's concept of the imagination suggests the intensely dynamic power which Coleridge avowed. By allowing the poet to see immortal existence, the imagination arrests mutability, however short a length of time its vision may be.

Such preoccupations are central in the poetry. The earlier poems attest the revelatory power of the imagination. But after *Endymion* the piping takes on a sad tone, for the power of the imagination becomes suspect. The great odes are concerned with the odd moments of intense imagina-tive activity in which beauty is perceived, but, deplorably, "beauty cannot keep her lustrous eyes." It must die; mutability conquers the ideal realm where "Truth is Beauty." "Ode on a Grecian Urn" and "Ode to a Nightingale" dramatize the contrast between the ideal world "forever happy and forever new" and the mutable world of the earth-bound listener who can never reach the realm of Beauty-Truth inhabited by the urn and the nightingale. Here is also a contrast of the permanence of art with the impermanence of life. Beauty is truth in the "Ode on a Grecian Urn" precisely because the poetic imagination has perceived an empirical

23. *Letters*, I, 185.

truth (here, the mutability of life) and has shaped an object of beauty from it in the form of art. Thus, truth becomes the means through which Beauty is cast into form. The imagination is the means by which Beauty and Truth are identified.

While the Romantic poets are interested in reconciling the polarities of the real and ideal worlds and acknowledge the role of the imagination as a unifying force, the critics generally speak of the poem as a thing achieved, as an equilibrium realized, and of ends met. To do so indicates that the means of reconciliation and the process involved are indifferently treated, if at all. Their concern is with product rather than process, with the being of a poem rather than its becoming. Yet the reconciling force of imagination and its vital process is, I think, Keats's main interest in most of his poems. He would, therefore, describe the immensely rich act of imagination, which we have already identified as a divine power prefiguring truth, with all of the appropriate figures he can devise. The odes are poems that speak metaphorically of the mysterious, unifying imagination, which like a catalyst makes something new and whole by a miraculous process. Of the genesis of *Endymion*, Keats states, "it was a regular stepping of the Imagination towards a Truth." [24] He would figure the steps in the creative process, as well as the vision of truth to which he ascends. Both the process and product of the imagination seem equally important in his poems about poetry.

III

Having explored the main significances of the letter to Bailey, we may now be able to see its import for some of the other critical attitudes toward poetry which appear in later letters. Keats's intention to pursue a life of sensations foreshadows some of his most sophisticated attitudes toward the poetical character. His idea of the "chameleon poet" and his celebrated idea of "negative capability" attempt to show that in true poetry the identity of the poet is obliterated by being invested in a suitable object, if first that object arouses the sympathetic imagination of the poet. The perception of the object and the projection of the poet's

24. *Ibid.*, p. 218.

ego into the object occur at the same moment. The peculiar "intensity" [25] (i.e., feeling) with which the poet sees the object ignites his imagination so that it becomes infused with his being. The more intense the perception, the more responsive the sympathetic imagination. In Keats the life of intense sensations leads to imaginative activity, and simultaneously the imagination finds its fit expression in the object it contemplates. The ability to animate an object by projecting one's feelings into it is the property of "gusto," which only the true (i.e., Keatsian) poet possesses. Shakespeare, losing his identity in the object, is the supreme poet of disinterestedness, for "he has no Identity—he is continually infor[ming] and filling some other Body—the Sun, the Moon, the Sea and Men and Women." [26]

When the sympathetic imagination, rooted in the affections, cannot project itself, the poetic powers wither. The loss of passion and sympathetic imagination explains the despondency in "Ode on Indolence." Like Coleridge's plight in "Dejection: An Ode," seeing and feeling are dissociated ("I see, not feel, how beautiful they are"). Both poets can no longer see a sparrow and "take part in its existence and pick about the Gravel." [27] Nature is nothing or everything depending on the state of the "shaping spirit": "we receive but what we give / And in our life alone does nature live."

The poetical character as described by Keats is common in Romantic critical theory. Hazlitt had talked about sympathy long before Keats attended his lectures. And Coleridge had said,

Imagination is the power of objectifying one's self, the Protean self-transforming power of genius. To become all things and yet remain the same, to make the changeful God be felt in the river, the lion, and the flame—that is true imagination. [28]

While showing an affinity with the critical ideas of Coleridge, Keats's aesthetic is at odds with the frequently direct subjectivism of the other major Romantic poets, Wordsworth, Byron, and Shelley. His ideas of

25. Art especially quickens the emotions, as Keats suggests to his brothers: "the excellence of every Art is its intensity" (*ibid.*, p. 192).
26. *Ibid.*, p. 387.   27. *Ibid.*, p. 186.
28. Quoted in René Wellek, *A History of Modern Criticism: 1750–1950* (New Haven, 1955), II, 163.

"negative capability" and of the "chameleon poet" are in a sense anti-Romantic, because they call for objectivity, not subjectivity. They repudiate the "egotistical sublime" of Wordsworth, who peacocks his way through poetry.[29] Wordsworth does not "look steadily at [his] subject"; moreover, his didacticism leads Keats to assert, "We hate poetry that has a palpable design upon us." [30] "Man should not dispute or assert but whisper results to his neighbour." [31] By "whisper" Keats means the devices of artistic indirection, the result of which is achieved by the poet's concern for the particular and not the general. Keats, often talking about the fundamentals of poetry in this way, stresses the concrete as essential in capturing the attention of the reader. Through immediately apprehended language, i.e., suitable imagery and metaphor, the superior or Keatsian poet suggests, embodies, or "whispers" his ideas. The concept of the "chameleon poet" attests to the essentially metaphorical nature of poetry, conceived as the habitual objectification of thought and feeling.

The stress upon objectivity in the letters strikes one as peculiarly modern. Eliot's idea of the objective correlative and Yeats's concept of the mask are nothing new, but rather derive from the Romantics' practice of finding in concrete language and in metaphor a way to talk about the imagination and art. The Grecian urn, for example, is a large metaphor objectifying the achievements of the imagination. Later poets writing poems about poetry and imagination root their thoughts and feelings in central analogues similar to Keats's urn, as for example in Yeats's "perne in a gyre" and in Stevens' "jar in Tennessee." We may observe that metaphor since the Romantic period has in general become the structure of poetry.[32] And Keats, it seems to me, is the only Romantic to cling consistently and scrupulously to an aesthetic rooted in metaphor; his addiction to it is so intense that he is considered virtually a metaphysical poet in some of his denser poems.[33]

We find other evidence in Keats's criticism for his preference of ob-

29. *Letters*, I, 223, 387.   30. *Ibid.*, p. 224.
31. *Ibid.*, p. 232.
32. In contrast to the Romantic attitude of the intrinsicality of metaphor to poetry, Dr. Johnson's lexical definition of metaphor as a "simile comprized in a word," and as a figure used for making an example reveals the general neoclassical attitude of the extrinsicality of metaphor to poetic structure. Even so recent a critic as R. A. Foakes argues incorrectly that Romantic poetry is not basically committed to metaphor. See *The Romantic Assertion* (New Haven, 1958), pp. 20–22.
33. See Wasserman, *The Finer Tone*, p. 99.

jectivity to subjectivity; indirection to statement; aesthetic distance to
personal intrusion; metaphor, symbol, and myth to exposition. A letter
to Reynolds (February 19, 1818) offers a clue to his basic attitude toward poetry. The poem, as the fixed product of imagination, makes the
beholder aware of its artistic richness and complexity:

I have an idea that a Man might pass a very pleasant life in this manner
—let him on any certain day read a certain Page of full Poesy or distilled
Prose and let him wander with it, and muse upon it, and reflect from it,
and bring home to it, and prophesy upon it, and dream upon it, untill it
becomes stale—but when will it do so? Never—When Man has arrived
at a certain ripeness in *intellect* any one grand and spiritual passage serves
him as a starting post towards all "the two-and thirty Pallaces." How
happy is such a "voyage of conception," what a delicious diligent Indolence! A doze upon a Sofa does not hinder it, and a nap upon Clover
engenders ethereal finger-pointings—the prattle of a child gives it wings,
and the converse of middle-age a strength to beat them—a strain of
musick conducts to "an odd angle of the Isle," and when the leaves
whisper it "puts a girdle around the earth...." [34]

In this letter, so little noted by critics, the poet is telling Reynolds
not only how to read, but also how the poet creates an endlessly evocative texture of words. Through metaphor words take on a world of possible connotations and, depending upon the precision with which they
are ordered in the poem, may precipitate new and surprising networks
of reference. The worth of a poem, therefore, lies in the number of
relationships perceived and in the several possible avenues of meaning.
For Keats the perfectly "distilled" poem is free of verbal impurities;
ideally every element of the poem serves some functional purpose. Thus
the true poet should be "Jealous of dead leaves in the bay wreath crown,"
as Keats says in "If by dull rhymes."

Such intentions of achieving formal purity are voiced throughout the
letters. We are reminded of Keats's admonition to Shelley to "curb your
magnanimity and be more of an artist, and 'load every rift' of your
subject with ore." [35] On occasion he uses the word "discipline" to describe
the artist's need of extreme awareness and care in selecting words and
arranging them in order to bring the poem to a richness of perfection.
The "Ode to Psyche" calls this skill in arranging and ordering "all the
gardener Fancy e'er could feign."

34. *Letters*, I, 231.   35. *Ibid.*, II, 323.

Keats clearly intends a highly evocative poetry of metaphor. The letter to Reynolds further spells out the character of "distilled" art. In re-enacting the poet's complex journey of fancy, the perceptive reader appreciates the beauty, diversity, and richness of art:

Now it appears to me that almost any Man may like the Spider spin from his own inwards his own airy Citadel—the points of leaves and twigs on which the Spider begins her work are few and she fills the Air with a beautiful circuiting: man should be content with as few points to tip with the fine Webb of his Soul and weave a tapestry empyrean—full of Symbols for his spiritual eye, of softness for his spiritual touch, of space for his wandering of distinctness for his Luxury—But the Minds of Mortals are so different and bent on such diverse Journeys that it may at first appear impossible for any common taste and fellowship to exist between two or three under these suppositions—It is however quite the contrary—Minds would leave each other in contrary directions, traverse each other in Numberless points, and at last greet each other at the Journey's end.[36]

The "man" spoken of is evidently Keats the poet, and the "tapestry empyrean" is the highly crafted fabric of his poem. It is no plain footmat but a Gobelin arras, wrought by the complex processes of imagination and reaching, in its intensity, the empyreal realm of Truth-Beauty. It is interesting to note that in another letter written two weeks after the one to Reynolds, Keats, again defining poetry, says it "should surprise by a fine excess and not by Singularity"; [37] here the textural richness of poetry seems analogous to the woven complexity of "a tapestry empyrean."

It is clear by now that Keats is suggesting that a poem is autonomous, complex, and highly unified. Furthermore, the poet in making "a beautiful circuiting" is creating his own world. Every poetic act of creation is a taming of the rough Heraclitean beast, flux or chaos. The merit of each poem resides in the number of perceived relationships in its parts, all of which should contribute functionally to the whole. Keats proposes an organic theory of poetry which has found its strongest adherent in Cleanth Brooks, whose well-known criterion for the worth of a poem is in the function and relation of its organic parts.[38] The neo-Romantic

36. *Ibid.*, I, 231–232.   37. *Ibid.*, p. 238.
38. Cleanth Brooks, "The Poem as Organism: Modern Critical Procedure," *English Institute Annual*, 1940 (New York, 1941), pp. 30–31, 37–38.

Wallace Stevens has grasped the essential intricacy of poetry so conceived: "Poetry is not the same thing as the imagination taken alone. Nothing is itself taken alone. Things are because of interrelations or interactions." [39]

Keats's organic theory of literature conforms basically to Coleridge's idea of beauty as "multeity in unity," for the degree of richness in a poem is proportional "to the variety of parts which it holds in unity." [40] Obviously the central aim of Keats and other poets was to achieve a high degree of unity in their poems (and in their lives). A poem should not only be highly integrated, part to part, and part to whole, but should exfoliate in a natural but orderly way. A letter to James Hessey remarks: "That which is creative must create itself." Indeed the unfolding of a poem and its progress lend to its overall order: "The rise, the progress, the setting of imagery should like the Sun come natural to him—shine over him and set soberly although in magnificence leaving him in the Luxury of twilight." [41] Does not "To Autumn" achieve this effect? The ideal poem describes a perfect, circular motion, which is for Keats but a metaphor for its unity. Coleridge had expressed this exact idea with the same figure: "The common end of . . . all poems is to convert a series into a whole: to make those events, which in real or imagined history move in a straight line assume to our Understanding a circular motion." [42]

Wholeness, harmony, radiance: these are Aristotelian terms for poetry, but they apply precisely to Romantic aesthetics. The integration which the perfectly executed poem achieves does not allow it to be unraveled into its formal and thematic elements. Its oneness makes such a separation as artificial as isolating the dancer from the dance, or the leaf and blossom from the bole. In short, art exists as a living, organic entity. Long before Archibald MacLeish stated the case for pure poetry ("A poem should not mean but be"), Keats, in viewing the poem as autonomous, had understood its perfect inviolability to dissection: "all poems

---

39. Wallace Stevens, *Opus Posthumous*, ed. Samuel French Morse (New York, 1957), p. 163.
40. *The Complete Works of Samuel Taylor Coleridge*, ed. William G. T. Shedd (New York, 1854), IV, 330.
41. *Letters*, I, 238.
42. *Unpublished Letters of Samuel Taylor Coleridge*, ed. E. L. Griggs (New Haven, 1933), II, 128.

should do without any comment," he said to George and Georgiana Keats.[43]

If we accept the fact that two of Keats's major themes involve the creative process, which includes poetic inspiration, and the perfect symmetry, tightness, and complexity of poetry, then we should be aware of the heavy burden which he bears as a poet. He is in continuous search for adequate metaphors for the most subjective, abstract, and personal of all experiences: the workings of the fancy and aesthetic intuitions. He must figure the various causes of poetry: the formal cause, or the initial, dim plan of the poem as it first appears to the imagination; the efficient cause, or the actual labors of the imagination as they attempt to achieve in words what is envisioned; and the final cause, or the completed, orderly poem itself. The continuous demands of invention pressing upon Keats suggest that any system of metaphors he might devise will be highly personal, even private in meaning. As we have noted elsewhere, he is not a poet who is willing to dilute his poetry with statement. He remains scrupulously metaphorical, with the result that meaning often remains hidden because of the extreme privacy of his figures.

Critics have only recently begun to read the poetry with the care that it demands. They have become aware that what appears at first to be diffuse verse is really highly crafted and meaningful in the smallest figurative details, a conclusion arrived at only after careful reading and collation of the recurrent, private metaphors for poetry and the imaginative process. One task of the modern critic has been to plumb the significance of each poet's private language. To be sure, there are many soundings still to be made. M. H. Abrams is one of the first critics to circumscribe some favorite Romantic analogues for the imaginative mind. It is important to note that *The Mirror and the Lamp* fails to mention Keats in its survey of these commonly used analogues. A reason can be given. In the poetry of Keats these metaphors are so allusive and so easily read into other contexts of meaning that their real significance is buried. Other more highly personal series of metaphors to describe his inner life of imagination are frequently carried to the limits of camouflage. Keats's life was his poetry, and each individual poem an "allegory" of the inner life of imagination, as he suggests in a letter to George and Georgiana Keats:

43. *Letters,* II, 21.

A Man's life of any worth is a continual allegory—and very few eyes
can see the Mystery of his life—a life like the scriptures, figurative....
Lord Byron cuts a figure—but he is not figurative—Shakespeare led a life
of Allegory; his works are the comments on it.—[44]

The poems figuratively describe that inner imaginative life repeatedly.
But in the letters he is consistently noncommital about the meaning of
his poetry. His humorous comments to his brother concerning the
"kisses four" in "La Belle Dame sans Merci" and his reticence about
remarking on *Lamia* are examples of his attitude that "all poems should
do without any comment." [45] It is left for the critic to fathom what
Keats chose to leave unsaid; that is to say, within the poetry we perceive
the dominant life which he chose to record, the life of imagination.
That is why he said with earnestness, "I find that I cannot exist without
poetry—without eternal poetry—half the day will not do—the whole of
it." [46]

Richard Woodhouse's manuscript commenting on Keats's method
of composition has a strong bearing on our understanding of the genesis
and recurrence of metaphors:

He has said that he has often not been aware of the beauty of some
thought or expression until after he had composed and written it down
—It has then struck him with astonishment and seemed rather the
production of another person than his own. He has wondered how he
came to hit upon it. This was the case with the description of Apollo
in the 3rd book of 'Hyperion' . . . It seemed to come by chance or magic—
to be as it were something given to him.[47]

The statement leads us to this important consideration: How does one
explain this apparently spontaneous method of writing poetry, or, to take
the most celebrated example of inspired writing, Coleridge's reputed
method of writing "Kubla Khan," "in which all the images rose up before
him as *things*, with a parallel production of the correspondent expres-
sions, without any sensation or consciousness of effort"? *Hyperion* and
"Kubla Khan" are the *ne plus ultra* of spontaneity and automaticism,
if we are to accept Woodhouse's and Coleridge's commentaries. But no

44. *Ibid.*, p. 67.   45. See *ibid.*, pp. 21, 97, and 189.
46. *Ibid.*, I, 133. Keats's trembling for "not having written anything of late" suggests an addiction to poetry that is not without anguish. We are reminded of Wordsworth's confession of extreme distress and sweating when he took his pen in hand.
47. Quoted in Amy Lowell, *John Keats* (Cambridge, Mass., 1925), I, 501–502.

poem is detached from the life of its author. Perhaps Wordsworth offers the best clue to explain the genesis of the images and metaphors coming to Keats with "a fine suddenness," or for that matter to any poet of genius, when he states that poems are produced by a man who "had . . . thought long and deeply" on his subject.[48]

However, Woodhouse and Coleridge admit to no conscious thought, at least not at the time of composition (although Coleridge was later to modify his claim of poetic genesis, arguing that judgment accompanies dream). One then conjectures: might not the poet's thinking, albeit in fragments, have already taken place in the past and then submerged below the level of consciousness? Any long and labored-over thinking—and we must agree that Keats thought long and deeply about poetry—will produce a network of corresponding images which may be retained by memory for possible future use.

According to Keats, inspiration comes after long periods of rumination, where different images and metaphors relating to a common thought are linked and associated, waiting for the proper moment of inspiration for release. He implies that Shelley would be a better poet if he kept his "wings furl'd for six Months together." [49] During this gestation period a kind of pregnant interchange of images and metaphors relating to a particular idea may develop below the level of consciousness. Thought and intellectual growth are a prelude to great poetry,[50] as he affirms on August 16 of his most productive year, 1819. By this time he says to Fanny Brawne: "My Mind is heap'd to the full; stuff'd like a cricket ball—if I strive to fill it more it would burst." [51]

The imaginative burst begins in a state of emotion where the poet recollects and recombines favorite images and metaphors associated with his predominant idea, which for our purposes involves the theme of poetry and the imaginative process. It may be an object that awakens the association of images with idea, as we have seen in considering Keats's concept of "negative capability." Thus after long states of absorp-

48. "Preface to the Second Edition . . . of *Lyrical Ballads*," *Poetical Works*, II, 388.
49. *Letters*, II, 323.
50. See John Livingston Lowes, *The Road to Xanadu: A Study in the Ways of the Imagination* (Cambridge, Mass., 1927), pp. 308 ff. for a discussion of the effects of Coleridge's reading and thinking on the creation of poetry, and on the windings of the imagination.
51. *Letters*, II, 141.

tion and preparation, poetry, when it comes, "should... appear almost a Remembrance," and that "by merely pulling an apron string we set a pretty peal of Chimes at work." [52] These statements refer to the associative imagination. Recurrences of images and metaphors in different poems suggest that when linkages of ideas with particular images are once formed the poet has habitual recourse to them. T. S. Eliot has pondered over this psychic phenomenon:

Why, for all of us, out of all that we have heard, seen, felt, in a lifetime, do certain images recur, charged with emotion, rather than others? The song of one bird, the leap of one fish, at a particular place and time.... such memories may have symbolic value, but of what we cannot tell, for they come to represent the depths of feeling into which we cannot peer.[53]

The answer to Eliot's question lies in his use of the word "emotion." A main reason for the poet's compulsion to reuse certain images in different poems is that the linkage of apparently heterogeneous images with an idea is born in passion, which seems to be the annealing force between the two. Poetry is the expression of "felt thoughts." We have seen in discussing Keats's idea of the "chameleon poet" that the poet, in projecting his feelings into an object, may create a lasting identification between object and emotion. If that emotion is sufficiently powerful, its equivalent objective expression, by association, may be etched in the surface of memory and may reappear when the poet has similar periods of emotional thinking. Coleridge perceives these relationships when he says, "images ... become proofs of original genius only as far as they are modified by a predominant passion; or by associated thoughts or images awakened by that passion." [54]

Edward A. Armstrong's study of Shakespeare's imagery demonstrates how highly private ideas and emotions are objectified in recurrent image clusters throughout a poet's corpus. For example, the reappearing goose is always linked in a cluster with images of disease, harlotry, and urination, because for Shakespeare the goose was habitually associated with the unsavoriness of the phrase "Winchester goose," which describes the

52. *Ibid.*, I, 238, 280.
53. T. S. Eliot, "The Use of Poetry and the Use of Criticism," *Selected Prose*, ed. John Hayward (Harmondsworth, England, 1953), p. 95.
54. Samuel Taylor Coleridge, *Biographia Literaria* (London, 1910), p. 169.

repulsive victim of venereal disease contracted at Bankside, the Bishop of Winchester's domain.[55] Armstrong demonstrates the tenacity of this particular image as it finds new and apt companions in several clusters of images describing bitterness, restraint, sauce, and music.

Like Shakespeare, Keats spins a web of associated images and metaphors around his central theme: poetry and imagination. Keats's letter on "distilled prose," to John Hamilton Reynolds (February 19, 1818), suggests that the poet's "voyage of conception" indeed moves by a process of association. The reader recreates for himself the emotion and thought of the poet by perceiving the "fine circuiting" of related images and metaphors within the tapestry of the poem. It is important to note that the "Life of Sensations" accompanies the poet while he is circuiting. To return again to that famous letter to Bailey (November 22, 1817), Keats clearly defines the workings of associative imagination as a process of sudden, intuitive linkages between image and idea, made in the emotional heat of creativity:

the simple imaginative Mind may have its rewards in the repeti[ti]on of its own silent Working coming continually on the spirit with a fine suddenness—to compare great things with small—have you never by being surprised with an old Melody—in a delicious place—by a delicious voice, felt over again your very speculations and surmises at the time it first operated on your soul—do you not remember forming to yourself the singer's face more beautiful [than] it was possible and yet with the elevation of the Moment you did not think so—even then you were mounted on the Wings of Imagination.[56]

Image (melody) and idea (speculations and surmises) are reassociated in an emotional state which is identified as an "elevation," that is, imaginative creativity which comes when the pre-established association is revived. The "silent Working" of the associative mind revives the image linked to the felt thought "with a fine suddenness." At that moment the image has risen up to consciousness as it is recalled from the past by the memory, the mind's historian.

55. Edward A. Armstrong, *Shakespeare's Imagination* (London, 1946), p. 62. Armstrong relies on two important works for his study: Caroline Spurgeon's *Shakespeare's Imagery* (Boston, 1958) and C. K. Ogden and I. A. Richards' *The Meaning of Meaning* (New York, 1959).
56. *Letters*, I, 185.

The mind in imaginative activity draws to a fixity of concentration, which in prolonged trains of associative thinking becomes trance. The state is somewhat hypnotic; the restrictions of consciousness are removed, allowing the mind free association. Wordsworth has described the silent working of the associative mind as

> That serene and blessed mood,
> In which the affections gently lead us on,—
> Until, the breath of this corporeal frame
> And even the motion of our human blood
> Almost suspended, we are laid asleep
> In body, and become a living soul:
> While with an eye made quiet by the power
> Of harmony, and the deep power of joy,
> We see into the life of things....

Keats never tired of repeating verses from "Tintern Abbey." It seems to me that these are germinal lines in a study of his poems about poetry, for his method and themes consistently focus on sleep, release, and the imaginative perception of truth. Highly charged images and metaphors repeatedly describe the "blessed" state of "soul."

I have perhaps overemphasized the emotional state of the poet in the moments of travail; trance, semi-consciousness, unconsciousness, and dream are certainly concomitant with poetic composition, but one must not ignore the rational and discretionary powers of the poet, who consciously prunes and alters so as to bring his poem to a final order. Poets, it is true, create "what they understand not," but the rational mind must finally judge, detect flaws, and reshape what the font of imagination may have imperfectly gushed. Keats considers judgment as giving a final imprimatur to a poem: "things which [I] do half at Random are afterwards confirmed by my judgment in a dozen features of Propriety." [57]

Later he speaks of joining "random" (i.e., spontaneous and unguided) poetic creativity with judgment. He suggests that he composes on two levels of mind simultaneously, the emotive and intellective; that is to say, he creates in associative meditation, yet can have his judg-

57. *Ibid.*, p. 142.

ment at hand to censor any inappropriate material in his poem as he goes along.[58] He says of *Endymion*, realizing its inadequacy, its raggedness, and its indiscriminate profusion of language:

I have written independently *without Judgment*—I may write independently & *with judgment* hereafter. The Genius of Poetry must work out its own salvation in a man: It cannot be matured by law & precept, but by sensation & watchfulness in itself.[59]

He finds satisfaction in *Lamia* because his discretionary powers, in addition to his imagination, have wrought the poem finely: "I have great hopes of success, because I make use of my Judgment more deliberately than I yet have done." [60]

Clearly, two psychic levels appear to be working with one another in the creative process. The mind in association must be free of intellectual interference, yet the judgment seems able to impose itself on the train of thought and make swift modifications wherever necessary. Let us now turn to the products of such imaginative activity and see with what metaphors describing the creative process and poetry Keats loaded every rift of his subject.

58. Keats would agree with Coleridge, who, surprisingly reversing his claim that the creation of "Kubla Khan" was automatic, remarks that although he acknowledges the pre-eminence of poetic feeling, he "cannot suspend the judgment even for a moment. A poem may in one sense be a dream, but it must be a waking dream." See *Coleridge's Miscellaneous Criticism*, ed. Thomas M. Raysor (London, 1936), p. 162.

59. *Letters*, I, 374.   60. *Ibid.*, II, 128.

Chapter two

Woman as poetry — The moon and sexuality — Enthralment

Woman as poetry

"I know not why Poetry and I have been so distant lately; I must make some advances soon or she will cut me entirely." [1] Keats's identification of the poet as lover and of woman as poetry—with all the admixture of feeling associated with so supreme an emotion as love—should be considered as the central metaphor throughout most of his work. The letters assert that his only real life is the ardent pursuit of poetry. With the intensity and seriousness of an impassioned lover, he avows, "I cannot exist without Poetry"; [2] and of Shakespeare's plays and *Paradise Lost* he says, "I look upon fine Phrases like a Lover." [3] He acknowledges "the yearning Passion I have for the beautiful," [4] and repeatedly identifies himself as the swain of poesy, which is consistently characterized as feminine. [5] One might say therefore that his relationship with poetry takes on all the attributes of a love affair. That amour is, however, no casual pursuit, but a total commitment in which he invests his life and emotions with almost the same ardor as the sublunary lover in quest of a real woman. Indeed, until Fanny Brawne enters Keats's life, poetry commands his deepest emotional attention. He apparently visualizes

---

1. *Letters*, II, 74.
2. *Ibid.*, I, 133.
3. *Ibid.*, II, 139.
4. *Ibid.*, I, 404.
5. "Maiden-Thought," for example, is poetry of simple, unthinking delight, the sensations found in "I stood tip-toe" and other early poems. We remember too the artful, feminine spider weaving her own "tapestry empyrean," whereby "*she* fills the Air with a beautiful circuiting" (*ibid.*, p. 232).

poetry as an evanescent, incredibly beautiful form when he says, "The faint conceptions I have of Poems to come brings the blood frequently into my forehead." [6]

It is not difficult to understand why Keats would choose the passion of love for a woman as his basic metaphor for poetry. Archetypally, the woman is the visible form of earthly beauty, whose presence arouses man's sensibility to supernal beauty. Recalling his idea that intense sensation (by which he meant both emotional and sensory experience) is the necessary prerequisite for poetry—"this . . . excitement in me is the only state for the best sort of poetry"—we understand that passionate love for a woman is a precise objective correlative for an excited, essentially poetic state, enabling the poet to transcend the world and to achieve the realm of Beauty-Truth. The famous letter to Bailey carefully singles out love over all other emotions: "I have the same Idea of all our Passions as of Love they are all in their sublime, creative of essential Beauty." [7]

Keats's consistent connection of the lover with the poet, both of whom are capable of intense imagination, is by no means original, but rooted in literary tradition. The analogue is brilliantly adapted and takes on wider significance when traced to its several sources. Shakespeare perhaps provided the major source of the metaphor, specifically A *Midsummer Night's Dream*, V. i. 7 (which Keats heavily underscored): "The Lunatic, the lover and the poet / Are of imagination all compact." In his romantic comedies, Shakespeare continually refers to "fancy," a word having the double meaning of projecting our visions or imaginings, and of falling in love. In *Twelfth Night*, for example, we find the ambiguous lines, "So full of shapes is fancy / That it alone is high-fantastical," meaning that the passion of love is so full of imagination that it is replete with fantasies. The poet's imagination, therefore, feeds on love and thrives. Claude L. Finney claims that Keats's equation of love with poetry may derive from *Love's Labours Lost*: [8]

> But love, first learned in a lady's eyes,
> Lives not alone immured in the brain,
> But with the motion of all elements,

6. *Ibid.*, pp. 387–388.　　　　　　　　7. *Ibid.*, p. 184.
8. Claude L. Finney, *The Evolution of Keats's Poetry* (Cambridge, Mass., 1936), I, 315–316.

Courses as swift as thought in every power,
And gives to every power a double power,
Above their functions and their offices.
It adds a precious seeing to the eye....

(IV. iii. 327–333).

Keats perhaps found a great degree of personal relevance in Biron's advice: "Never durst poet touch a pen to write / Until his ink were tempered with love's sighs" (346–347).

We find yet another source in Petrarch, referred to directly in "Sleep and Poetry." The poet's love for Laura provides the origins of poetic inspiration:

Petrarch, outstepping from the shady green,
Starts at the sight of Laura; nor can wean
His eyes from her sweet face. Most happy they!
For over them was seen a free display
Of out-spread wings, and from between them shone
The face of Poesy....[9]

The tradition of identifying poetry as love appears also in Spenser. The poet calls Elizabeth Boyle his "helicon" in the first sonnet of *Amoretti*, suggesting that imagination and poetry derive from inspiring gushes of passion. *Amoretti* is not merely focused on Spenser's earthly passion, but also on his imagination, which is symbolized by a woman. Keats's in-depth reading of Spenser, as well as Shakespeare, offered him a metaphorical convention which he modified to his own needs. The evident difference between his treatment of love as poetry and that of the Renaissance writers is that woman serves, not occasionally but rather consistently, as a metaphor for poetry.

Milton, in providing yet another source for Keats's basic metaphor, offers a helpful clue in identifying woman as the imparter of the highest poetic inspiration. The muse spoken of in the early lines of several books of *Paradise Lost* was the agent of the loftiest visionary poetry,

---

9. Ll. 389–394. The edition used is *The Poetical Works of John Keats*, ed. H. W. Garrod (2nd ed.; Oxford, 1958). Hereinafter, references to lines of poetry will be noted in parentheses within the text.

admired profoundly by the young Keats. Milton celebrates the visitation
of Urania, calling her

> ... my celestial patroness, who deigns
> Her nightly visitation unimplored,
> And dictates to me slumbering, or inspires
> Easy my unpremeditated verse. . . .
>
> (IX, 21–24)

The reality of such imaginative moments, as Maud Bodkin points out
in *Archetypal Patterns in Poetry*, forces the poet to represent his poetic
experience: "The access of power or inspiration is attributed to a figure
related both to the muse mother or Orpheus and to that wisdom that
had part in the cosmic mystery of creation." [10]

And lastly, to bring the tradition down to Keats's time, we note that
Wordsworth is conscious of the baleful effect on the poet-lover when
the muse in nature absents herself:

> The Poet, gentle creature as he is,
> Hath, like the Lover, his unruly times;
> His fits when he is neither sick nor well,
> Though no distress be near him but his own
> Unmanageable thoughts. . . .
>
> (*Prelude*, I, 135–139)

In summary, then, Keats's statement that the passion of love is creative
of essential beauty stands in a firmly rooted poetic tradition of which
he was consciously aware and, indeed, which he worked meaningfully
and subtly into his poetry.

The paean to love in the introduction to Book II of *Endymion* points
to the meaning of the poem in its suggestion that the presence of love
occasions the release of poetry:

> O sovereign power of love! O grief! O balm!
> All records, saving thine, come cool, and calm
> And shadowy, through the mist of passed years:
> For others, good or bad, hatred and tears
> Have become indolent; but touching thine,
> One sigh doth echo, one poor sob doth pine,
> One kiss brings honey-dew from buried days. . . .

10. Maud Bodkin, *Archetypal Patterns in Poetry* (New York, 1961), p. 150.

A sigh, a sob, and a kiss revive the "records" of past emotions of love, the "records" being poetry of the romance. Love serves as the poet's guide, leading him to beauty wherever it may be found:

> O Love! how potent hast thou been to teach
> Strange journeyings! Wherever beauty dwells,
> In gulf or aerie, mountains or deep dells,
> In light, in gloom, in star or blazing sun,
> Thou pointest out the way, and straight 'tis won. . . .
>
> (III, 92–96)

Since love is "creative of essential beauty," or poetry, Keats's heroes, accordingly, are lovers who, in embarking on amatory experience, "tread . . . the path of love *and* poesy" (II, 36, 38). "I stood tip-toe" describes Endymion as "a poet, sure a lover too" (193). Lycius in *Lamia* and the knight-at-arms in "La Belle Dame sans Merci" are also lovers pursuing poetry, as I shall have occasion to demonstrate later.

Necessarily, then, the basic idea of the poet as lover has strong consequences for the imagery in many of Keats's poems about poetry; this imagery, it will be seen, is essentially sexual.

The early poems directly characterize the imagination as a woman. "Sleep and Poetry" offers the most explicit example in the lines, "As she was wont, th' imagination / Into most lovely labyrinths will be gone" (265–266). The same poem describes "Poesy" as "might" and "the supreme of power," yet gently feminine:

> The very archings of her eye-lids charm
> A thousand willing agents to obey,
> And still she governs with the mildest sway.
>
> (238–240)

The "shapes of delight" and the "lovely wreath of girls" (138, 149), sweeping across Keats's vision most enchantingly "as they would chase / Some ever-fleeting music" (140–141), can thus be identified as muses. Keats is here following classical tradition in identifying the muses, the inspirers of poetic vision, as women. They reappear later in the poem as the attendants, if not the governors, of spontaneous music to quicken Keats's poetic imagination. The linkage of women and music generally recurs as a part of his perception of essential beauty. He says,

> Scarce can I scribble on; for lovely airs
> Are fluttering round the room like doves in pairs; [11]
> Many delights of that glad day recalling,
> When first my senses caught their tender falling.
> And with these airs come forms of elegance
> Stooping their shoulders....
>
> (327–332)

Keats is less certain in other poems that the feminine imagination will favor him with song. The epistle "To My Brother George" expresses anxiety that "the bright glance from beauty's eyelids slanting" may not honor him by making "a lay of [his] enchanting / Or warm [his] breast with ardour" (15–17). "To George Felton Mathew" expresses hope that he and his fellow poet, Mathew, "may greet the maid— / Where we may soft humanity put on / And sit, and rhyme and think on Chatterton" (54–56). At the end of this poem the maid appropriately becomes a Naiad, inspiring Mathew with her "daily food," which he kisses from her "pearly hands." In a similar manner, "To Some Ladies" presents the muses as nymphs, stingily imparting inspiration; like Cynthia, "the enthusiast's friend," they have the power to instil poetic fervor in the poet.

The later poetry, as well, straightforwardly characterizes the imagination as feminine. The lissome fancy is addressed as "a mistress to thy mind" ("Fancy," 80). Keats very deftly explains in *Lamia* why he must present the insubstantial imagination as a woman; he does so in order to avoid the dullness of abstract and literal language which plagued Wordsworth and other poets who failed to find the proper organizing metaphor in writing poems about poetry and imagination. One of the last poems suggests how tenaciously he held his early metaphor for poetry, a beautiful woman:

> There is not such a treat among them all,
> Haunters of cavern, lake, and waterfall,
> As a real woman, lineal indeed
> From Pyrrha's pebbles, or old Adam's seed.
> Thus gentle Lamia judg'd and judg'd aright,

11. These lines may be a clever reference to the beauty of the very couplets which Keats uses in "Sleep and Poetry."

That Lycius could not love in half a fright,
So threw the goddess off, and won his heart
More pleasantly by playing woman's part,
With no more awe than what her beauty gave. . . .

(I, 330–338)

Similarly, Mnemosyne and Moneta in the "Hyperion" fragments, La
Belle Dame sans Merci, and Psyche play the woman's part of the poetic
imagination. Like Lamia, Mnemosyne moves invisibly to all but the
poet, who sees her as "the supreme shape" (*Hyperion*, III, 61). Moneta,
of "accent feminine" (*The Fall of Hyperion*, I, 215), is cast as the
stepmother of Apollo and, therefore, the arch-muse or "prophetess" of
poets. She is to be distinguished from the merely coy and mute forms
of loveliness of earlier poetry by virtue of her role as a sage, warning the
poet that he no longer be a dreamer, but a "humanist, physician to all
men" (90). And Psyche, the feminine soul of imagination and a fallen
goddess like Mnemosyne and Moneta, provides a more indirect yet
still considerable influence on the poet, who resolves to worship her
memory in poetry.

These feminine muses, however, cannot be actively solicited by the
poet-lover. In "To George Felton Mathew" the poet frets, "How vain
for me the niggard muse to tease"; yet for Mathew "she will [his] every
dwelling grace." The uncertainty of the poetic visitation constitutes a
part of the poet's fear in "When I have fears," for the "fair creature of an
hour" promises no constancy. She alone guarantees power of "unreflecting
love," or noncontemplative, spontaneous emotion which Keats prescribes
for the best sort of poetry. But his flirtation with poetry often fails to
move the coy muse to respond. In "To George Felton Mathew" the
"fine-eyed maid" is not easily attainable. Such fickleness is like the inconstancy of the changing moon, which in fact becomes a favorite
metaphor for the fickle imagination.

The moon and sexuality

Keats calls the moon the "maker of sweet poets" ("I stood tip-toe,"
116) for an apparent, though generally overlooked, reason. The moon,
or Cynthia, is the sister of Phoebus Apollo, the god of poetry, music,

and eloquence, whose powers Keats attributes to her. We can understand his purpose in making Cynthia the ministering spirit of poetry;
if he is to maintain the basic metaphors which had dominated his earliest poetry—the poet as lover and feminine presences as imparters of
poetic inspiration—Cynthia must succeed to Apollo's throne.

In seeking Cynthia's presence, the poet-lover in *Endymion* and other
poems hopes to assume her Apollonian imagination and perhaps even
raise himself to an "immortality of passion" (II, 808). But she is not
easily confronted; she waxes and wanes with an inconstancy befitting the
uncertain imagination, and for want of more regular visitations Endymion
becomes lunatic. In addition, Cynthia's natural reticence remains a
further hindrance to the poet, who must actively overcome it by persistent invocation in order to achieve her gift of inspiration. Endymion,
"the wanderer by moonlight," becomes the ideal poet in "I stood tip-
toe," for at rare moments he (as well as the earthly poet) is brought
"shapes from the invisible world, unearthly singing" (186), i.e., poetry
itself, by the archmuse Cynthia. The effect of the moon's presence on
the poet is clearly inspirational in "To Charles Cowden Clarke," she
being central in a cluster of delights:

> When Cynthia smiles upon a summer's night
>
> .   .   .   .
>
> No sooner had I stepp'd into these pleasures
> Than I began to think of rhymes and measures. . . .
>
> (93, 97–98)

Because of her benevolent, if periodic, influence, Endymion apostro-
phizes the moon:

> And I grew in years, still didst thou blend
> With all my ardours: thou wast . . .
>
> .   .   .   .
>
> . . . my topmost deed:—
> Thou wast the charm of woman, lovely Moon!
> O what a wild and harmonized tune
> My spirit struck from all the beautiful!
> On some bright essence could I lean, and lull
> Myself to immortality. . . .
>
> (*Endymion*, III, 162–163, 168–173)

His "topmost deed" is the creative, poetic act, made possible only by Cynthia's influence, if not her presence. Since she signifies the generative force behind poetry, the poet-lover resolves to write poems about her divine power to inspire. In this same address to the moon, Endymion voices what we understand to be Keats's own aim, writing poems about poetry and imagination:

> No one but thee hath heard me blithely sing
>
> . . . .
> No melody was like a passing spright
> If it went not to solemnize thy reign.
>
> (156, 158–159)

Cynthia's dominion over poetry or "melody" is to be solemnized almost exclusively, for she alone has heard him sing; and she alone will remain his theme. We may therefore consider this passage as expressive of Keats's primary poetic intention.

With chaste and retiring demeanor, Cynthia sits queenlike on "her throne . . . most meek and most alone" (III, 45–46), a description of her royalty made previously in "I stood tip-toe," where she is hailed "Queen of the wide air; thou most lovely queen" (205). In "Sleep and Poetry" we find "the face of Poesy" as yet another instance of the feminine moon shining imperially and approvingly between Petrarch and Laura: "from off her throne / She overlook'd things that I scarce could tell" (394–395), as Keats reverently admits. With these three passages in mind, we can now be certain that Keats means to figure Cynthia, in all her regality, as poetry.

The three main characteristics of Cynthia as a metaphor for the poetic imagination, namely, her inconstancy, meekness, and royalty, recur in the later poems, but with altered meaning. "Ode on Indolence" presents a state of languor directly opposite to imaginative frenzy. The poet cares nothing now for the mercurial changes of feeling which the creation of poetry excites, and especially the eventual, sapping effect of such activity; he wants not to know the waxing and waning of the moon, that is to say, of poetry:

> For Poesy!—no,—she has not a joy,—
> At least for me,—so sweet as drowsy noons,
>
> . . . .

O, for an age so shelter'd from annoy,
That I may never know how change the moons.

(45–46, 48–49)

If the speaker in the ode clearly desires to avoid the influence of the moon, or "the passion poesy" (a phrase describing the moon in *Endymion*, I, 29), he consciously wills to ascend to the sovereign realm of "the Queen-Moon" in "Ode to a Nightingale." Unhappily, he fails in his attempt. We see in these two odes, then, the inability of the infirm, constrained poet to touch the royal imagination; between the writing of *Endymion* and the writing of these odes, clearly, something has altered Keats's attitude toward poetry and the power of imagination.

The recurrent association of the luminescent moon with poetic imagination appears later in *Lamia*. Lamia's compelling influence upon Lycius has its unmistakable parallel in Cynthia's domination of Endymion; like Cynthia, she is crescented with "silver moons" (*Lamia*, I, 51), and charged with a "dazzling hue."[12] Moreover, like the moon goddess, she is royal in appearance, "regal dressed" (II, 133), when enthroned with her lover in a palace ambiguously described as "sweet-sin." Her royalty is further and more subtly suggested in the reference to her "azure vein[s]," an attribute not unlike Cynthia's "more bluely vein'd, more soft, more whitely sweet" majesty (*Endymion*, I, 625).

She can also be identified with Cynthia in her meekness toward the mortal poet, Lycius. In Part I of *Lamia*, he is enthroned with his Queen-Moon and experiences a fulfilment unknown to the equally aspiring, but mortal, poet in "Ode to a Nightingale." And although Lamia's ability to inspire vision in her favorite is also like Cynthia's, her equal reign with Lycius leads to his eventual tyranny over her and, paradoxically, to her destruction of him. This fate is unknown to Endymion because the

---

12. Wasserman has noted this similarity in *The Finer Tone*, p. 166. Keats obviously means to invest Lamia with the attributes of Cynthia, although when Lycius calls Lamia "my silver planet both of eve and morn" (II, 48), the suggestion is that she be identified with Venus, the love-goddess, and not merely the staid and chaste Cynthia. Lemprière's description of Diana, another name for Cynthia, provides a positive clue in identifying her with Lamia; she is a goddess "generally known in the figures that represent her by the crescent on her head. . . ." (J. Lemprière, *Bibliothela Classica* [Dublin, 1792], see "Diana.") Keats's reading of Lemprière was close and thorough, as this and other footnotes suggest. Of all the sources from which he culled classical myth, this dictionary is undoubtedly the richest.

moon, or imagination, though inconstant and meek, is finally the poet's salvation rather than his ruin.

It should be evident by now that the moon assumes a central position in Keats's poems about poetry by virtue of its possessing several metaphorical values, the most important of which is its sexual influence upon the poet. Special notice must be taken of the feminine moon's power to fertilize the earth and its poets. In this regard we must credit Keats with being particularly aware of the traditional association of the cycles of the moon with human fertility.[13] As Cynthia waxes, so do the poet's own fecund powers of imagination. The earth, bathed in the light of common day, is totally changed when she arrives to "bless everywhere, with silver lip / Kissing dead things to life" (*Endymion*, III, 56–57). Endymion eagerly awaits her presence, for poetic creation (put in terms of sexual conception) depends upon her. He avows that

> In sowing time ne'er would I dibble take,
> Or drop a seed, till thou wast wide awake;
> And, in the summer tide of blossoming,
> No one but thee hath heard me blithely sing. . . .
>
> (153–156)

"Sowing time" suggests the period of imaginative fertility that leads to song; the poet's "seed," or germ of poetic conception, grows by an organic process and blossoms into song. It is therefore quite apparent why Endymion identifies Cynthia with Ceres: both goddesses have powers of creativity to be bestowed upon the poet possessed of a "constant spell" (III, 24). Elevated to the ethereal realm of primary creation, he is able to "watch the abysm-birth of elements" (28). In this realm of what Coleridge calls "the infinite I AM,"

> A thousand Powers keep religious state,
> In water, fiery realm, and airy bourne;
> And, silent as a consecrated urn,
> Hold sphery sessions for a season due.

13. Originally the Greek moon goddess, Artemis, influenced erotic and organic life, as well as childbirth. These roles were not wholly obscured by the Homeric modifications of older myths; mythographers identify her contrasting roles of virgin huntress and patroness of chastity, and goddess of childbirth.

Yet few of these far majesties, ah, few!
Have bared their operations to this globe—
Few, who with gorgeous pageantry enrobe
Our piece of heaven—whose benevolence
Shakes hand with our own Ceres; every sense
Filling with spiritual sweets to plenitude. . . .

(30–39)

Keats is talking here of the rare poet blessed with the power of entering the realm of the primary imagination (where the "abysm-birth of elements" takes place) at the times when Cynthia's waxing is strongest. Ceres and Tellus (III, 71) are but earthly equivalents of these heavenly gods of creativity, such as the moon, whose powers are comparable to the infinite fecundity of the poetic imagination. Cynthia alone allows it to be released; of all the divinely creative powers she is "the gentlier-mightiest" (43), for she "bare[s]" to the poet the divine "operations" of primary creation. She is, metaphorically, the supernal imagination who, like Ceres, fills every human sense "with spiritual sweets to plenitude." And because Cynthia causes sense and soul to teem, the poet, Endymion, swears that "by the feud 'twixt Nothing and Creation" (which through Cynthia's help he has just witnessed) she is "the mightiest fair" (41, 43), for she allows the poet to perform a like, secondary act of creating from nothing by fertilizing his seeds of imagination "in sowing time."

How then does the poet put on the poetic knowledge which Cynthia and her feminine counterparts possess? The concept of the "chameleon poet" pursuing a life of sensory experience offers us an answer to the question. Keats suggests that the poet by identifying himself with the object he contemplates and projecting himself into it so that he has "no identity" is finally united with it. That is to say, the more intense the poet's perception of the object of beauty—and we have established that for Keats a woman is the supreme embodiment of beauty—the more stimulated is his sympathetic imagination through the most intense form of sensory experience, sexual love. The "chameleon poet" completely loses his "self" and is elevated to the heights of imaginative activity. The sexual act in Keats's poems therefore figures the ultimate imaginative intensity and is consequently "creative of essential beauty." The frenzied creative act of the poet finds its fit analogue in sexual union, where the woman, playing the part of the imagination, *conceives*, bestowing her knowledge upon the aroused poet at the supreme moment. The union of poet and woman, the one providing passion and the other providing imagination, figures the creative act, wherein poetry is born. Complete loss of self and achievement of unity with his imagination allow the poet to command universal knowledge; Truth and Beauty are reached in the few moments of sexual-imaginative experience.

For fuller understanding of this spectacular metaphor an account of its origin and adaptation needs to be made before tracing its development throughout the poetry. Keats was influenced, in all probability, by a key section of verse in the Preface to *The Excursion*, a poem which he admired as one of "three things superior in the modern world." [14] A part of his admiration undoubtedly stems from its example of metaphor, which suggested how he himself might be able to continue to talk about poetry in his poems and yet avoid the untoward diffuseness and directness of early poems such as "I stood tip-toe." In his Preface Wordsworth suggests the necessity of the poet to wed his mind to the external universe in order to arrive at truth. The product of such fruitful mental intercourse he terms his "spousal verse," a figure which Keats seized upon and dramatized in *Endymion* by making Endymion the poet, and Cynthia the imagination or "empyreal mind." The metaphor of sexual wedding of the poet's imagination with nature, the issue being poetic truth, is expressed by Wordsworth as follows:

> . . . the discerning intellect of Man,
> When wedded to this goodly universe
> In love and holy passion, shall find these
> A simple produce of the common day.
> —I, long before the blissful hour arrives,
> Would chant, in lonely peace, the spousal verse
> Of this great consummation:—and, by words
> Which speak of nothing more than what we are,
> Would I arouse the sensual from their sleep
> Of Death, and win the vacant and the vain
> To noble raptures; while my voice proclaims

---

14. *Letters*, I, 204.

How exquisitely the individual Mind
(And the progressive powers perhaps no less
Of the whole species) to the external World
Is fitted:—and how exquisitely, too—
Theme this but little heard of among men—
The external World is fitted to the Mind
And the creation (by no lower name
Can it be called) which they with blended might
Accomplish:—this is our high argument. . . .[15]

Wordsworth's gathering, sexual metaphor, in which the wedding, consummation, and creation are parts of the poetic process, is changed by Keats to a greater level of indirection by making the empyreal, imaginative mind a woman, and the "spousal verse" the result of sexual union.[16]

Prefiguring the recurrent metaphor of sexual union as fertile imaginative experience (which appears in *Endymion* and later poems), "Sleep and Poetry" introduces Keats's poetic intentions in uncommonly subtle sexual terms:

O for ten years, that I may overwhelm
Myself in poesy; so I may do the deed
That my own soul has to itself decreed.

. . . .

Catch the white-handed nymphs in shady places,
To woo sweet kisses from averted faces,—
Play with their fingers, touch their shoulders white
Into a pretty shrinking with a bite
As hard as lips can make it: till agreed,
A lovely tale of human life we'll read.

. . . .

Another will entice me on, and on

. . . .

15. "Preface to the Edition of 1814 of *The Excursion*," *Poetical Works*, V, 4–5.
16. Keats's use of the sexual act as a metaphor for poetic creation seems consistent with the Romantic poets' quest for unity. Thus, hermaphroditism in Shelley's poetry, Wordsworth's wedding of the human mind with nature, and Coleridge's concept that the imagination reconciles opposites are identifiable with Keats's metaphor of sexuality; all attempt to describe that oneness perceived in supreme imaginative vision. Keats's quest for unity uses sex not as an end, but rather as a means to that end; for the issue of passion is poetry and vision.

> Till in the bosom of a leafy world
> We rest in silence, like two gems upcurl'd
> In the recesses of a pearly shell. . . .
>
> (96–98, 105–110, 117, 119–121)

There is a strong, though unapparent, relationship between the first three lines of this passage and the final nine lines: Keats desires to immerse ("overwhelm") himself completely in "Poesy" in the same manner that he would like to plunge himself, sexually, in the "white-handed nymphs." His identification of the act of writing poetry with sexual activity is further suggested in his curiously ambiguous phrase "do the deed," [17] which overtly means "perform the poetic act," and, covertly, "to have sexual intercourse." The last nine lines of this passage, therefore, metaphorically dramatize the statement of poetic intention in the first three lines; that is to say, sexual pursuit represents poetic pursuit.

Scenes of flirtation, suggestions of sexual play, and final consummation ("In the recesses of a pearly shell") recur in *Endymion* and even later in "Ode to Psyche." Almost every sexual encounter in *Endymion* involves some sort of "lovely tale of human life," or truth, a tale mysteriously and passionately uttered by Cynthia (whom we have seen investing the earth with her fertile power) during and after sexual union.

The "pleasure thermometer" passage of Book I of *Endymion* prepares us for a further understanding of Keats's sexual metaphor. Poetic fulfilment comprises a series of sensory intensities annihilating the self and leading to love and friendship.

> . . . there are
> Richer entanglements, enthralments far
> More self-destroying, leading, by degrees,
> To the chief intensity: the crown of these
> Is made of love and friendship. . . .
>
> (797–801)

"Fellowship with essence" describes the state of buoyancy "like a floating spirit's," whereby the poet achieves "a sort of oneness." At the

---

17. This phrase is a manifest Cockneyism, used in the low idiom then as today. Keats might have found justification in using it after example in Shakespeare, where the expression is used freely. See Eric Partridge, *Shakespeare's Bawdy* (New York, 1960), p. 103.

supreme peak of winged, spiritual communion, the poet draws nourishment from love:

> . . . at the tip-top,
> There hangs by unseen film, an orbed drop
> Of light, and that is love: its influence
> Thrown in our eyes, genders a novel sense,
> At which we start and fret; till in the end,
> Melting into its radiance, we blend,
> Mingle, and so become a part of it,—
> Nor with aught else can our souls interknit
> So wingedly: when we combine therewith,
> Life's self is nourish'd by its proper pith,
> And we are nurtured like a pelican brood.
> Aye, so delicious is the unsating food,
> That men . . .
>
> . . . .
>
> . . . wipe away all slime . . .
>
> . . . .
>
> Whilst they did sleep in love's Elysium. . . .
>
> (805–817, 820, 823)

The sexual connotations of "entanglements," "melting," "blend," "mingle," "interknit," "combine," and "sleep" become apparent when we realize that the "tip-top drop of light . . . that is love" is yet another metaphor for Cynthia, or poetry, both having been described elsewhere as light-giving: in his first dream, Endymion describes the moon as soaring "so passionately bright" that his soul is "dazzled" (II, 594); "Sleep and Poetry" characterizes poesy as "a drainless shower / Of light" (235–236); Endymion himself "cons / Sweet poesy by moonlight" (I, 369), whose influence is clearly inspirational. Since Cynthia is the vessel of light and love, the poet's act of blending or melting into her serves as Keats's basic metaphor describing imaginative or poetic fulfilment; in attaining supreme sexual intensity, the poet is "nourished by [her] proper pith," which is "the unsating food" of extreme imaginative power providing the poet with vision and giving him words and music to record that vision. Like the legendary pelican brood feeding on its mother's blood, the poet is nourished by the very "pith," or vital, creative interior of life, which Keats leads us to understand is the fertile womb of imaginative power possessed by Cynthia. In a related manner of figurative expression revealing the interdependency of head and heart in the creative soul, Keats writes to the George Keatses on April 21, 1819, "The Heart . . . is the teat from which the Mind or intelligence sucks its identity." In thus maintaining his metaphor of the poetic mind as a suckling nourished from the seat of love, that is, the heart, he provides a clue to the proper interpretation of the lines in the "pleasure thermometer" section of *Endymion*, "Life's self is nourish'd by its proper pith": the poetic mind fulfils itself through love.

The "pleasure thermometer" section should be read as a statement in sexual terms of imaginative fulfilment; further, it helps to define recurrent acts of sexuality in *Endymion* and other poems. The union of Keats's poet-lovers with Cynthia, Lamia, Psyche, or Circe, who are the agents of inspiration, quickens the poets' latent capacity for poetic creativity; music, or poetry, is indeed the food of love. For example, the culmination of Endymion's dream-union with Cynthia in Book I suggests that the "unsating food" which she provides is similar to the fruits of supreme imaginative activity:[18]

> I was distracted; madly did I kiss
> The wooing arms which held me, and did give
> My eyes at once to death: but 'twas to live,
> To take in draughts of life from the gold fount
> Of kind and passionate looks; to count, and count
> The moments, by some greedy help that seem'd
> A second self, that each might be redeem'd
> And plunder'd of its load of blessedness. . . .
>
> (653–660)

18. I am in agreement with Stuart M. Sperry in his doctoral dissertation (Harvard, 1959), "The Concept of the Imagination in Keats's Narrative Poems," (published in part as "The Allegory of 'Endymion,' " *Studies in Romanticism*, II [1962], 38–53), where he effectively debates the exclusiveness of Finney's Neo-Platonic thesis and Newell Ford's interpretation of *Endymion* as the pursuit of eroticism. He correctly interprets the sexual metaphor as imaginative activity and is aware of the inspiration which Cynthia provides. He sees Cynthia as Endymion's unconscious passions given release; but in his attempt to perceive thematic unity in *Endymion*, he pays insufficient attention to important metaphors clustering around the erotic passages in recurrent patterns and giving these passages their particular character as acts of the creation of poetry. These metaphors then, demand a more thorough analysis than Sperry has been able to make. Since he is limited to four long narrative poems, he has little opportunity to extend his observations to the shorter works (see pp. 32, 46–47 of the dissertation).

Sexual union immediately results in "draughts" from the font of imagination;[19] the poet counts the "moments" or periods, both temporal and poetic, by which the active imagination allows truth to be realized in form, that is to say, in metrical regularity. Endymion's "moments" of poetic knowledge, imparted by his teeming, feminine imagination, are as brief and precious as his concomitant sexual fulfilment. Raised to the heights of sexual-imaginative experience, he finds himself capable of a spontaneous overflow of divine speech which Cynthia controls and allows to be "plundered." In Endymion's dream in Book II, for example, his wedding with Cynthia, which represents the union of the mortal poet with the divine imagination, leads to "words" that fountain forth from the lips of both:

> These lovers did embrace . . .
>
> . . . .
>
> Long time in silence did their anxious fears
> Question that thus it was; long time they lay
> Fondling and kissing every doubt away;
> Long time ere soft caressing sobs began
> To mellow into words, and then there ran
> Two bubbling springs of talk from their sweet lips.
> O known Unknown! from whom my being sips
> Such darling essence. . . .
>
> (730, 733–740)

Endymion's act of drinking in Cynthia's "essence," in this context meaning her vitalizing words, should recall the important lines in the "pleasure thermometer" passage—"Life's self is nourish'd by its proper pith." In both instances the poet is wholly inspired. Sexual love leads to the creation of "essential beauty" (i.e., the "darling essence" of "talk" or poetry), as Cynthia's final promise in the dream-tryst of Book II suggests:

> . . . I vow an endless bliss,
> An immortality of passion's thine.
>
> . . . .

---

19. Unconscious imaginative activity, metaphorized by the "gold fount," should remind us of "Kubla Khan" and its fountain "momently forced." This reservoir of power, the "second self," Sperry has perceptively interpreted as the unconscious mind (see *ibid.*, p. 28).

And I will tell thee stories of the sky,
And breathe thee whispers of its minstrelsy
My happy love will overwing all bounds!
O let me melt into thee; let the sounds
Of our close voices marry at their birth;
Let us entwine hoveringly—O dearth
Of human words! roughness of mortal speech!
Lispings empyrean will I sometimes teach
Thine honied tongue—lute-breathings, which I gasp
To have thee understand, now while I clasp
Thee thus. . . .

(807–808, 812–822)

The crudeness of speech in the mortal, and therefore deficient, poet is corrected by the marriage of his voice with Cynthia's; passionate utterance, a blending of her "lute breathings" and the poet's "roughness of mortal speech," is therefore the child of sexual love. His perfect melting into the supernal imagination provides him with a "honied tongue" after example of her "lispings empyrean." Physical union again figures the passionate genesis of poetry; melting and intertwining allow the poet to put on divine knowledge in poetic form, i.e., in "lispings empyrean." Cynthia's love clasp is a fertilizing, productive act releasing the lovers' otherwise mute and perhaps inarticulate "sounds" to "marry at their birth."

We may now understand more fully the important lines which end the "pleasure thermometer" section of Book I; love is not to be pursued as "the chief intensity" for its own sake, but rather as it leads to "richer entanglements, enthralments far / More self destroying," or in other words, the sexual-imaginative encounter (an "entanglement") leads to the richest union of divine and human utterance—what Coleridge would call the "mingled measure," or poetry.

In addition to connoting physical involvement and verbal union, the word "entanglements" also suggests psychic perplexity; "enthralments" underscores this tertiary meaning. Both words point to the spellbound state into which love and imaginative creativity cast the poet; his rational, conscious mind is overborne by the feminine, seductive imagination as she clasps the poet in an impassioned, beatific embrace. In imparting poetic inspiration to her poet-lover, Cynthia may be compared to the unthinking, spontaneous nightingale.

> . . . upperched high,
> And cloister'd among cool and bunched leaves—
> She sings but to her love, nor e'er conceives
> How tiptoe Night holds back her dark-grey hood.
> *Just so say love, although 'tis understood*
> *The mere commingling of passionate breath,*
> Produce more than our searching witnesseth. . . .

(I, 828–834; italics mine)

The italicized lines perhaps most clearly reveal passion as an analogue for poetic inspiration. *Endymion* assuredly is not concerned with sexual passion as an end in itself, but rather as a means of allowing the poet-lover to experience Cynthia's passionate breath:

> . . . wherefore may I not
> Be ever in these arms? in this sweet spot
> Pillow my chin for ever? ever press
> These toying hands and kiss their smooth excess?
> Why not for ever and for ever feel
> That breath about my eyes? . . .[20]

(II, 740–745)

The two passages above are typical of the manner in which the poet-lovers receive poetic inspiration. As a metaphor for poetic inspiration, sexual union with a muse contrasts sharply with Wordsworth's unspectacular figurative description of the poet's moment of imaginative feeling. The Wordsworthian poet receives his inspiration from nature asexually and half-passively, usually from a "correspondent breeze." Keats's metaphor is archetypal[21] but not characteristic of Romantic poetry, for among the other poets inspiration had rarely been represented in sexual terms. Keats, however, actually does conform to the romantic tradition of using "the correspondent breeze" as a metaphor for what M. H. Abrams calls "a persistent Romantic analogue of the poetic mind," [22] but it is invariably so disguised or buried in an ostensibly erotic

20. These lines compare closely with the "Bright Star" sonnet, which may also be read as a poem about poetic inspiration.

21. See Bodkin, pp. 148–210.

22. For full discussions of this metaphor in Wordsworth and Coleridge, see M. H. Abrams, "The Correspondent Breeze: A Romantic Metaphor," *English Romantic Poets: Modern Essays in Criticism* (New York, 1960), pp. 37–54, and *The Mirror and the Lamp* (New York, 1960), pp. 187–198.

context that its real meaning is missed by even the best of critics. The allusiveness of this metaphor is no less diminished in Keats's other metaphors for poetry, as I shall have occasion to suggest.

Enthralment

The sexual-imaginative encounters of Keats's poet-lovers are "enthralling" in two senses of the word: they are both charmed and enslaved. We have seen the beneficent effects of sexual union between Endymion and Cynthia, and between the poet and the maiden-muses in the early poetry: such union leads to golden fountains of speech, music, truth, and finally, for Endymion, immortality. Yet Endymion's passionate bliss is not without its ill effects, since it is transitory. Cynthia's final words, ending her long marriage of body and breath with him, pronounce an attendant distress:

> . . . I am pain'd,
> Endymion: woe! woe! is grief contain'd
> In the very deeps of pleasure, my sole life? . . .[23]
>   (II, 822–824)

Grief assuredly lodges in the boll of pleasure, just as melancholy shares the "temple of Delight" with Joy (i.e., pleasure) and Beauty. He who has the ability to experience with a "palate fine" and a "strenuous tongue" must also taste melancholy as sensory pleasure vanishes. And since sensory pleasure attends imaginative experience,[24] as we have already seen, it follows that pain must be an inevitable part of the poetic process in its waning stages. Poetry and pain are inextricably bound together. Further, we note that beauty, melancholy, and joy are addressed as feminine and that just as the poet's soul has tasted of each—and most intensely of "melancholy's might"—so too has Endymion tasted, sexually, Cynthia's "sweet soul to the core"; "all other depths are shallow" to him thereafter (II, 904–905).

Since Keats regards poetic intensity as painful, because evanescent,

23. Sperry has noted the parallel with "Ode on Melancholy" but has not pursued its implications. See "The Concept of the Imagination . . . ," p. 49.
24. This idea is subtly implied in the ode. The palate and tongue are the origins of the gustatory sense and also of utterance—poetic and musical.

he uses desertion and lovesickness as metaphors for the withdrawal of poetry. Cynthia's departure, for example, signifies the literal expiration of poetry, for as she leaves, her sounds of unearthly beauty, voiced in the sexual embrace, die out:

> Anon the strange voice is upon the wane—
> And 'tis but echo'd from departing sound,
> That the fair visitant at last unwound
> Her gentle limbs, and left the youth asleep. . . .
>
> (II, 849–852)

Sound and sex (that is, poetry and passion) cannot exist without each other; loss of Cynthia, then, is equivalent to the loss of the intense joy of poetic creativity:

> Endymion awoke, that grief of hers
> Sweet-paining on his ear: he sickly guess'd
> How lone he was once more, and sadly press'd
> His empty arms together, hung his head,
> And most forlorn upon that widow'd bed
> Sat silently. Love's madness he had known. . . .
>
> (855–860)

Endymion's search for Cynthia is, metaphorically, the poet's search for his sustaining poetic imagination; in an unusual moment of literal statement, Keats defines Endymion's frustration as "imagination's struggles":

> . . . and then he foams,
> And onward to another city speeds.
> But this is human life: the war, the deeds,
> The disappointment, the anxiety,
> Imagination's struggles. . . .
>
> (151–155)

Endymion's slavish dependence on Cynthia takes its toll from the poet. His divorce from the sweets of sexual-imaginative experience drives him into madness. The struggles of imagination leave their mark on an exhausted Endymion, "whose cheek is pale" repeatedly (III, 76). One is reminded of the pallor of the knight-at-arms, of the wizened hoariness of Glaucus, and of "heart-struck" Lycius, "pale with pain." Such physical debility occurs when each lover is unable to achieve poetic vision because of his estrangement from his fickle mistress, an estrangement that casts the poet into a painful enthralment from which she alone can guarantee relief.

We must read the poet-lover's enthralment as yet another metaphor describing the destructive rather than the vitalizing force of poetry. Not only is the poet tormented by the absence of poetic vision, but also by the expense of spirit required in the very act of achieving poetic intensity. For poetry remains for Keats the coyest of mistresses, who must be cajoled and wrestled with before he can gain her ultimate gift. Yet the favors of poetry remain uncertain; she offers the poet no guarantee of fulfilment after all his ardor, and frequently leaves him exhausted and despairing.

The letters voice misgivings over these long, almost compulsive bouts with poetry. To Fanny Brawne he complains despairingly of the baleful effect of poetry on his constitution: "What hope is there if I should be recoverd ever so soon—my very health [will] not suffer me to make any great exertion. I am recommended not even to read poetry, much less write it."[25] Keats earlier remarked about the feverish effect of poetry on him, saying, "The faint conceptions I have of Poems to come brings the blood frequently into my forehead." Somewhat later he realizes the dangerously sapping, because enthralling, effect of poetry. He wishes "to be able [to bear] unhurt the shock of extreme thought and sensation without weariness." With resignation he says in the same letter,

But I feel my Body too weak to support me to the height; I am obliged continually to check myself. . . . I have nothing to speak of but myself —and what can I say but what I feel? If you [John Hamilton Reynolds] should have any reason to regret this state of excitement in me, I will turn the tide of your feelings in the right channel by mentioning that it is the only state for the best sort of Poetry—that is all I care for, all I live for.[26]

The last words in this quotation—of caring for and living for poetry— again remind us of how an enthralled lover could speak of his mistress. The total suggestion seems to be that poetry will not relent; it will not release him from his restless captivity.

25. *Letters*, II, 257.   26. *Ibid.*, pp. 146–147.

In yet another revealing letter we notice Keats confounding poetry, death, and a bewitching woman; all three subjects course through his mind at the same time:

the voice and the shape of a woman ["Charmian," or Jane Cox, of whom Keats said to Georgiana Keats, "I should like her to ruin me, and I should like you to save me"] has haunted me these two days—at such a time when the relief, the feverous relief of Poetry seems a much less crime— This morning Poetry has conquered—I have relapsed into those abstractions[27] which are my only life. . . . Poor Tom—that woman—and Poetry were ringing changes in my senses.[28]

The letter is highly significant, for in recording a kind of semi-conscious thinking, Keats seems to be equating three apparently different ideas, i.e., Tom Keats's death, Charmian's destructiveness, and the "feverousness" of poetry. But his thoughts are not so different as to be refractive; they are all focused on ruination. Just as the voice and shape of a seductress can enthral and "ruin" Keats, so too can the attractions of poetry. If a woman and poetry can ring changes in Keats's senses, and haunt him to a feverous pitch, it seems fairly apparent that they should be identified as allied forces of torment.

More than a tax on Keats's health, compulsive poetic activity seems to have as virulent an effect as the consequences of extreme lovesickness: "When I have succeeded in doing so [writing poetry] all day and as far as midnight, you [Fanny Brawne] return as soon as this artificial excitement goes off more severely from the fever I am left in."[29] Here Keats admits to Fanny Brawne that he is alternately *victimized* by his feverish addiction to poetry and then by equally tormenting thoughts of her.

Because poetry is demanding, enervating, and even enthralling, Keats identifies his poetic "demon" in "Ode on Indolence" as a "maiden most unmeek." As Keats's attitude toward poetry changes, the women in his poetry change from the innocent, kindly maidens of the earliest poems to the beautiful *femmes fatales* of his middle and late poems. The very choice of the ambiguous term "demon" to describe poetry invites comment. We find an extended definition in Lemprière:

27. "Abstractions" here means imaginative activity. See Clarence D. Thorpe, *The Mind of John Keats* (New York, 1926), p. 35.
28. *Letters*, I, 370.   29. *Ibid.*, II, 137.

A kind of spirit, which, as the ancients supposed, presided over the actions of mankind, gave them their private counsels, and carefully watched over their most secret intentions. Some of the antient philosophers maintained that every man had two of these Daemons, the one bad and the other good. These Daemons had the power of changing themselves into whatever they pleased, and of assuming whatever shapes were most subservient to their intentions.[30]

"Demon Poesy" could therefore be either a Cynthia or a Circe, that is to say, a guardian divinity or a malevolent spirit. She could delight yet sap, bestow her favors yet withhold them, show passionate concern or bland indifference, and ultimately guarantee immortality or destruction. Of all Keats's women, Lamia best characterizes this twofold spirit of poetry; as Lycius' "demon mistress or the demon self" (I, 56), she first raises him to the heights of imaginative life and then leaves him to his death. However, she is not so intentionally malevolent as Circe, who is yet another representative of "demon Poesy."

Keats's choice of Circe as the grimmer, evil visage of his two-headed demon is appropriate, not only because she is the cruel enchantress of the *Odyssey*, but also because she is known as the daughter of Phoebus Apollo, and like Cynthia, who is Apollo's sister, can claim membership in the household of divine poetry.[31] Keats considers Circe as Apollo's bad seed, for by the perverted use of her divine power of poetry she is able to seduce and enthral Glaucus.

The Circe-Glaucus episode in Book III of *Endymion* may be considered as Keats's first extended treatment of the pernicious effect of poetry on an unsuspecting mortal. It should be noted that Circe's appeal to Glaucus is at once poetic *and* sexual, an observation that reminds us of Keats's consistent identification of poetry and passion. Glaucus' sexual

30. Lemprière, see "Daemon." Keats talks of a "good genius" presiding over Haydon and feels a like demon guiding his pen into "a dozen features of propriety" (see *Letters*, I, 142).

31. Glaucus' words faintly associate Circe with her meeker aunt, Cynthia, and at the same time suggest their opposition in spatial terms. Floundering in the sea and desirous of "relief," he says,

> ... So above the water
> I rear'd my head, and look'd for Phoebus' daughter.
> Aeaea's isle was wondering at the moon. ...
> (III, 413–415)

In meeting the "most unmeek" of all of Keats's demon-women, Glaucus is not so fortunate as his counterpart, Endymion.

enslavement is brought about by Circe almost immediately; he admits being enthralled by the beauty of her features, "the fairest face that morn e'er look'd upon," and also by the beauty of her words: "The dew of her rich speech, . . . whose thraldom was more bliss than all / The range of flower'd Elysium" (429, 427–28). Her promises of love, beauty, and music—in short, inspiration—are suspiciously like Cynthia's oaths to Endymion:

> ". . . I will pour
> "From these devoted eyes their silver store,
> "Until exhausted of the latest drop,
> "So it will pleasure thee, and force thee stop
> "Here, that I too may live. . . ."
>
> (433–437)

The rhythm of Circe's "rich speech" (429), which is clearly poetry, holds Glaucus in hypnotic infatuation as "Thus she link'd / Her charming syllables" (444); having entranced Glaucus she eventually leads him to the closest union possible, sexual intercourse:

> And then she hover'd over me, and stole
> So near, that if no nearer it had been
> This furrow'd visage thou hadst never seen. . . .
>
> (446–448)

In overwhelming Glaucus in passion, Circe proves fruitful, at least for the moment. He avows: "She took me like a child of suckling time" (456). The metaphor used here is especially appropriate in suggesting that Circe provides the teat of inspiration whose nourishment is as life-giving to Glaucus' imaginative powers as real milk is to the life of a child. Just as Cynthia pours forth "lispings empyrean" to inspire Endymion, Circe suckles Glaucus by "breath[ing] ambrosia" (454) on him so as to "immerse / [His] fine existence in a golden clime" (455–456). Her breath is, therefore, literally inspiring; the "ambrosia" which constitutes it has the power to make immortal those who drink this substance of the gods.

The reward of love is transcendent imaginative vision for Glaucus. For the moment, he assumes the consciousness of Apollo, perceiving the infinite variety and beauty of nature:

> For as Apollo each eve doth devise
> A new appareling for western skies;

So every eve, nay every spendthrift hour
Shed balmy consciousness within that bower. . . .

$$(463-466)$$

His "fine existence in a golden clime" (455), which Circe's ambrosia
has allowed, may now be interpreted as his life of imagination in the
golden realm of the sun god and arch-poet, Apollo. The giddiness of
imaginative vision is no less intensified by Circe's ambrosia. Glaucus'
description of his mental state as "balmy consciousness" suggests that
he is overwhelmed in soothing warmth and fragrances, which disarm
him completely.

In experiencing the varieties of sensory experience, suggested in the
imagery of eating, drinking, singing, and breathing, Glaucus is ascending
the different degrees of the "pleasure thermometer" until he attains the
chief intensity, sexual union, during which imaginative vision is open
to him. And since these pleasures flow from Circe, he accurately calls
her "the banquet of my arms" (498), an appellation with a thinly disguised sexual implication.

The sexual encounter with Circe, though at first life-giving, soon
leaves him a "tranced vassal" (460). For she is not Cynthia, the true,
beneficent imagination, but the profane and apostate "arbitrary queen
of sense." Glaucus' grim realization of his enslavement to her occurs
only after she withholds her sexual favors. As the dull sublunary lover,
whose soul is sense, he cannot endure her absence, for he has become
wholly addicted to her "ambrosia," "breath," and "rich speech":

One morn she left me sleeping: half awake
I sought for her smooth arms and lips, to slake
My greedy thirst with nectarous camel-draughts;
But she was gone. Whereat the barbed shafts
Of disappointment stuck in me so sore,
That out I ran and search'd the forest o'er. . . .

$$(477-482)$$

Glaucus is condemned to suffer, as are his successors in other poems.[32]
We are reminded of similar fates befalling the knight-at-arms and Lycius,

32. What Sperry fails to realize in his comments on the Circe-Glaucus episode is
that Glaucus is not a poet, and is therefore defenseless against the enthralling, overwhelming, seductive beauty of poetry, represented by Circe. At the outset Glaucus

both of whom are enthralled by the beauty and sexuality of their women-muses and then grieved by their withdrawal. Because of the tyrannical streak in Lamia, for example, Keats fittingly calls her "cruel lady" (I, 290) and "Some demon's mistress or the demon's self" (57) with the same ambivalence of feeling that he shows to his "unmeek" "demon Poesy" in "Ode on Indolence." Like Circe, who victimizes a mortal, Lamia entrammels her lover in a net of sexual pleasures until he is enslaved. Once again the sexual metaphor demonstrates the rule of the feminine imagination over the poet.

Lycius should not be considered an arbitrary representative of the poet. Keats, as always, selects his names extremely carefully. In Lemprière we discover that the name "Lycius" is an alias of Apollo; and of Lamia we read of her kinship to

certain monsters of Africa who had the face and breasts of a woman, and the rest of the body like that of a serpent. They allured strangers to come to them, that they might devour them, and though they were not endowed with the faculty of speech, yet their hissings were pleasing and agreeable. Some believed them to be witches, or rather evil spirits . . . under the form of a beautiful woman.[33]

Keats must have been struck by the usefulness of this passage for his own poetic purpose, for it objectifies so well his own ideas about the ambiguous character of his "demon Poesy," at once destructive and fair, enthralling and pleasing in its utterance of melodious sounds. Lamia's first words are indeed pleasing. Her "syllabling" (I, 244), like Circe's "link[ing] . . . charming syllables," soon overcomes him:

> For so delicious were the words she sung,
> It seem'd he had lov'd them a whole summer long. . . .
> (249–250)

---

admits to Endymion that in his earthly life "I touch'd no lute, I sang not, trod no measures: / I was a lonely youth on desert shores" (III, 338–339). The perils of an unprepared, unsponsored, would-be visionary are soon all too clear to Glaucus. Furthermore, Sperry does not see that Glaucus' enslavement is sexual in nature, a fact of cardinal importance in interpreting the episode, for, like other passages involving the union of Endymion and Cynthia, sexual experience remains in the gathering, structural metaphor for poetic experience.

33. Lemprière, see "Lamia." Critics have unanimously agreed that Burton's *Anatomy of Melancholy* provided the source for Lamia; however, this quotation should suggest that Lemprière is at least equally important for providing Keats with the germinal facts for his main character.

The hypnotic effect of her poetry renders him defenseless:

> . . . every word she spake entic'd him on
> To unperplex'd delight and pleasure known. . . .
>
> (326–327)

As with Glaucus and the knight-at-arms, Lycius' eyes are fixed on the enchantress with eager and almost monomaniacal attention as he drinks in her beauty. Once again Keats suggests the life-giving power of such ocular contact. The motif of eye-drinking tends to indicate that Lamia is an inexhaustible source of inspiration. Described as "a Naiad of the rivers," she is allied with the guardian spirit of the fount of imagination, which we have already noted to be a common recurrent metaphor in the earlier poetry. Fearing that she may vanish, Lycius feels the absolute necessity of retaining her in his vision; and in compelling him to feel this need of her, Lamia, as the force of poetry, easily contrives his seduction and enslavement:

> And soon his eyes had drunk her beauty up,
> Leaving no drop in the bewildering cup,
> And still the cup was full,—while he, afraid
> Lest she should vanish ere his lip had paid
> Due adoration, thus began to adore;
> Her soft look growing coy, she saw his chain so sure:
> 'Leave thee alone! look back! Ah, Goddess, see
> 'Whether my eyes can ever turn from thee!
> 'For pity do not this sad heart belie—
> 'Even as thou vanishest so shall I die. . . .'
>
> (251–260)

By alluding to the Orpheus myth, Keats suggests the essentially poetic nature of the enthralment and imminent destruction. Lamia coyly states: "Lycius, look back! and be some pity shown." He does, "not with cold wonder fearingly, / But Orpheus-like at an Eurydice" (246–248). Just as the poet Orpheus looked back to his beloved against Pluto's advice and thereby fashioned his own disaster, Lycius compulsively fastens his eyes on Lamia and initiates his own ruin.

Hypnotized by her eyes and singing, he finds imaginative fulfilment in sexual union with Lamia, who, after a delicate and perhaps maddening withholding of her divine breath, at last whispers inspiration to him at the supreme moment of their long love embrace.[34] She

> Put her new lips to his, and gave afresh
> The life she had so tangled in her mesh:
> And as he from one trance was wakening
> Into another, she began to sing,
> Happy in beauty, life, and love, and every thing,
> A song of love, too sweet for earthly lyres,
> While, like held breath, the stars drew in their
>   panting fires.
> And then she whisper'd in such trembling tone,
> As those who, safe together met alone
> For the first time through many anguish'd days,
> Use other speech than looks. . . .
>
> (I, 294–304)

The issue of passion is some kind of divine knowledge put in the form of poetry, that is, in words and music. Lycius is at first an enraptured auditor:

> . . . every word she spake entic'd him on
> To unperplex'd delight and pleasure known.
>
> (326–327)

But Lamia, as the controlling, feminine imagination, releases her lover's own latent capacity for poetic utterance:

> Lycius to all made eloquent reply,
> Marrying to every word a twinborn sigh.
>
> (340–341)

The marriage of true imaginative minds is here a verbal one, and is occasioned by a concomitant physical union.

In calling Lamia's influence an "empery of joys" (II, 35–36) Keats suggests her absolute, royal dominion over Lycius, a dominion that slowly wanes in Part II of the poem as he foolishly insists on showing her off to the vulgar Corinthians against her better judgment. He fails to realize that her beauty, while enthralling, is at the same time life-

---

34. The poet, in turn, "must *whisper* results to his neighbor," as Keats writes to Reynolds (*Letters*, I, 232).

sustaining. His addiction to her is like Glaucus' dependence on Circe; both demon-women provide sensory pleasures that eventually lead to sexual-imaginative experience. Lycius' enthralment suggests the paradox of imaginative fulfilment that is both creative and at the same time destructive. Of Lamia's inspiring beauty Keats ambiguously states that "while it smote still guaranteed to save" (I, 339). Lycius' "demon Poesy" offers him imaginative fulfilment and poetic vision while wounding and destroying.

Lamia's power to inspire imaginative vision rests in passion and kind looks; both disintegrate under Apollonius' withering, rationalistic gaze (significantly "without a twinkle"). The light and heat of poetic inspiration which she radiates are wholly extinguished:[35]

> 'Begone, foul dream!' he cried, gazing again
> In the bride's face, where now . . .
>
>   .   .   .   .
> . . . [was] no passion to illume
> The deep-recessed vision:—all was blight.
>
> $\qquad$ (II, 271–272, 274–275)

As the spontaneous, non-rational, poetic imagination, breeding in the passion of love, she cannot exist but in Lycius' dream-like trance where vision is accommodated. Her power to enthral on the wane, she understands her imminent fate as Lycius begins to awaken from their love-sleep:

> . . . she began to moan and sigh
> Because he mus'd beyond her, knowing well
> That but a moment's thought is passion's passing bell.
>
> $\qquad$ (37–39)

Her light, passion, and ability to provoke "the deep-recessed vision" are all blighted. Robbed of her life-giving warmth, light, music, and sexual

35. Lamia's eyes, as the source of light and heat, have a special significance here. As Lycius looks into Lamia's eyes he sees himself "mirror'd small in Paradise" (II, 47), a detail which may clarify the important statement that Keats made in his letter to Bailey, concerning the imagination's power of "empyreal reflection." Keats suggests that the imagination mirrors the highest heaven of fire and light (the literal meaning of "empyreal"). In mirroring Lycius in Paradise, Lamia is identified as imagination, for she gives back to him an image of his own transcendent status in an "empyreal reflection." As a mirror of Lycius, Lamia is a part of the poet himself; that is to say, she is his imagination.

passion that jointly sustain his poetic vision, Lycius, too, ceases to exist. The almost simultaneous demise of both sounds the death knell for poetry.

Having discussed at length one of the dominant metaphors for poetry, I should now like to suggest what consequence this investigation may have in estimating Keats as a poet. Too frequently critics have charged him with being mawkish and puerile in passages involving sexual encounters:[36] "piss-a-bed poetry" according to the literalistic Byron. More often the reaction is not a sneer, but embarrassment. The tremor of Endymion's and other lovers' voices, when speaking of their love, is supposedly too sentimental and overwrought to be acceptable and convincing. *Endymion* may jar the modern sensibility when read on the literal level of meaning. But to read in this limited manner cheats the reader of the richness and complexity of the poem, wherein sexual love is a brilliantly conceived and executed metaphor for transcendent poetic experience. The poems which employ this gathering metaphor can hardly be considered mawkish, but rather ingeniously subtle and sophisticated. One feels that Keats's search for an adequate metaphor succeeds, even though he was less than satisfied with the total achievement of *Endymion*. Although Keats's greatness rests mainly on the excellence of the odes, I should like to suggest that he achieves a similar brilliance and richness in those poems presenting sexual experience as the large gathering metaphor for poetic experience. This metaphor incorporates and carries the meaning of such poems as *Lamia* and *Endymion*, and, as shall be seen, "Ode to Psyche" and "La Belle Dame sans Merci."

36. See, for example, J. Middleton Murry's *Studies in Keats, New and Old* (London, 1939), p. 38.

Chapter three

Sleep and dreams — Flight and wings — The elf
— The steeds — The boat — Swimming

Though sexual experience remains in Keats's hierarchy of metaphors the most effective analogue for intense poetic experience, dreams and sleep, flight, riding the steed or boat of poetry, and swimming are varying, apt metaphors to suggest the excitement, release, and freedom which the poet feels when the poetic process begins to unfold. Logically related to one another, these metaphors represent Keats's attitude toward poetic creativity as transcendent adventure and uncertain exploration of strange seas, giddy heights, or unknown watery depths. Sleep and dreams are appropriate metaphors for the spontaneous shaping spirit of imagination stirred to life and given full release once the restraints of consciousness are thrown off. Only then may the poetic soul take flight on wings of imagination. Dream and flight form, therefore, a natural linkage in the poetry. Generally they are figurative of the initial, excited kindling of imagination and its progress to poetic vision.

The means of attaining vision, however, may be also described in terms of the winged steed of poetry, which the poet rides in cavalier fashion. Sometimes he describes poetic adventure as a perilous or facile sea voyage on the bark of poetry. And finally, swimming may also suggest the search for vision; for as a metaphor closely allied to flying or sailing, it suggests the element of risk and adventure.

These, then, are the larger organizing metaphors for poetic experience; around them Keats weaves smaller, local metaphors just as he does in clustering figures of breathing and music around the sexual act to suggest their inspirational nature. These smaller, yet significant, clusters of images and metaphors further inform us of the essentially poetic nature of flight, dreaming, and sailing—for example, the linkage of fire and light imagery to winged flight and impassioned dreaming.

Sleep and dreams

Keats's comparison of imagination to Adam's dream celebrates man's primal dream as a god-given vision of beauty—Eve. Milton's account of the birth of Eve in Adam's fancy and at the same time in the actual garden identifies the truth-making capability of dream. According to Keats's reading of the episode, beauty and truth coalesce. Beauty is fleshed; its real presence is also truth. Eve in a sense is a perfect work of art.

Although it is understandable then why *Paradise Lost* may be acknowledged a main source of the two metaphors under investigation here, it is in Shakespeare[1] that we find the most revealing, traceable origin of sleep and dreams as they figure the artistic process and specifically poetry. The controlling idea that dreams analogize the working of imagination derives from Prospero's speech in *The Tempest* announcing the dissolution of the Ceres masque. Speaking as both the author of the gorgeous pageant-within-a-play and as a character among other dramatis personae, Prospero states that the dramatic vision of the playwright ("the baseless fabric of this vision"), the settings and other spectacles ("cloud-capp'd towers, the gorgeous palaces, / The solemn temples"), and the stage

1. The comment "Shakespeare and the *Paradise Lost* every day become greater wonders to me" reveals the twin, abiding interests of Keats's reading. Although Shakespeare's influence on him has been widely commented upon, there has been no estimate of the degree to which Keats assimilated and used Shakespeare's passages on imagination and poetry. Finney tells us that he not only studied but absorbed the plays to the extent that his developing style found its character from them (*The Evolution of Keats's Poetry*, p. 205). "Thank God I can read and perhaps understand Shakespeare to his depths," wrote Keats in 1818 (*Letters*, I, 239). As this paragraph and others will suggest, Keats made Shakespeare's metaphors for poetry a part of his general hoard; for example, the relation between love and fancy in *A Midsummer Night's Dream* and in *Love's Labour's Lost* provides him a ready-made metaphor for poetry.

itself—i.e., London's "great globe"—are "such stuff as dreams are made
on." Prospero's use of the sovereign "we" refers to the spirits enacting
the pageant and, as well, to all the actors in the play proper, both of
whom he is manipulating by his "art." They are the "stuff" of imagination and their "little life" upon the stage is "rounded"—i.e., shaped,
completed, and finished[2]—with a sleep. Shakespeare is using dreams and
sleep as organizing metaphors for the imaginative process. The imagination creates actors and action in the same manner as dreamwork. And
like the visions of dreams, the creations of the imagination—actors, setting, staging—shall all inevitably dissolve. All the elements of theater
that the globe possesses ("all which it inherit")[3] shall dissolve as the
poetic imagination returns from its extravagant "little life" of dream
played out on the stage. Only the memory is left to puzzle over the
"insubstantial pageant faded."

Keats's profound admiration for Prospero's speech, marked heavily in
his copy of Shakespeare and quoted frequently in the letters, suggests
the special metaphorical relevance it had for him. And while the lines
assuredly assert that life is a dream, Keats, fathoming Shakespeare to his
depths, saw them as a statement on the artistic process as dream.[4] Echoes
of Prospero's speech ring noticeably in *Endymion*, as for example in the
description of the tenuousness and evanescence of dreams and fancies:

> . . . The Morphean fount
> Of that fine element that visions, dreams,
> And fitful whims of sleep are made of, streams
> Into its airy channels . . .
>
> . . . .
>
> . . . how light
> Must dreams themselves be; seeing they're more slight
> Than the mere nothing that engenders them! . . .
> (I, 747–750, 754–756)

2. A *New Variorum Edition of Shakespeare*, ed. H. H. Furness *et al.* (Philadelphia,
1892), IX (*The Tempest*), 218.
3. *Ibid.*, p. 212.
4. Poems are made of dreams also in Milton, the second important poet to influence Keats's poetic practice. Milton's muse or "celestial patroness deigns / Her
nightly visitation unimplored / And dictates to me slumbering" (*Paradise Lost*,
IX, 21–23). Here obviously his divine muse takes the role of Morpheus.

Sleep and dreams form the main framework upon which other metaphors for poetry depend. To appreciate their importance let us consider a passage in *Endymion*:

> O magic sleep! O comfortable bird
> That broodest o'er the troubled sea of the mind
> Till it is hush'd and smooth! O unconfin'd
> Restraint! imprisoned liberty! great key
> To golden palaces, strange minstrelsy,
> Fountains grotesque, new trees, bespangled caves,
> Echoing grottos, full of tumbling waves
> And moonlight; aye, to all the mazy world
> Of silvery enchantment! . . .
>
> (I, 453–461)

As a "key" to further wonders, sleep magically sets free the mind to flee to the realm of "enchantment." As suggested in this passage, sleep is the first stage of release of the poetic imagination, whereby the poet becomes a "living soul" to "see into the life of things," as Wordsworth had said in "Tintern Abbey." As the instrument of spontaneous vision, sleep has its roots in the feelings and not in the reason. If then sleep occasions or invokes the poetic imagination, dreaming signifies the imaginative process unfolding. We understand, therefore, the paradox of the sonnet, "O thou whose face hath felt the Winter's wind": "he's awake who thinks himself asleep"; for the entranced, imaginative poet sees most acutely where the conscious man perceives only dimly or not at all.

This consistent contrast of the merits of dreaming and the deficiencies of consciousness is well dramatized in both "Ode to a Nightingale" and *Lamia*. The speaker in the ode, despite his earnest desire to "fade away" into dream, to "leave the world unseen," not through the intoxication of wine but rather through poetry, remains "darkling"; he cannot lapse fully into the dream state and thereby achieve vision in the bright realm of the "Queen-Moon" and the nightingale, who are the agents of poetry; for the "dull," conscious "brain perplexes and retards." The real world— "where but to think is to be full of sorrow"—remains too much with him. The consistent, though paradoxical, association of light with dreams, and darkness with consciousness, suggests that vision is to be achieved only in dreaming.

In contrast to the speaker in "Ode to a Nightingale," Lycius reaches the realm of silvery enchantment or total imagination in the depths of dream. Having attained "the deep-recessed vision" (i.e., perception of beauty and truth in poetic form while he is in a profound trance), Lycius quite justifiably rejects the wide-awake and critical rationalist, Apollonius: "to-night he seems / The ghost of folly haunting my sweet dreams" (I, 377). Indeed in "To J. H. Reynolds, Esq." Keats himself admits to a similar sweetness in dreaming, for dream involves vision and divine eloquence that come but rarely. Only as a dreaming Apollo might he adequately describe the "Enchanted Castle" of imagination to Reynolds:

> O Phoebus! that I had thy sacred word
> To shew this Castle, in fair dreaming wise.
>
> (30–31)

In one of the earliest and most explicit poems on the nature of sleep, "Sleep and Poetry" (which might well have been entitled "Sleep *as* Poetry"), we note the observation that "for what there may be worthy in these rhymes / I partly owe to him [i.e., sleep]" (347–348). Keats's meaning seems clear enough: because the slumbering mind has the ability to create spontaneously and effortlessly, sleep is poetry. Reverie, drowsing, trances, and the like consistently evoke the romantic ideal of spontaneity.[5] Keats can be extremely subtle in identifying "poesy" as trance, as in the following example:

> . . . 'Tis the supreme of power;
> 'Tis might half slumb'ring on its own right arm. . . .
>
> (236–237)

These figures, repeated throughout his works, indicate the musing, leisurely, semi-conscious yet powerful mental state which the poet must assume for his numbers to flow. Similarly, in *Lamia* we find the perfectly withdrawn imaginative state in the two lovers:

> . . . with eyelids clos'd,
> Saving a tythe which love still open kept,
> That they might see each other while they almost slept. . . .
>
> (II, 23–25)

5. See James R. Caldwell, *John Keats' Fancy* (Ithaca, 1945), p. 117. Caldwell is one of the first critics to comment at length on "the kinship between imagination and the sleep work of the mind"; his criticism is, however, general and not closely critical. Its aim is to prove the associationalist influence on Keats's poetry.

Also important to note, in this regard, is the fact that Lamia can begin
to seduce Lycius to the delights of poetic vision only after he strays from
the real world and lapses into a state of reverie bordering on dream:

> His phantasy was lost, where reason fades
> In the calm'd twilight of Platonic shades. . . .
>
> (I, 235–236)

Lamia has the power of sending her own dreams anywhere and of controlling her spirit at will, just as the mobile, godlike imagination is
capable of mastering the limitations of time and space:

> . . . she could muse
> And dream . . .
> Of all she list, strange or magnificent:
> How, ever, where she will'd her spirit went. . . .[6]
>
> (202–205)

She gains entrance into Lycius' mortal imagination, blending into and
enlivening his daydream. Dominated by Lamia, his initial fantasies become a prolonged, ideal dream-vision.

A long apostrophe in *Endymion* identifies sleep as the "great key . . .
to all the mazy world / Of silvery enchantment" (I, 456, 460–461).
The domain of sleep is, more particularly, bathed in "moonlight" (460),
and therefore invested with all the enchantments of Cynthia (as we
have previously noted); the relation between sleep and Cynthia (or the
moon) is a close one: in many instances of sexual-poetic activity, sleep
is a consistent prerequisite (or "key") and the erotic dream the inevitable
attendant. Endymion's anticipation of sexual delight in dreaming—"O
let me then by some sweet dreaming flee / To her entrancements" (II,
703–704)—finds fulfilment only after he has achieved "power to dream
deliciously" (708), a state leading to the rapturous touch of Cynthia's
"naked waist" and ultimately to sexual-poetic fulfilment with her.

As the most powerful source of poetic vision,[7] the moon would quite

6. Lamia's ability to create and project her dreams at will parallels very closely
Ovid's descriptions of the power of Sleep to send his dreams, "resembling truth,"
anywhere. See George Sandys, *Ovid's Metamorphoses Englished* (London, 1626),
pp. 231–232.
7. The words "power," "might," and "strength" describe poetic capability and
recur throughout the poetry.

naturally be linked, metaphorically, with the one appropriate mental state that accommodates spontaneous invention: dreaming. The identification of the moon and dreams as like forces recurs throughout the poetry. In "I stood tip-toe," the moon is the "closer of lovely eyes to lovely dreams" (120), and in *Endymion* "my daintest dream" (IV, 656). Similarly, Lycius considers Lamia his "silver moon[ed]" bringer of dreams, while Apollonius regards her as anything but "dainty." He calls her a "foul dream," thereby suggesting the most hated state of mind to the rationalist, and bids her "begone." It is evident that all the women-muses have the power to inspire dreams within their poet-lovers for good or ill purpose. Most pernicious is Circe, who is a kind of false Cynthia in promising Glaucus "a long love dream" which turns out, however, to be a nightmare.

In contrast to the poems demonstrating the fertility of imagination in moonlight-bathed dreams, the "Ode on Indolence" presents the inertness of imagination in languid sleep or reverie: "My sleep has been embroider'd with dim dreams," that is, sleep with sparse imaginative "brede" and character. The absence of generative light, or even moonlight, confirms this interpretation, for the day is "clouded," "full of faint visions"; the poet's soul is "sprinkled with stirring shades and baffled beams," not the intensely burning light of creativity, nor the oblique light of lunar inspiration. Similarly, in the sonnet "On Sitting Down to Read King Lear Once Again," Keats uses the dream as a metaphor for poetic imagination in imploring his patron saints, the great poets of England, "Let me not wander in a barren dream"; and in "On Receiving a Laurel Crown from Leigh Hunt," the failure to reach the dream state signifies a failure to create as he would like to.

While sleep and dreams are fit analogues for spontaneous poetic creation, Keats finds it necessary, in developing his metaphor, to resort to myth in an attempt to characterize more fully and concretely the plastic power of the active dreaming mind. Morpheus, the vicar of sleep, offers us an additional insight into the metaphor. The Greeks, according to Ovid in the *Metamorphoses*, regarded Morpheus not merely as the scatterer of poppy seed but as a supreme artist and counterfeiter of form; furthermore, they esteemed him as the most skilful speaker in manner and tone:

Shape-faining *Morpheus* . . .
with subtler cunning can
Usurp the gesture, visage, voice of man,
His habit and knowne phrase.[8]

He is, in a word, poet. Having known Ovid through Sandys (as Finney
has shown), Keats very early in his poetic career was aware of the appropriateness of sleep and dream as metaphors for the artistic process;
for like the vital imagination they shape, recombine, and compress the
materials of conscious experience in a subconscious state of mind. No
better example of this shaping, protean process can be found than in
the description of Morpheus completing his task of fashioning a prefigurative dream of Endymion's wedding with Cynthia:

His litter of smooth semilucent mist,
Diversely ting'd with rose and amethyst,
Puzzled those eyes that for the centre sought;
And scarcely for one moment could be caught
His sluggish form reposing motionless.
Those two on winged steeds, with all the stress
Of vision search'd for him [i.e., Morpheus], as one would look
Athwart the sallows of a river nook
To catch a glance at silver-throated eels,—
Or from old Skiddaw's top, when fog conceals
His rugged forehead in a mantle pale,
With an eye-guess towards some pleasant vale
Descry a favourite hamlet faint and far. . . .

(IV, 385–397)

The baffling haze of light, diluted with the changeful polar colors, the
uncertainty of dimension to this realm, the intangible, fleeting, and
barely perceptible form of Morpheus, whose movements the beholders
are unable to arrest, suggest the essentially kinetic quality of the poetic
imagination. The reason cannot comprehend and fix its flux. In suggesting
its constant change, Keats is consistent in his definition of the poetical
character as "chameleon." "A Poet . . . has no Identity—he is continually infor[ming] and filling some other Body—The Sun, the Moon,

8. Sandys, p. 232.

the Sea and Men and Women who are creatures of impulse are poetical and have about them an unchangeable attribute—the poet has none; no identity." [9]

While the imagination is possessed of infinite freedom to shape forms in sleep, there is also within the poetic process a strongly limiting and ordering faculty. Just as dreams shape experience into meaningful (although apparently occult) metaphorical patterns,[10] the protean imagination shapes into significant and recognizable form the abstract and chaotic feelings and ideas of the poet by means of meter, rhyme, rhetorical patterns, stanza forms, etc. Keats suggests both the license and restriction of the poetic imagination in his paradoxical definition of sleep as "unconfin'd / Restraint! imprison'd liberty!" (*Endymion*, I, 455–456). In summary, then, imagination and poetry are severely limited to the form which their content will take, although the possibilities of formal expression are infinite (as are dreams).

In relation to our discussion of sleep as a metaphor for poetry, we must consider death. To Keats and many others in the nineteenth century, death was not the cessation of mental activity, but the ultimate intensity.[11] For example, the "Bright Star" sonnet equates swooning to death with sexual culmination, suggesting that eternal sleep achieves for the poet-lover a perpetual intensity of feeling. And in the sonnet

9. *Letters*, I, 387. Compare with Coleridge's definition of imagination as "the Protean self-transforming power of genius . . . to make the changeful God be felt in the river, the lion and the flame." Quoted in Wellek, II, 163.

10. Freud calls the process by which a wish or physical drive (i.e., the raw "material") is ordered into recognizable form the "dream process." The shaping force of dreams he terms the "censor," which, through "substitution of the part for the whole, hints or allusions, symbolic connection, and plastic word representation (images)," artistically reshapes and disguises these latent drives "without offending the ethical and *aesthetic* tendencies of the ego." See Sigmund Freud, *A General Introduction to Psychoanalysis* (New York, 1949), pp. 128, 151, *et passim*. Freud's concept of "dream work" and the "censor" is closely identifiable with Keats's idea of the shaping spirit of imagination in dreams.

11. Caroline Hogue's comment on Emily Dickinson's "I Heard a Fly Buzz When I Died" is revealing in suggesting that the moment of death involved, for the nineteenth century, a perception of ultimate truth in intense sensation; the dying person "await[s] expectantly a burst of dying energy to bring on the grand act of passing . . . as climax the dying one gave witness in words to the Redeemer's presence in the room, how He hovered, transplendent in the upper air, with open arms outstretched to receive the departing soul. This was death's great moment." *The Explicator*, XX (1961), art. 26. See also David Perkins, *The Quest for Permanence* (Cambridge, Mass., 1959), pp. 251–253.

"Why did I laugh?" death is "Life's high meed," or the avenue to continuous sensation. Death forever erases the fretting and palsy of imagination during consciousness. Implicit in Keats's longing for death in the "Ode to a Nightingale"—"Now more than ever seems it rich to die"—is the desire for perpetual poetic intensity. The release of the human soul which occurs in death is analogous to the nightingale's "pouring forth [its] soul abroad / In such an ecstasy" of song. The poet expects to find a similar poetic ecstasy in dying. Death is, therefore, a subtle and mutant form of the basic metaphor of sleep as poetry.

Some of the later poems reveal an uncertainty that sleep and dreams can adumbrate a vision of truth as Adam's dream did. Suspicious of his own imagination, Keats frequently poses a question such as that found at the end of the "Ode to a Nightingale": "Was it a vision, or a waking dream. . . . Do I wake or sleep?" We can interpret this fruitful rhetorical question as an inquiry into real and false dreaming; it asks whether the imaginative experience is merely an airy nothing, a trick of the slumbering mind playing actively in that twilight area between sleep and consciousness, or whether it has revealed truth in a vision.

The distinction made between the dreamer and the poet reveals a meaningful sea-change in Keats's thought. The awe-struck mortal of "the dreamer tribe" in *The Fall of Hyperion* learns that "the poet and the dreamer are distinct" (I, 199), that the dreamer "venoms all his days" (175); for only the true poet brings philosophical depth to his poems, which the baseless fabric of dreams cannot alone provide. The poet must identify himself with the problems of humanity and serve as a "humanist, physician to all men" (190). Yet it should be noted that *The Fall of Hyperion* is cast in the form of a dream, apparently suggesting that Keats still believes in its power to reveal truth. The poet hears Moneta's advice while he is asleep; and it is very specific advice, not "lispings empyrean" or the even vaguer "lute breathings" of Cynthia: the poet must be responsible to his fellow man, a humanitarian rather than an aesthetic hermit. Thus Keats reaffirms one of the earliest poetic resolutions arrived at in "Sleep and Poetry": that the poet should pursue a "noble life, / Where [he] may find the agonies, the strife / Of human hearts" (123–125). This "nobler life" identifies the true visionary poet. It repudiates the merely sensory dreaming in the realm of "Flora and Old Pan."

Sleep has its inseparable companion in the metaphor of flight, which represents the soaring, coursing, mobile imagination, "free of space"; as the poet's "ready mind is" alchemized into a state "like a floating spirit's" (i.e., the poet's imagination is transmuted from base metal into gold as he approaches Apollo's golden realm), it grows wings of fancy. The recurrent use of winged flights is easily explainable: because flight defies the restrictions of time and space, it serves as an appropriate metaphor for the active poetic imagination, which, like dreams, carries the poet beyond the limits of earthly reality. Further, wings with their connotations of swiftness, nimbleness, and sublimity work easily as a metaphor for imagination; they serve as the agent for poetic flight. For example, in the profound letter of February 19, 1818, to Reynolds, we find the poet talking of a winged "voyage of conception" (i.e., imagination) that "puts a girdle round the earth" with the swiftness of Shakespeare's Puck.[12] Mindful of such supernatural license in the poem "Fancy," Keats desires to "let the winged fancy wander."

He often underscores the vital, empyrean nature of the imagination by linking his wings of poesy with fire imagery, as in the sonnet, "To Spenser," where, in the act of writing, Keats would like "To rise like Phoebus with a golden quill / Fire wing'd." [13] These lines recall two lines in the prologue of Henry V, quoted in a letter to John Taylor:

> O for a muse of fire, that would ascend
> The brightest heaven of invention. . . .

The fire-wings cluster again appears in "To George Felton Mathew," where the great poets "who have left streaks of light athwart their ages" possess "the bright golden wing / Of genius" (60, 63–64). By such recurrent linkages Keats suggests the intensity and radiance of imaginative activity as well as its range and mobility.

Often, "when streams of light pour down the golden west," thoughts

12. *Letters*, I, 231. See A *Midsummer Night's Dream*, II. i. 175. The nimbleness and dispatch of Ariel, Puck, and other sprites remained a fascination to Keats. His letters and annotations of the plays suggest that these sprites reminded him of the properties of his own fancy.

13. Fire and light, as Abrams has pointed out, are two common romantic "metaphors for mind." See Chapter III, "Romantic Analogues of Art and Mind" in *The Mirror and the Lamp*, and specifically pp. 59–60.

of past poets such as Milton and Sidney (as well as of Apollo, the sun god) may be strong enough to occasion a flight "on wing of Poesy" ("Oh! How I love, on a fair summer's eve," 12, 14). Like his soaring predecessors, Keats is always poised and ready to take flight; "I stood tip-toe upon a little hill," as the very title line suggests, presents the physical position taken by the poet before his pinions of imagination spread; the poem is not a "hill poem," but a poem of the tiptoe stance before the expected soaring:

> I gazed awhile, and felt as light, and free
> As though the fanning wings of Mercury
> Had play'd upon my heels. . . .
>
> (23–25)

If the youthful Keats is telling his audience that he is preparing for flight in this early poem, his later poetry traces that extensive soaring.

In addition to the intensity, speed, and supernatural power connoted in the metaphor of the winged flight of imagination, Keats develops another salient attribute. The dream-flight conveys a sense of intense excitement, "adventure," and anticipation of discovery, as evidenced in "Notes on Milton's *Paradise Lost*"; creating poetry is an intrepid pioneering flight: "The spirit of mounting and adventure can never be unfruitful or unrewarded: had he [Milton] not broken through the clouds which envelope so deliciously the Elysian field of verse, and committed himself to the Extreme, we should never have seen Satan." [14] Flight on wings serves as one of Keats's chief intensities, as J. R. Caldwell has noted in explaining the "awful mission," the "worldly fear," and "the affrighted . . . gaze" of the fledged poet, terrorized in his soaring, in the poem "God of the Meridian":

Keats' creative reverie often reached to this depth; he knew panic, fear as well as elation in his coursings. On this point we have the evidence, not only of the often expressed feeling of terror at the metaphorical height to which the wings of bardic fury bring him. [15]

But we do not need the critic to explain what Keats himself will admit; a letter to Reynolds sufficiently reveals the panic of his metaphorical flight:

14. John Keats, "Notes on Milton's *Paradise Lost*," *The Poetical Works and Other Writings of John Keats*, ed. Harry Buxton Forman (London, 1883), III, 19.
15. Caldwell, p. 38.

The difference of high Sensations with and without knowledge appears to me this—in the latter case we are falling continually ten thousand fathoms deep and being blown up again without wings and with all [the] horror of a bare shouldered Creature—in the former case, our shoulders are fledge, and we go thro' the same air and space without fear.[16]

Strong, sure wings are made of philosophical knowledge; frail wings of weak "maiden thought," though zealous enough, are inadequate. Keats very early anticipates the problems of the poet lacking wings of "spanning wisdom" ("Sleep and Poetry," 285). Realizing he has "Daedalian wings" (303), he understands the perils of flying and falling, and though fearful and uncertain ("I do not know / The shiftings of the mighty winds that blow," 285–286) he resolves not to be a "coward."

Notwithstanding this lack of confidence, in "What can I do to drive away" (as in "I stood tip-toe") he is prepared to fly at any poetic occasion:

> My muse had wings
> And ever ready was to take her course
> Whither I bent her force
> Unintellectual, yet divine to me. . . .
>
> (11–14)

And though the Icarian poetic fall looms large, he is willing to risk imaginative flights: "I do not see why it is a greater crime in me than in another to let the verses of a half-fledged brain tumble into the reading-rooms." [17]

Having established that flight, like dreaming, is an experience involving intense sensation,[18] we should not fail to perceive its close metaphorical relationship to sexual adventure. Flight or other acts of mounting in dreams are either the inevitable precursor of or the attendant upon sexual activity. A compact example of this linkage can be seen in the revealing commentary on the genesis of the sonnet, "On a Dream":

The dream was one of the most delightful enjoyments I ever had in my life—I floated about the whirling atmosphere as it is described with a

---

16. *Letters*, I, 277.   17. *Ibid.*, II, 130.
18. Of the "extreme thought and sensation" necessary "for the best sort of Poetry," Keats says: "I feel my Body too weak to support me to the *height*," thereby linking, in a submerged manner, poetic intensity with winged flight (*ibid.*, pp. 146–147).

beautiful figure to whose lips mine were joined [as] it seem'd for an age—and in the midst of all this cold and darkness I was warm—even flowery tree tops sprung up and we rested on them sometimes with the lightness of a cloud till the wind blew us away again . . . o that I could dream it every night.[19]

Keats is candid enough here, but he is perhaps innocent of the submerged meaning of this experience. It is a sexual dream, to be sure,[20] but the intensity of feeling is sublimated, in a strikingly Freudian manner, as flight and movement. In this and other poems we may read acts of flying and mounting on wings to great airy heights, and other acts of ascension on ladders, stairs, and steep inclines, as sexual intercourse, and therefore an integral part of poetic experience.

The "pleasure thermometer" passage in *Endymion* itself, always a helpful instrument in gauging Keats's metaphors for poetry, marks the degrees of increasingly intense sensations whereby the "floating spirit" is led "into a sort of oneness." [21] Book II shows most revealingly the metaphors of dreams, wings, and flight, all clustered together, as a sublimated expression of Endymion's most intense sexual sensation:

> . . . tie
> Large wings upon my shoulders, and point out
> My love's far dwelling . . .
>   . . . .
> O be propitious, nor severely deem
> My madness impious; for, by all the stars
> That tend thy bidding, I do think the bars
> That kept my spirit in are burst—that I
> Am sailing with thee through the dizzy sky!
> How beautiful thou art! . . .
>
>   (177–179, 183–188)

But within the metaphorical pattern of withdrawal, sleep, flight, and the rapture of sexual union, there is fear and terror in such adventure:

19. *Ibid.*, p. 91.
20. Sperry, in "The Concept of the Imagination in Keats's Narrative Poems," p. 175, sees the experience as an imaginative love-dream, but does not mention the significance of flight in this cluster of metaphors.
21. A thorough explanation of the steps to "oneness" can be found in Wasserman, *The Finer Tone*, pp. 23–27.

>   . . . My spirit fails—
> Dear goddess, help! or the wide-gaping air
> Will gulph me—help!—At this with madden'd stare,
> And lifted hands, and trembling lips he stood. . . .
>
>   (193–196)

Endymion, being mortal, can sustain only temporary flight; he must inevitably fall back to earth, just as in dreaming he must eventually wake to the sublunary world. But more distressing than plummeting back to reality is not being able to fly at all.

We have already seen the significance of barren dreams; they are unfruitful imaginative experiences. Similarly, the poet who cannot achieve flight shows a creative infirmity. The speaker's languor and inertia in the "Ode on Indolence" are directly opposite to the coursings which characterize poetic fervor. He laments,

>   . . . I burn'd
> And ach'd for wings . . .
>
>   .   .   .   .
>   . . . I wanted wings. . . .

And in "What can I do to drive away," his inert imagination, its feathers shed, provokes a similar despondency:

>   How shall I do
>   To get anew
> Those moulted feathers, and so mount once more. . . .

The heaviness of mortality remains as the consistent enemy of the youthful, buoyant, and aggressive poetic imagination. In perceiving the pinnacles of art which the creator of the Elgin marbles has reached, Keats can only vicariously sense the giddy heights of achieved imaginative soaring—"these wonders [bring] a most dizzy pain." His own poetic spirit, "like a sick eagle looking at the sky," remains, unhappily, grounded. The comparison of his own imaginative infirmity to a "sick eagle" is appropriate, for what was once powerful in flight, keen in vision, graceful, and aggressive is now quite inadequate.

And in another poem on the failure of flight and the weakness of mortal wings, "Ode to a Nightingale," the speaker desires to "fly . . . on the viewless wings of Poesy, / Though the dull brain perplexes and

retards." The confined poet cannot ascend to the upper realm of immortal song and light where the Queen-Moon sits on her throne. Only
the night accompanies the nightingale ("Already with thee! tender is
the night").[22] The unfledged poet is left in darkness, guessing at the
heaven of immortal poetry. He is no winged Lycius or Endymion, both
of whom are able to take winged flight to the sacred realm of primary
creation. This upper domain can be reached only with the aid of their
divine muses, as the early lines of Book III of *Endymion* state. In this
realm of "the abysm-birth of elements . . . A thousand Powers keep
religious state"; their "throned seats" are "unscalable / But by a patient
wing" that "can make a ladder of the eternal wind" (23 ff.).[23] Endymion's
wings of poesy are the gift of Cynthia, one of the primary "powers" of
creation.

Although winged flight serves as the basic recurrent metaphor for
facile, almost involuntary poetic adventure, Keats occasionally regards
the ascent to the throne of poetry as a struggle afoot and therefore much
more difficult. A central incident in *The Fall of Hyperion*, as an example
of this significant variation on a metaphor, involves a deliberate and
painful poetic mounting as the poet approaches Moneta's throne. In
taking up Moneta's challenge—

> None can usurp this height . . .
> But those to whom the miseries of the world
> Are misery, and will not let them rest. . . .
>
> (I, 147–149)

—the poet, as he ascends on foot, puts on the knowledge of human
sympathy and philosophy necessary for the most superior kind of poetry.
In short, he becomes "A humanist, physician to all men" (190) by tem-
pering knowledge with imagination. Gone are his poetic wings. Keats

22. Wasserman (*ibid.*, pp. 198–199) suggests that this important line must not be
interpreted to mean that the poet attains the level of the nightingale.
23. The invocation to Book III is undeniably similar to Milton's invocation to
Book I of *Paradise Lost*, where the poet hopes to take poetic flight and "soar /
Above the Aonian mount" (14–15) so that he too may create like the Holy Spirit,
who "with mighty wings outspread / Dove-like satest brooding on the vast abyss
/ And made it pregnant." As in "Kubla Khan," primary creation is comparable to
poetic creativity. Coleridge's chasm and Milton's "pregnant abyss" have the same
metaphorical significance as Keats's realm of the "abysm-birth of elements," which
can be attained by Cynthia's gift of poetic wings. Cynthia, or the Queen-Moon,
may therefore be considered as Keats's equivalent to Milton's Holy Ghost or
Coleridge's Kubla Khan.

felt himself struggling well below the poetic eminence long before *The Fall of Hyperion*; his painful metaphorical ascent, accompanied by feelings of inadequacy and unworthiness, manifests itself in an early letter to Haydon: "I am 'one that gathers Samphire dreadful trade' the Cliff of Poesy Towers above me." [24] And in another letter (to Hunt) he talks of the "continual uphill journeying," suggesting again the wingless, poetic struggle dramatized in *The Fall of Hyperion*.

The steps and cliffs of poetry over which the unfledged poet struggles lead to the one desired summit—poetic attainment. We are now able to interpret the seemingly gratuitous epithets by which Endymion addresses the moon—"Thou wast the mountain top . . . my topmost deed" (III, 164, 168). They are meant to suggest exclusiveness, strenuous pursuit and sublimity in the poet's attainment of the throne of poesy.[25] "Sleep and Poetry," anticipating *Endymion*, places the shrine of poetry at the highest and most difficult earthly elevation—"Upon some mountain-top"—where the poet may kneel and wait for inspiration "until I feel / A glowing splendor round about me hung" (50–51). Similarly, the peak of imaginative attainment symbolized by the Elgin marbles further impresses upon Keats the severity of the poetic ascent:

> . . . each imagin'd pinnacle and steep
> Of godlike hardship tells me I must die
> Like a sick Eagle. . . .

It should be apparent at this point that the two types of metaphors describing poetic ascent—whether it be winged flight to suggest wholly intuitive, spontaneous soaring or the more deliberate, difficult uphill climbing to signify a more realistic, philosophical poetry that wrestles with the problems of humanity—are dependent upon Keats's attitude toward poetry at the time he is composing. In general, winged flight represents a highly romantic, internal poetic coursing toward some private vision of truth-beauty, while the deliberate trudge upwards represents the poet's difficult search for vision turned outward in an attempt to aid men to truth. The latter attitude toward poetry accounts for Keats's significant variation of the winged flight metaphor.

24. *Letters*, I, 141.
25. *The Prelude*, Bk. XIV, likewise demonstrates the poet's uphill journey of imagination.

The elf

The workings of the imagination may be described as magical. The strangely alchemic power of sexual passion on the imagination, as revealed in the "pleasure thermometer" passage in *Endymion*, suggests how closely allied is the poet's art to sorcery. The poet's winged dream-flights of fancy, defying time and space, further identify the poetic act as supernatural. Since Keats continually implies that the creation of poetry demands more than human powers, he quite appropriately attributes feats of imagination to elves, gnomes, sprites, and fairies; and indeed, the whole poetic domain he identifies as "fairy land." The sonnet, "On a Dream," written after reading Dante's episode of Paolo and Francesca, provides a useful example of the metaphor of the sprightly imagination as at once industrious and creative:

> As Hermes once took to his feathers light,
>   When lulled Argus, baffled, swoon'd and slept,
> So on a Delphic reed, my idle spright
>   So play'd, so charm'd, so conquer'd, so bereft
> The dragon-world of all its hundred eyes;
>   And, seeing it asleep, so flew away
>
>   . . . .
>   . . . to that second circle of sad hell
>
>   . . . .
> Pale were the lips I kiss'd, and fair the form
> I floated with, about that melancholy storm. . . .

The entire waking experience of reading Dante provides the source for Keats's dream. Playing music on an Apollonian reed, his "idle spright" of imagination stirs itself to life, takes flight, and achieves ecstatic union with the womanly embodiment of truth-beauty, Francesca. He perhaps chose the word "spright" in this poem, as in "Ode on Indolence"—"Vanish, ye Phantoms! from my idle spright"—with special care, for it means not only "spirit" but also "vital essence," "elf," "fairy," "goblin," "the mind," and "mental faculties." All of these meanings, and particularly the term "vital essence," apply to the imagination. In this sonnet, as well as in *Endymion*, the "spright" would achieve supreme poetic happiness in "fellowship with essence," i.e., in the union of mortal and immortal minds.

The whole of *Endymion* comprises a sequence of elfin voyages not unlike that of Keats's sprite in the sonnet on Paolo and Francesca and the "fire-wing'd" ascension of Phoebus in the sonnet to Spenser; for Endymion spans earth, heaven, and ocean in his elfin search for poetic vision. His voyage is recurrently described as a "fairy journey" conquering time and space with the swiftness and precision of a Puck or Ariel on a magical errand for his master.

The letter to Reynolds on "a voyage of conception" demands special attention here, for it suggests that the poetic imagination performs the same amazing feats as Shakespeare's ministering fairies: "How happy is such a 'voyage of conception' . . . a strain of musick conducts to 'an odd angle of the Isle' and when the leaves whisper it [i.e., the voyage of conception] puts a 'girdle round the earth.' " [26] Both of these quoted phrases, the first from *The Tempest* and the second from *A Midsummer Night's Dream*, allude to the magical deeds of Puck and Ariel, who are at the point of executing their masters' wishes. These fairies are able to change their shapes at will, to haunt the woods with music, and to move instantaneously wherever Prospero and Oberon command. Keats interprets Oberon and Prospero as poet-conjurors, and their fairy slaves as the industrious fancy.

His very special reading of key parts of these two plays I have noted elsewhere. But as the source for the metaphor of the elf of poetry, these romantic comedies require a wider discussion in order that we may appreciate just how private and literary is Keats's use of figures. *The Tempest* provides sufficient evidence for us to fathom his special interpretation of Ariel as the imagination. Prospero calls Ariel "My tricksy spirit . . . my diligence" (V. i. 227, 241). Further, he commands his elf as a magician would his own fancy:

> Go make thyself like a nymph o' the sea:
> Be subject to no sight but thine and mine,
> Invisible to every eyeball else.
>
> (I. ii. 301–303)

26. *Letters*, I, 231.

And if Ariel is capable of fanciful deceit, Puck too has the power to roam invisibly and practice the deceptions that his master commands. Further, both fairies possess the industriousness of the honeybee, an insect which Keats specifically identifies as a figure for the active poetic imagination in his letter to Reynolds. Though arguing that passiveness has its rewards for the poet, he also suggests that Hermes, the god of eloquence and the messenger of Apollo, like the bee, can engender in the receptive poet imaginative knowledge:

Now it is more noble to sit like Jove [than] to fly like Mercury—let us not therefore go hurrying about and collecting honey-bee like, buzzing here and there impatiently from a knowledge of what is to be arrived at: but let us open our leaves like a flower and be passive and receptive— budding patiently under the eye of Apollo and taking hints from every noble insect that favors us with a visit.[27]

The passage most likely derives from Ariel's song,

> Where the bee sucks, there suck I:
> In a cowslip's bell I lie. . . .

(V. i. 88–89)

Keats's adaptation of this song seems yet another indication of a persistent association of imagination with fairies, flight, fertility, and nourishment.

Though the elfin imagination serves its master faithfully in Shakespeare, it plays falsely with those mortals whom it is assigned to deceive, mortals too weak and defenseless to withstand the magic and incantations of Prospero and Oberon. Keats often feels that he is a victim, an abused Trinculo, rather than the ruler of his poetic elf. We have already noted in the poems an awareness of the dangers of the false poetic muse who casts the doting, beguiled poet into a deathly thraldom. The mischievous elf practices a like treachery on the mortal poet. "Ode to a Nightingale," for example, repines over the deceptions of the elfin fancy:

> . . . the fancy cannot cheat so well
> As she is fam'd to do, deceiving elf. . . .

Endymion voices a similar mistrust of the cheating fancy as his imaginative vision weakens:

27. *Ibid.*, p. 232.

And thoughts of self came on, how crude and sore
The journey homeward to habitual self!
A mad-pursuing of the fog-born elf,
Whose flitting lantern . . .
Cheats us into a swamp.[28]

(II, 275–279)

Endymion's pursuit of the elf's deceptive lantern involves the same kind of madness that Keats himself was aware of in pursuing a poetry which he suspected was unreal, a wisp or shadow of truth: "I am sometimes so very sceptical as to think Poetry itself a mere Jack a lanthern to amuse whoever may chance to be struck with its brilliance." [29] Once again poetry is identified as an elf, a "Jack a lanthern," whose annoyance and deceit the poet forswears, in "Ode on Indolence." His "maiden most unmeek," or "demon Poesy," love, and ambition all remain phantoms incapable of arousing his indolent poetic spirit:

Vanish, ye Phantoms from my idle spright,
Into the clouds, and never more return!

Here we find the elfin poetic capability associated with the woman-muse. This linkage might be expected, for Keats frequently joins his large gathering metaphor with lesser ones, as we have seen, for example, in the clustering of sexual passion, dream, flight, music, and light.

In the sonnet "When I have fears that I may cease to be," death's dateless night forebodes, chiefly, the loss of "the faery power," i.e., fancy. The lines,

And when I feel, fair creature of an hour,
That I shall never look upon thee more,

28. Spurgeon has noted the parallel between Keats's "fog-born elf" and Shakespeare's description of Ariel leading mortals into a wilderness (p. 13).

29. *Letters,* I, 242. Compare Endymion's complete skepticism of the beguiling fancy in Book IV:

...No, never more
Shall airy voices cheat me to the shore
Of tangled wonder, breathless and aghast.
Adieu, my daintiest Dream! ...

(IV, 653–656)

The "airy voices" suggest the special talent of Ariel, who, playing on his tabor and singing, lures Trinculo, Stephano, and Caliban into briars and swamps and then abandons them.

> Never have relish in the faery power
>   Of unreflecting love. . . .

suggest that the imagination as a woman, the "fair creature" of one precious hour, provides him with the "faery power" of spontaneous fancy that thrives in passion. As with the visitations of Lamia and Cynthia, these gifts of fancy are ephemeral, the blessing of an hour.

In other poems, Keats clearly invests his women-muses with elfin powers. Lamia, for example, is at first no wanton meddler in human affairs as are ordinary fairies. She is a "penanced lady elf" (I, 55). In metamorphosing from serpent to woman, "her elfin blood in madness ran" (147). Freed from her prison tree, she enjoys the mobility of an elf and directs her way to Corinth where she chooses "so fairily / By the wayside to linger" (200–201), until Lycius passes. By entering Lycius' world and rewarding him with a life of sensations, Lamia, metamorphosed into a woman, performs precisely the same magical role as Puck. For she too inspires a mortal with heightened fancy and unearthly visions of beauty. As she sleeps with Lycius in her fairy palace, their intensifying passion and dreaming dramatize a central tenet held by Keats: "I have the same Idea of all our Passions as of Love they are all in their sublime, creative of essential Beauty."[30] The elfin Lamia, therefore, represents the imaginative force searching for and finding fulfilment in sexual passion.

Keats's women-muses are often attended by elfin yeomen. Lamia, for example, missions "her viewless servants" to decorate her palace (I, 136). The "Queen-Moon" of "Ode to a Nightingale" reigns on her poetic throne "cluster'd around by all her starry fays," who presumably are able to carry out her royal ministrations in moonlight. Similarly, in the poem "Fancy," the reigning poetic imagination "has vassals to attend her." Through their embassy

> She will bring, in spite of frost,
> Beauties that the earth hath lost. . . .
>
> (29–30)

Through her elfin servants, the Queen-Moon has the power to change the real world into a fairy land of imagination. Bathing the earth in her light, she releases her elves of fancy, who invest the landscape and

30. *Letters*, I, 184.

air with untold beauties. Keats describes that fairy land of poetry in his epistle "To George Felton Mathew":

> . . . witness what with thee I've seen,
> The dew by fairy feet swept from the green,
> After a night of some quaint jubilee
> Which every elf and fay had come to see:
> When bright processions took their airy march
> Beneath the curved moon's triumphal arch. . . .
>
> (25–30)

From Keats's first efforts in *Poems*, (1817), to his very last work, the figure of the elf and the poetic fairy land recur. Interestingly, at the very end of his career, November and December of 1819, he was at work on "The Cap and Bells," an allegorical satire of his literary circle. The various elves are characterizations of his rival poets, and Panthea, the fairy capital of poetry, represents London. Elfinan, the fairy emperor reluctantly betrothed to Berthea, appears to be a portrayal of both Keats and Byron; Hum represents the obnoxious Hunt and perhaps Lamb also.[31] And Crafticanto suggests the characters of Wordsworth and Southey. The intrigues and backbiting of each of these elfin-poets seem an honest estimation on Keats's part of the extreme vanity and egotism of his literary rivals. He himself is none too charitable in his description of Crafticanto, or Wordsworth, practicing his metaphysics:

> Show him a mouse's tail, and he will guess,
> With metaphysic swiftness, at the mouse;
> Show him a garden, and with speed no less,
> He'll surmise sagely of a dwelling house. . . .
>
> (VII)

Keats's poetic fairy-land harbors all manner of meddlesome and vain elfin poets. Like Puck, Ariel, the "Jack a lanthern" of poetry, and Endymion's "fog-born elf," they are cheats and deceivers. The suggestion is that the poets' cunning and dishonesty, like the tricksy elves, seem a natural circumstance of the literary world of London. The use of the elf as the large metaphor for "The Cap and Bells" therefore is appropriate.

31. Robert Gittings, *The Mask of Keats* (London, 1956), pp. 136, 138–139.

The persistent association of the elf with poetry throughout an entire career suggests how ingrained this figure remained in Keats's memory. Indeed, the very next poem he had hoped to begin after landing in Italy involved another elfin spirit, Milton's Sabrina.[32] At sea Keats told Severn that he would begin her story.[33] One might venture a guess on the nature and theme of his newly proposed poem: Might Sabrina represent a beneficent Lamia who guides the mortal poet to a safe and complete poetic vision rather than to his death? For unlike the deceiving elves whom Endymion falls victim to, Sabrina is guileless and protective; and yet she possesses all the magical art to lift the poet-lover to imaginative vision.

The steeds

We note an even more important variation within the organizing metaphor of the adventurous poetic flight. The poet is recurrently borne aloft not on his own wings, but rather by winged steeds. The metaphorical link between steed and imagination is explicit in "Sleep and Poetry," which asks:

> . . . Is there so small a range
> In the present strength of manhood, that the high
> Imagination cannot freely fly
> As she was wont of old? prepare her steeds,
> Paw up against the light, and do strange deeds
> Upon the clouds? . . .
>
> (162–167)

32. In a previous poem, Keats associates the poetry of Beaumont and Fletcher with Comus, the elf of sensuality and drink:

> Spirit here that laughest!
> Spirit here that quaffest!
> Spirit here that dancest!
> Noble soul that prancest!
>
> . . . .
>
> Spirit, I flush
> With a Bacchanal blush
> Just fresh from the Banquet of Comus!

("Song" [Written on a blank page in Beaumont and Fletcher's works]).

33. Sir Sidney Colvin, *John Keats: His Life and Poetry, His Friends, Critics and After Fame* (New York, 1917), p. 79.

Other examples of the recurrent association of winged steeds with the "strange deeds" of imagination might be cited to show that this early-conceived metaphor is hardly isolated but an intrinsic part of Keats's stock. Peona admits to Endymion that her fanciful visions see "horses prancing" in the sunset (I, 744). And similarly, the epistle "To My Brother George" records these "strange deeds" of fancy's steeds:

> . . . when a Poet is in such a trance
> In air he sees white coursers paw, and prance. . . .
>
> (26–27)

The letters speak of imaginative flight in equestrian imagery. To Taylor Keats says, "I have been endeavouring to persuade myself to untether Fancy and let her manage for herself.[34] And to James Rice he asserts that the steed of imagination cannot maintain his upward coursings, for the mounted poet, as "spiritual cottager, has knowledge of the terra semi incognita of things unearthly; and cannot for his Life, keep in the check rein." [35]

All these examples subtly associate poetic flight with Pegasus, the winged horse closely linked to poetry by virtue of its having dwelled on Mount Helicon and having created the sacred fountain of imagination, Hippocrene, by striking its hoof in the earth. According to Lemprière, Pegasus "became the favorite of the Muses," perhaps for these reasons.

In addition we must not overlook the close association between Pegasus and Cynthia. How are we to interpret, for example, Endymion's address to the moon—"thou wast my steed" (III, 167)—or the description in "Sleep and Poetry" of the maiden-muses in saddle—"Stooping their shoulders o'er a horse's prance" (332)—but as significantly linked metaphors indicating that moon and muse and steed all provide imaginative experience for the poet. Both of the quoted lines allude to the poetic vitality associated with Pegasus.

The steeds are also associated with Apollo and quite obviously, therefore, with poetry. Under the masterly control of the supreme poet, the harnessed steeds of imagination draw his chariot across the sky and respond to his bidding. In "Sleep and Poetry," Keats would like to hold the reins to Apollo's steeds, to assume that god's rapt concentration and poetic "glow," and to put on his divine knowledge; in short, the mortal

34. *Letters*, II, 234.   35. *Ibid.*, I, 255.

poet would like to tame his imagination through the skill and knowledge of poetic horsemanship which only the divine poet possesses consummately:

> And now broad wings. Most awfully intent
> The driver of those steeds is forward bent,
> And seems to listen: O that I might know
> All that he writes with such a hurrying glow. . . .
>
> (151–154)

Prompted by a picture by Poussin entitled "L'Empire de Flore," Keats intends the coursing steeds and driver to be an analogue for the strength of high imagination ranging beyond mere luxurious poetry (represented by Flora) toward the realm of philosophy and "Soul-making."[36] Further, the passage serves to inform us of the meaning of Apollo's words in *Hyperion*: "Knowledge enormous makes a god of me" (III, 113). That is to say, Apollo possesses supreme poetic knowledge by which he is able to order his steeds of imagination on a course that brings light to the universe. If Apollo's intentness and skill at the reins is a fairly apparent metaphor for poetic knowledge, this figure seems less obvious in *Lamia*. Lycius, the intent, Platonic dreamer, "charioting foremost in the envious race" (I, 217), must be identified (by collation of Keats's recurrent equestrian imagery) as an Apollo figure mastering his own imagination in the race for poetic eminence."[37] Indeed, it is partly through his fine horsemanship that Lamia decides to grant him her poetic "knowledge enormous."

The most extensive Pegasian flight in all of the poetry appears in Book IV of *Endymion*, where Endymion, soaring to heaven with the Indian Maid on "two steeds jet-black, / Each with large dark blue wings upon his back" (343–344), finally does put on the knowledge of Apollo. The episode bears analysis, for the metaphorical nature of this flight differs significantly from horseless flights, in that Endymion's handling of his steeds shows a confidence, control, and strength which are ordinarily

36. Ian Jack's informative essay on the pictorial source of this episode and other parts of "Sleep and Poetry" supports and amplifies my interpretation of the Apollonian chariot. Keats saw in "L'Empire de Flore" "the nobler life" of poetic endeavor, represented in the steeds, chariot, and charioteer. See " 'The Realm of Flora' in Keats and Poussin," *Times Literary Supplement* (April 10, 1959), p. 212.

37. "Envious race" could also mean here "rivalrous group of people," a not altogether charitable allusion to his fellow poets.

unknown to the poet using his own frail pinions of imagination. Here very little sense of the fear of soaring seems to predominate as in Endymion's other flights. Endymion places the Indian Maid on one of the steeds "and felt himself in spleen to tame / The other's fierceness" (346–347). As master of the steeds, he holds their speed, range and course in check as the expert poet wilfully controls and directs his imagination:

> . . . Through the air they flew,
> High as the eagles. Like two drops of dew
> Exhal'd to Phoebus' lips, away they are gone,
> Far from the earth away—unseen, alone,
> Among cool clouds and winds, but that the free,
> The buoyant life of song can floating be
> Above their heads, and follow them untir'd. . . .
> (347–353)

The images clustering around the central metaphor of flight further dramatize the poetic nature of the adventure. The steeds are taking the flight which the aspiring eagle-poet of "On Seeing the Elgin Marbles" would like to take. The comparison of the flight to breath "exhaled to Phoebus' lips" suggests the poetic nature of the journey, for the flight itself is to be identified as poetic utterance in honor of the god of poetry. The "untir'd" life of song, following the steeds and their passengers, seems to be the sustaining, "buoyant" force which always accompanies or issues from successful imaginative flight. Keats himself intrudes to speak of his imaginative intoxication and to avow that he is the source of the song which provides the buoyancy for Endymion and his steeds:

> Muse of my native land, am I inspir'd?
> This is the giddy air, and I must spread
> Wide pinions to keep here; nor do I dread
> Or height, or depth, or width, or any chance
> Precipitous: I have beneath my glance
> Those towering horses and their mournful freight.
> Could I thus sail, and see, and thus await
> Fearless for power of thought, without thine aid? . . .
> (354–361)

Passing through Sleep's purple mist, Endymion is lulled; flight and dream become one:

Endymion sleepeth and the lady fair.
Slowly they sail, slowly as icy isle
Upon a calm sea drifting: and meanwhile
The mournful wanderer dreams. . . .

(404–407)

The joining of two metaphors for poetic experience has the force of intensifying Endymion's perceptions and inner creative life and suggests that his imaginative ascension is about to result in vision. He has a rare prefigurative dream wherein he "walks / On heaven's pavement, . . . talks / To divine powers," and is upstart enough to try Phoebus Apollo's bow (408–411). He then meets Cynthia, wakes up, and "beheld awake his very dream." Dream and flight on the spanning horse of imagination have raised Endymion to the realm of truth-beauty for the moment. In this particular dream-flight, Endymion's most successful achievement of Cynthia's realm must be credited to the sturdy, supporting, obedient, winged horses of imagination. In suggesting the strength of imagination by this figure, Keats reminds his reader of an earlier statement that poetry is "the supreme of power; / 'Tis might" ("Sleep and Poetry," 236–237). The vigor and deftness of Endymion's horsemanship is no less responsible for the success of his flight. Here then is the poet in complete control of his poetic imagination.

Keats moves toward an entirely different theme in using the Pegasus metaphor as a means to comment in a highly satiric manner on his own and contemporary poetry. He compares the grandeur of Pegasus' swift and powerful flight with the feeble, plodding, earth-bound movements of the poets of his own day. In attacking the inanities of contemporary poetry, he has Apollo blush at his bardic progeny, the dunces who "swayed about upon a rocking horse, / And thought it Pegasus" ("Sleep and Poetry," 186–187). And in one of the most humorous letters on his failure in imaginative flight during the composition of *Otho the Great*, Keats ironically uses Apollo's steeds and chariot as a submerged metaphor in admitting to Dilke, "Brown and I are pretty well harnessed again to our dog-cart. I mean the Tragedy which goes on sinkingly." [38] This description aptly suggests the dullness felt: the two men in place of Pegasus, a cart for a chariot, and a sinking movement instead of flight. An additional example of the satiric use of the Pegasus metaphor appears in

38. *Letters*, II, 135.

The Cap and Bells, where Crafticanto's[39] poetic style is described as strangely elegant:

> Gentle and tender, full of soft conceits,
>
> . . . .
>
> O, little faery Pegasus! rear—prance—
> Trot round the quarto—ordinary time!
> March, little Pegasus, with pawing hoof sublime! . . .
>
> (LXXI)

The poetic steed is here a pretty little verse-plaything, a circus pony delicately prancing instead of soaring powerfully. In prancing, trotting, and marching in "ordinary time," Pegasus' hoofs beat out a regular monotonous measure, like the unvaried, rocking-horse rhythm of the poet-dunces in "Sleep and Poetry," to suggest the mediocrity of Crafticanto's meter. The metaphorical linkage between the pacing of horses and metrical monotony is evident in this stanza. The winged horse, therefore, conveys to Keats not only the attribute of imaginative flight, but because it is one of the most regular of pacing animals, also represents the quality of meter in poetry. Thus we may be justified in interpreting the equine gaits both in Peona's vision of "horses prancing" (I, 744) and in Keats's trance in which "white coursers paw, and prance" ("To My Brother George," 26–27) as metrical regularity that brings order to the flights of imagination.

Further justification for this reading of the horse-metaphor can be made by citing the diction Keats used in talking about meter in poetry, meter being, as Bailey told Lord Houghton, "one of Keats's favorite topics of conversation." Bailey said,

> The principle of melody in verse . . . he believed to consist in the adroit management of open and close vowels. . . . In 'Endymion,' indeed there was much which not only seemed, but was, experimental, and it is impossible not to observe the superior mastery of melody, and sure-footedness of the poetic paces, in 'Hyperion.' [40]

Other examples from the poetry might be given to demonstrate that the horse put through its paces serves as a recurrent metaphor for the poetic imagination put to meter. The domineering Lycius would like to

39. Identified as both Wordsworth and Southey by Gittings. The prosiness of both poets' blank verse is, in part, the subject of the satire (see pp. 131–134).
40. Forman, *Works,* III, 123, n. 1.

show the rabble what a prize he owns. He proposes a public display of
Lamia, his own imagination, whereby he may proudly lead or ride her
about, in complete control of her gait:

> '. . . . Listen then!
> 'What mortal hath a prize, that other men
> 'May be confounded and abash'd withal,
> 'But lets it sometimes pace abroad majestical,
> 'And triumph, as in thee I should rejoice. . . .
>
> (II, 56–60)

Lamia does become a kind of obedient horse. The cadences of Cynthia
are equally majestic as she radiates "silver-footed messages" throughout
the universe (III, 51). With a similar quality of ceremonious gesture,
Circe first entices Glaucus with her "light footsteps," which significantly
accompany her music and "rich speech" (III, 423). In all these examples,
such pacing movement may be read as the necessary attribute of the
imagination manifesting itself as cadenced verse.

The boat

Although the imagination for the most part sallies upward on wings,
poetic adventure and discovery are often expressed by the metaphor of
the sea voyage.[41] The early poetry records the perils of launching out on
uncertain poetic voyages; for lack of skilful control, the boat of poetry
drifts aimlessly:

> Whene'er I venture on the stream of rhyme;
> With shatter'd boat, oar snapt, and canvass rent,
> I slowly sail, scarce knowing my intent. . . .
>
> ("To Charles Cowden Clarke," 16–18)

This fearful hesitance to sail is similar to his terror of poetic flight; un-
skilful handling may end in disaster. Realizing the danger, he is re-
luctant to set an early sail without first acquiring the craft of the poet-

---

41. This metaphor has a long poetic tradition. Keats perhaps borrowed it from the
first and last stanzas of Canto XII of *The Faerie Queene*, Bk. I. *Alastor*, among other
poems by Shelley, uses the voyage as a metaphor for the poetic quest, and may be
considered as another possible source.

mariner and the philosophical knowledge necessary for safe, lengthy voyaging:

> . . . my flag is not unfurl'd
> On the Admiral-staff,—and so philosophize
> I dare not yet. . . .
>
> ("To J. H. Reynolds, Esq.," 72–74)

His task is, therefore, to become a kind of apprentice seaman.

Despite his sense of poetic inadequacy, and despite examples of other poets' innumerable poetic launchings that have ended in wreckage, Keats steadfastly embarks on his most ambitious poetic voyage, *Endymion*. Speaking directly to his readers, in the introduction to Book II, he characteristically maintains that love provides the buoyant force for true poetic voyaging and scores as inferior those epic poems immersed in battle (called "pageant history") by referring to them, metaphorically, as wrecked poetic barks:

> Many old rotten-timber'd boats there be
> Upon thy [the sea's] vaporous bosom. . . .
>
> (18–19)

And many poetic conceptions have never been floated, out of vaingloriousness or fear of failure:

> . . . many a sail of pride,
> And golden keel'd, is left unlaunch'd and dry. . . .
>
> (20–21)

The significance of Endymion's recurrent sea-voyages[42] should now be apparent. They are attempts to master the craft of poetry, despite the winds and tides that may steer him off course and wreck his voyage of imagination. Endymion is firm in his resolution that

> . . . nothing base
> . . . could unlace
> The stubborn canvas for my voyage prepar'd—
> Though now 'tis tatter'd; leaving my bark bar'd
> And sullenly drifting: yet my higher hope

42. Newell F. Ford's investigation of Keats's meaning behind "perilous seas" identifies the sea as the realm of romance, mystery, and fancy. See "Keats's Romantic Seas: 'Ruthless' or 'Keelless'?" *Keats-Shelley Journal*, I (1952), 11–22.

Is of too wide, too rainbow-large a scope,
To fret at myriads of earthly wrecks. . . .

(I, 770–776)

We can be certain that Keats is talking metaphorically of the mariner-poet not in complete control of his headway, by comparing the nautical figures he uses here to those used in a letter to Bailey, written at the time he was bringing *Endymion* to completion: "a long Poem is a test of Invention which I take to be the Polar Star of Poetry, as Fancy is the Sails, and Imagination the Rudder." [43] Endymion's derelict boat lacks a sound canvas of fancy and rudder of imagination, yet he is determined to drift on uncertainly. In repeatedly using the boat metaphor, Keats is estimating his skill as a poet—a skill that is sorely lacking in the first book of *Endymion*, where he is trying out his newly rigged canvas and rudder. Less than two years later the metaphor reappears, not to describe his foundering, but to indicate his supreme skill in poetic seamanship in the great months of the odes: "I would feign [fain], as my sails are set, sail on without an interruption for a Brace of Months longer—I am in complete cue . . . ; and shall in these four Months do an immense deal." [44]

We may now easily identify the metaphor of the boat as a variation of the figure of winged flight, yet closely allied in tenor. The sails of the poet's boat serve as the means by which the poet rides the wind of inspiration in the same way that the poet's wings of imagination or those of Pegasus, catching the wind, bear him aloft. Both metaphors appropriately suggest the proficiency and control needed by the poet in order to maintain his voyaging to unknown realms. And though he is borne afloat by an outside, inspirational power (either the wind or the sea) his success is determined by his own skill in sailing, flying, or riding. These metaphors imply that art derives from the perfect interaction of poet and nature; for although wind, sea, or beast carry the poet, control, direction, and range—in short, artistic helmsmanship—depend ultimately upon the poet.

The excitement that Keats feels in his own voyages of imagination is as high-pitched in his exploration of the works of other poets. It is no whim that he would compare himself to the explorer, Cortez, or that

43. *Letters*, I, 170.   44. *Ibid.*, II, 141.

he would construct his poem, "On First Looking into Chapman's Homer," on the nautical voyage of discovery. To be sure, the concern here is with personal critical discovery, but it becomes an occasion of imaginative involvement that launches him on his own "voyage of conception."[45] Reading Chapman is no ordinary cruise to smaller, "western islands," but a voyage to a new unexplored continent where he first discovers in "wild surmise" the vastness of a new ocean of poetry. As a mariner with "eagle eyes," Keats fixes his rapt and unerring attention on transfixing beauty.

Swimming

In addition to flying and sailing, we find a third and less important metaphor for imaginative journeying. Swimming is, in many ways, more adventurous than sailing in the boat of poetry and, when performed beneath the sea, proves the most explorative of all voyages of imagination. Like the dizzy heights through which Endymion ranges, the sea is a place of wonder, charmed by mysterious voices. Like the empyrean heaven the sea is an "unimaginable lodge" that can only be guessed at by the terrestrial poet.

> Its voice mysterious, which whoso hears
> Must think on what will be, and what has been. . . .
> ("To My Brother George")

The fathomless sea, therefore, is a suitable realm for poetic voyages of discovery.

The poet as fish is little different from the poet as fledged bird in Keats's metaphorical schema. One of the significances of "To George Felton Mathew" arises out of this similarity. The swimming fish, like the flying poet, is indeed "alchemized and free of space," which for Keats is one of the first conditions of creativity. Swimming is therefore metaphorically linked to dream and flight. In the poem, Diana plucks Mathew, who is first a flower, and throws him into the stream of song "To

---

45. The letter of February 19, 1818, a veritable prose-poem, uses as its organizing metaphor the aesthetic voyage. Keats's idea of a "voyage of conception" regards the imaginative "Minds of Mortals" as "different and bent upon . . . diverse Journeys" (*ibid.*, I, 232).

meet her glorious brother's greeting beam." Apollo then metamorphoses him into a fish of gold, whereupon Mathew swims on "travels strange," seeing "all the wonders of the mazy range / O'er pebbly crystal, and o'er golden sands"; and to suggest further that the immersion is poetic in nature, the last line introduces a muse-nymph, a kind of watery Cynthia, who inspires Mathew by offering nourishment and love. "Kissing [his] daily food from Naiad's pearly hands," he is the inspired poet-fish in the "mazy" stream of song.

Endymion's fantastic adventure at the bottom of the sea, in the third book of *Endymion*, represents, metaphorically, the poetic exploration of one of the three realms of beauty over which Cynthia's suzerainty extends: "water, fiery realm, and airy bourne." The moon goddess alone, the most benevolent of the "thousand Powers [that] keep religious state" (30–31), allows the poet to penetrate these depths and heights and by this immersion guides him to imaginative vision. Endymion literally sees beneath the world of appearance and into the life of things as he swims in the sea of imagination, which, appropriately, is ruled and moved by the moon's influence. He credits his superhuman power of total immersion to Cynthia:

> O Love! how potent hast thou been to teach
> Strange journeyings! Wherever beauty dwells,
> In gulf or aerie, mountains or deep dells,
> In light, in gloom, in star or blazing sun,
> Thou pointest out the way, and straight 'tis won.
> Amid his toil thou gav'st Leander breath. . . .
>
> (92–97)

Swimming, then, is an act of imagination by which the poet can know one of Cynthia's realms; whether penetrating the airy stream of purple sleep on Pegasus or Cimmerian depths, Endymion is repeatedly buoyed up because he is one of the "elect"; Cynthia's fidelity to him remains constant no matter what kind of element he chooses to immerse himself in.

Endymion's immersion in the ocean, in Book III, may have profound archetypal implications; for if the ocean symbolizes the source of life and the beginning of knowledge—i.e., the womb of all creation—his plunge and subaqueous wanderings suggest the quest for primary creation that exists beyond the ken of mortal man. That creative force behind all existence is at once sexual, imaginative, and divine; and in Cynthia reside these three levels of creativity, levels discriminated by the sensibility of Keats, who is the questing Endymion.

Chapter four

The fine frenzy — Manna — Flower dew — The laurel and oak — Wine

The fine frenzy

We have already noted Keats's identification of love with fancy and the absolute necessity of passion or excitement as "the only state for the best sort of poetry." Most often the woman-muse excites the poet into a perceptive, impassioned, creative state, which, as suggested in the last chapter, is associated with dream and flight.

Another basic metaphor, very closely related to dreams and love, describes that state of poetic excitement which Plato termed "madness" and which Shakespeare described as "a fine frenzy." [1] Around this parent metaphor cluster four kindred metaphors, all of which serve as vehicles of communicating the poetic fine frenzy almost in the same capacity as the women-muses. These metaphors are expressive of varieties of poetic stimulants not unlike aphrodisiacs, for each has the special power of raising the poet to transcendent passion, which Keats identifies as Platonic lunacy.

The frenzied poet is a common figure in his poetry. An early poem speaks of the poet winning "in fine wrath some golden sounds" ("I stood tip-toe," 203). Another calls Cynthia's face "the *enthusiast's* friend" ("To Some Ladies," 4; italics mine), intending to convey the literal meaning in this carefully chosen word, that is, *en theos*, to be possessed

1. See "Phaedrus," 245, and "Ion," 534, in *The Dialogues of Plato*, ed. B. Jowett (New York, 1937), I, 249, 289; and *A Midsummer Night's Dream*, V. i. 12.

of the gods with unmeasurable ardor. In a similar vein, the conceptions of poems to come make Keats "mad with glimpses of futurity" in "Lines on Seeing a Lock of Milton's Hair." And when these glimpses or visions are being fixed in poetry, the very process of incantation which the lunatic, spellbound poet feels is transferred in successful composition:

> For Poesy alone can tell her dreams,
> With the fine spell of words alone can save
> Imagination from the sable chain
> And dumb enchantment. . . .
>
> (*The Fall of Hyperion*, I, 8–11)

In the first of two sonnets "On Fame" the poet is explicitly called a madman; the line, "Ye artists, lovelorn! madmen that ye are!" gives evidence of a consistent association of lovesickness with poetic madness. The lunatic poet's fit quite appropriately waxes in moonlight, whose influence "often must have seen a poet frantic" ("To George Felton Mathew," 38).

Frequently the poet's frantic state is compared with fever that borders on illness. In the middle of writing *Lamia*, Keats avows, "I am in complete cue—in the fever," [2] suggesting an excessive excitement or derangement that he was aware of in his fellow poet, Charles Armitage Brown, of whom he says, "he will write when the *fit* comes on him." [3] Keats invests these metaphorical fever-fits with appropriate physical details characteristic of illness; the "pangs," "burning and strife," and "forehead hot and flush'd" recorded in "Lines on Seeing a Lock of Milton's Hair" reveal the inward fire of the poet, which a letter to Hunt describes as a "continual burning of thought." [4] As we have seen in Chapter two, the joy of such imaginative frenzy is not without its noxious effect; [5] yet, ac-

---

2. *Letters*, II, 141.   3. *Ibid.*, p. 136.
4. *Ibid.*, I, 139.
5. Keats admits to James Rice, "I may say that for 6 Months before I was taken ill I had not passed a tranquil day—Either that gloom overspred me or I was suffering under some passionate feeling, or if I turn'd to versify that acerbated the poison of either sensation" (*Letters*, II, 260). The giddiness that he felt in poetic frenzy and the resulting depression as the spell waned can be tentatively explained as the effects of tuberculosis, which Keats contracted in 1818, according to Aileen Ward (*John Keats: The Making of a Poet* [New York, 1963], p. 257). But see also Sir William Hale-White, *Keats as Doctor and Patient* (London, 1938), pp. 68–69. The extreme dizziness which the tubercular feels is frequently accompanied by a period of vision and strong sensation. This psychic phenomenon in tuberculars,

cording to Keats, such frenzy is wholly necessary for the best sort of poetry. Indeed, the state of mind in which poetry can never be produced—
indolence—is a significantly unfeverished one: "my pulse grew less and
less; / Pain had no sting" ("Ode on Indolence"). His head does not
feel flushed, but is "cool-bedded in the flowery grass." This state of poetic
languor comes as inexplicably as the state of imaginative furor. All that
the poet can hope to do is wait for the return of his fine frenzy, as a
letter to Bailey admits: "I have this morning such a Lethargy that I
cannot write—the reason of my delaying is oftentimes from this feeling—
I wait for a proper temper," [6] that is, the "short fever-fit" of poetry described in "Ode on Indolence."

In addition to the recurrent imagery of fever, burning, and lunacy,
strongly religious diction describes the fine poetic frenzy because of
Keats's belief in the essentially holy function of the poet. Like all of the
other Romantics, he considers the poet in the ancient, Platonic sense
as priest or prophet. According to Wordsworth and Coleridge he is an
oracle, according to Shelley, a hierophant. At times when Keats is seized
by holy frenzy he feels that he, as maker, may be competing with God
himself. A letter to the artist, Haydon, gives evidence of such a presumption:

I know no one but you who can be fully sensible of the turmoil and anxiety, the sacrifice of all what is called comfort the readiness to Measure
time by what is done and to die in 6 hours could plans be brought to
conclusions.—the looking upon the Sun the Moon the Stars, the Earth
and its contents as materials to form greater things—that is to say ethereal
things—but here I am talking like a Madman greater things that our
Creator himself made!! [7]

The poet can be a secondary god, a kind of votary to the Supreme Creator in those rare and blessed moments of divine frenzy when vision and
prophecy are granted to him. Since Keats considers the poet as an elected

---

called *spes phthisica* has long been known. (See, e.g., René and Jean Dubos, *The
White Plague: Tuberculosis, Man and Society* [Boston, 1952], pp. 59–63). The
application of medical facts is, I think, valid and useful. Critics and biographers, so
far as I have been able to determine, have overlooked what appears to be a strong
relationship between Keats's physical infirmity and imaginative stimulation leading to
creative bursts of poetry. One might venture to say that tuberculosis is the source of
his frenzied states of poetic imagination.

6. *Letters*, I, 287.   7. *Ibid.*, p. 143.

being (a notion that is particularly classical), his descriptions of the fine frenzy make repeated reference to the archetypal poet of rapt vision, the Delphian priest in Apollo's service. A repeated theme in the poetry is Apollo, his power, knowledge, and beauty. In worshipping the god of poetry, Keats would naturally identify himself with the Delphic oracles,[8] whose function was at once poetic and religious. The "Delphian pain" in "Song" ("Hence Burgundy . . .") alludes to the holy, frenzied state of the poet in the moments immediately preceding the flight of his soul to Apollo. The identification of poetic experience as "Delphian" in several poems intends to evoke the full mythological lore of an ancient poetic rite. The worship of Apollo at the Oracle of Delphi was performed by priests and priestesses who gave prophecies in frenzy after having breathed in vapors rising out of the chasm directly under the oracle. These prophets spoke their truths in melodious but enigmatic hexameters. Delphic madness seemed to Keats (as it did to Shelley) a proper account of his own fits of poetic inspiration, not unlike flights in dreams or the supreme moments of impassioned sexuality. At one significant point in *Endymion*, for example, the poet-lover, in addressing Cynthia as his "Delphos," anticipates the frenzy and the poetry that she may impart to him in their union:

> Those lips shall be my Delphos, and shall speak
> Laws to my footsteps, colour to my cheek,
> Trembling or steadfastness to this same voice,
>
> . . . .
> Say, is not bliss within our perfect seisure?
>
> (IV, 713–715, 720)

In this cluster of metaphors we see the identification of Delphian frenzy, sexual passion, and poetic utterance, all of which taken singly or together represent the supreme experience of acquiring divine, poetic knowledge, an experience known only by the incanting, erotically possessed and poetically frenzied priestesses at Delphi. The Delphic gift from Cynthia of "footsteps" and "color," i.e., meter and frenzy, becomes apparent if the reader sees her as a Delphic priestess uttering oracles in hexameters. She is his example and inspiration, and the poetry unleashed

8. In this regard, Haydon said of Keats: "[he had] an eye that had an inward look, perfectly divine, like a Delphian priestess who saw visions" (quoted in Colvin, p. 79).

in Endymion's own voice may be either quivering or firm (i.e., either imperfect or perfect) depending on his and Cynthia's "perfect seisure." The words "perfect seisure" refer to the perfection of their union and also to their consummate Delphic frenzy. In sum, Keats identifies sexual experience and the fine poetic frenzy as one and the same. Fully realized poetry is voiced spontaneously in that perfectly impassioned state wherein the poet is united with his imagination.

Manna

Although the woman as muse may excite the Delphic frenzy, the poetry frequently refers to other agents that inspire the rare and usually unexpected moments of impassioned vision. In writing poems about poetry, Keats continually seeks appropriate metaphors for these unfathomable and gratuitous moments. One of the basic questions which he, like many other intuitive artists, attempts to answer through metaphor is "Whence come these imaginative fits?" Shakespeare best posed the problem in these lines:

> Such tricks hath strong imagination,
> That, if it would but apprehend some joy,
> It comprehends some bringer of that joy. . . .
> (A Midsummer Night's Dream, V. i. 18–20)

One of the bringers of poetic rapture is manna, the divine food dropping miraculously from heaven to sustain God's chosen few, the poets.[9] In using this metaphor, Keats repeatedly suggests the eucharistic effect of manna upon the poet. Miraculously inspiring poetic vitality, it brings him to a kind of frenzied, imaginative holy communion with Truth-Beauty.

Most commonly in the poetry, the manna of inspiration is bestowed

9. The Biblical allusion need not be labored here. Obviously Keats had his own idea of who God's favored race was and uses the Biblical source to his own clever purpose here. Equally significant as a source for Keats's metaphor is Plato's "Ion," which talks about the divinely inspired poet receiving honey from heaven. Nor should another classical source in myth be overlooked in accounting for recurrent association of manna with poetry. We find the Greeks and Romans worshipping Mercury, the inventor of the lyre (and therefore venerated by poets), with "offerings of milk and honey," because, as Lemprière reports, "he was the god of eloquence whose powers were sweet and persuasive."

upon the poet by the muse-goddesses in "honey-words" or honeyed breath. Lamia drops verbal manna: "the words she spake / Came, as through bubbling honey" (I, 64–65). All the divinities responsible for primary creation, the "far majesties" (of whom Cynthia is a member), provide for "every sense / Filling with spiritual sweets to plenitude / As bees gorge full their cells" (*Endymion*, III, 38–40). Recalling that poetic frenzy is achieved when all of the senses are brought into activity, we understand that manna serves to fill "every sense . . . to plenitude," and is therefore one of the chief "spiritual sweets." In their intimate moments, Cynthia's manna-giving power provides Endymion with "a honeyed tongue," as evidenced in her promise:

> Ere long I will exalt thee to the shine
> Of heaven ambrosial . . .
>
> . . . .
> Lispings empyrean will I sometimes teach
> Thine honied tongue. . . .[10]
>
> (II, 809–810, 819–820)

The honey metaphor is frequently linked synesthetically with other metaphors for poetry—such as sexual experience—to suggest further the extremely sensory nature of poetic experience. Cynthia's inspiring sexual embraces are recurrently described as "sweet." If Keats seems to confuse the taste of manna and the touch of sex, his particular purpose is to identify moments of poetic experience as at once divinely inspired and sensually frenzied; in short, he demonstrates once again that "a life of sensations" serves as the necessary prerequisite for intuitive aesthetic perception. Endymion describes his moment of inspiration thus:

> The same bright face I tasted in my sleep,
>
> . . . .
> . . . such a breathless honey-feel of bliss
>
> (I, 895, 903)

Once again we notice the compounding of feeling through synesthesia, the "honey-feel" being the important figurative device through which the sexual metaphor and the dream metaphor are linked. We also note

---

10. Keats's essay in the *Champion* uses the honey metaphor to describe Kean's voice: "his tongue must seem to have robbed the Hybla bees and left them honey-less! There is an indescribable *gusto* in his voice" (quoted in Colvin, p. 243).

light issuing from Cynthia's face; as a part of the cluster it suggests, once again, the radiance of poetic inspiration.

That love is closely related to the manna-dew of poetic inspiration is clearly established in yet another example. The introduction to Book II of *Endymion* avows that strong feelings of love generated by one kiss result in a train of remembrances of poetic inspiration from past days: "One kiss brings honey-dew from buried days" (7). In its context "honey-dew" represents the poetry of the past which the power of love can release in the memory. Once again the linkage of the metaphors of love and manna suggests the perfect complicity of intense emotion (love) and inspired poetry (honey). Keats's ability to unleash poetry, we may therefore conclude, depends on acute sensation alone; both metaphors convey that state of sensation, which is to be identified with poetic frenzy.

In the Circe episode, too, we find this significant conjoining of the two metaphors. Like Endymion, Glaucus is overwhelmed by Circe's "honey-words" (III, 426); the "ambrosia" she breathes intoxicates and eventually transfixes his "o'er-sweeten'd soul." By cruelly perverting her divine power to drop the manna of inspiration and by withholding her sexual favors from the unsuspecting Glaucus, she victimizes him completely.

Occasionally the blessing of manna-dew comes gratuitously upon the poet as "dew-dropping melody" (II, 373). More significantly, its wondrous fall gives Endymion the breath and eloquence to define rather extensively to Peona the nature of poetic happiness. He is quite clearly flushed with inspiration in the lines immediately preceding his credo on the "pleasure thermometer":

> . . . his eyelids
> Widened a little, as when Zephyr bids
> A little breeze to creep between the fans
> Of careless butterflies: amid his pains
> He seem'd to taste a drop of manna-dew,
> Full palatable; and a colour grew
> Upon his cheek, while thus he lifeful spake. . . .
>
> (I, 762–768)

Lest we mistake Keats's drift here, we must be aware that he takes pains to link Endymion's inspiration from manna-dew with the literal inspiration provided by Zephyr's "little breeze." Endymion consequently becomes flushed in a mild frenzy as he sets out to explain, "lifefully," poetic happiness in terms of a thermometer of graded poetic intensities.

If manna-dew is the companion to poetic enthusiasm, its absence portends dejection of poetic feeling. Endymion recurrently feels the hurtful drought of the imagination. In his search for poetic vision, he flies from place to place like a honeyless bee in hope of sipping inspiration:

> Another city he doth set about,
> Free from the smallest pebble-bead of doubt
> That he will seize on trickling honey-combs:
> Alas, he finds them dry; and then he foams,
> And onward to another city speeds. . . .
>
> (II, 148–152)

This passage suggests the distinction between the transcendent life in imagination, when the poet is divinely inspired by the manna from "trickling honeycombs," and the gnawing anxiety and pain when the inspiration is wanting. Endymion's failure to find the honeycombs is a failure to strike on the food of poetic vision, which alone sustains him. Resignedly then, Keats says of Endymion's frustration,

> But this is human life: the war, the deeds,
> The disappointment, the anxiety,
> Imagination's struggles, far and nigh,
> All human. . . .
>
> (153–156)

Endymion's active search for manna is, perhaps, too deliberate and pressing. According to Keats passivity has its virtues, for it often results in unexpected inspiration. To express this attitude toward passivity, a large portion of the letter on "distilled prose" develops, somewhat indirectly, the manna-dew metaphor: "Man should not dispute or assert but whisper results to his neighbour, and thus by every germ of Spirit sucking the Sap from mould ethereal every human might become great." [11] Further, it states that sensitive humanity, like a flower, should be "passive and receptive—budding patiently under the eye of Apollo and taking hints from [every] noble insect that favors us with a visit—

11. *Letters*, I, 232.

sap will be given us for Meat and dew for drink." [12] The "sap from mould ethereal" and the sap from Apollo's bee are manna-dew in disguise, dropping from heaven to inspire humanity, or more particularly, the most sensitive of men, the poet J. H. Reynolds, as well as Keats himself.

The importance of manna-dew in *The Fall of Hyperion* cannot be ignored. Quite by accident, the visionary hero stumbles across

> . . . a cool vessel of transparent juice,
> Sipp'd by the wander'd bee. . . .

> (I, 42–43)

By drinking this intoxicant, the speaker swoons into dream and the subsequent vision which Moneta provides. The line, "That full draught is parent of my theme," suggests that manna-dew, in providing imaginative release, is the parent of the entire poem.

Yet other "parents" of poetry can be found in Keats's array of metaphors. The divine "sap" and "dew" mentioned in the letter to Reynolds refer, in other passages in his poetry, to yet another and more esoteric metaphor for poetic inspiration, as we shall now see.

Flower dew

Two rather puzzling recurrent images, the petals of the flower and the dew upon it, often appear in striking episodes of imaginative vision or in fruitful reverie. By some powerful and private association born in Keats's past and retained in his memory, these inseparable images are linked with poetic experience. Why should he refer again and again to the feel of "Fair dewy roses [that] brush against our faces" when he is in the midst of reading or writing a poetic tale? In "I stood tip-toe," he places the image "dewy roses" in the midst of other metaphors for poetry, as for example, "luxurious wings." In *Endymion* the poet-lover dreams of Cynthia and starts up in expectation of receiving her, when the same dewy and petaled delight smothers his face:

> I started up, when lo! refreshfully,
> There came upon my face, in plenteous showers,
> Dew-drops, and dewy buds, and leaves, and flowers,

12. *Ibid*.

Wrapping all objects from my smothered sight,
Bathing my spirit in a new delight.
Aye, such a breathless honey-feel of bliss. . . .

(I, 898–903)

This joy is tantamount to the excitement of flight, sexual embrace, and dream, and in fact is preliminary to these sensory delights. The image recurs in the Adonis episode of Book II, where Cupids shake dew and violets in Adonis' eyes while he dreams immortal visions (458), the whole ritual being called "enchantments." Here the linkage of dew and flowers with ecstatic dreaming is apparent; nor is Adonis' dream tainted with human failing; it is like the dreams of gods, real and everlasting, as *Lamia* states:

Real are the dreams of Gods, and smoothly pass
Their pleasures in a long immortal dream. . . .

(I, 127–128)

If, as the evidence of these three examples indicates, imaginative experience derives from the feel of dew and flower petals, the question arises: Are these linkages of flower petals and flower dew with other metaphors for poetry arbitrary, merely accidental, or should we take them as meaningful? That is to say, is there some real linkage of the image with an idea powerfully engrained in Keats's memory? [13] One can understand the meaning behind these images by examining their source in a key section in *A Midsummer Night's Dream*. One can conjecture about the intensity with which Keats read Shakespeare; undoubtedly it was uncommonly sharp and responsive. The entire dramatic incident in which Oberon talks about dreams, fancy, and love, and then instructs Puck on how to take his revenge on Titania, shows that Keats found in Shakespeare a metaphor ready-made for his own poetic purpose. Oberon says to Puck,

Fetch me that flower; the herb I shew'd thee once:
The juice of it on sleeping eye-lids laid

13. We have already seen that Keats rarely uses a metaphor gratuitously, but rather in a highly meaningful fashion. As I have suggested in Chapter one when discussing Armstrong's theory of recurrent imagery, images may have a special, private significance for a poet because of some personal experience—aesthetic, emotional, or intellectual—which forms the link between idea and image. Such is the case with this particular imagery.

Will make or man or woman madly dote
Upon the next live creature that it sees. . . .[14]

(II. i. 169–172)

The juice of Oberon's flower has the power to affect the fancy greatly, as Keats recognized in Shakespeare's equating of love, fancy, and imagination.[15] For the Elizabethan, nothing else stimulated the imagination quite as much as the passion of love. In *Love's Labour's Lost*, for example, "Love . . . adds a precious seeing to the eye" of the poet. Indeed,

Never durst poet touch a pen to write
Until his ink were temper'd with love's sighs:
O, then his lines would ravage savage ears. . . .

(IV. iii. 346–348)

In flower dew, then, Keats finds a useful, if highly esoteric, figure for poetic inspiration. Puck's flower juice, like manna, serves to stimulate the imagination to poetic vision.

Keats so artfully disguises Shakespeare's flower-dew that neither its source nor its meaning is remotely apparent. Thus in the "pleasure thermometer" section of *Endymion*, the "orbed *drop* / Of light . . . that is love" can be identified very closely with Puck's dew-drops which he throws on Titania's eye-lids to inspire her fancy. The lines,

. . . its influence [i.e., the orbed drop of light's]
Thrown in our eyes, genders a novel sense,
At which we start and fret. . . .

signify that a like stimulation of the imagination and subsequent poetic frenzy (i.e., "fret") within the poet derive from the "orbed drop of light." The culmination of this manna-like stimulation is sexual union, which we have identified as supreme imaginative fulfilment. The dew-drop is, then, the food of love or fancy. A late letter confessing Keats's intense feeling for Fanny Brawne employs the figure of dew to describe impassioned love and racing fancy:

I never knew before, what such a love as you have made me feel, was; I

14. Spurgeon notes that in his copy of Shakespeare, Keats "marks or underlines nearly the whole of Act II, Sc. i" of *A Midsummer Night's Dream* (p. 19; see also p. 92).

15. See Chapter two above, p. 27 for a fuller discussion of Shakespeare's use of the word "fancy."

did not believe in it; my Fancy was affraid of it lest it should burn me up. But if you will fully love me, though there may be some fire, 't will not be more than we can bear when moistened and bedewed with Pleasures.[16]

Cynthia herself becomes the Puckish agent who sprinkles the dew of inspiration on Endymion's eyes. The poet-lover acknowledges that

> There is no lightning, no authentic dew
> But in the eye of love. . . .

> (IV, 78–79)

We are now able to see the irony in Circe's ministration to the "brutes" and "deformities" whom she has enslaved. They, like Glaucus, desire a "long love dream" (III, 440) and expect to be pleasurably alchemized by "the dew of her rich speech" and by her "honey words" (429, 426). But instead "She whisk'd against their eyes the sooty oil . . . , black [and] dull-gurgling" (521, 515), which immediately excites their pain and rage and then throws them into an agonizing silence, whereupon they vanish. The entire ritual, and especially the effects of Circe's flower-dew, must be read as an ironic inversion of Cynthia's benign act of throwing the dew of inspiration into Endymion's eyes to engender an ecstatic imaginative experience. It suggests enslavement by a false poetic muse who inflicts the pains of reality on those whose pursuit of poetry lacks the authentic dew of inspiration from a propitiating guardian. Deluded, they are doomed to eternal suffering.

The laurel and oak

The laurel, also known as the bay, has been a common symbol for poetry ever since Apollo chose it as his favorite tree in commemoration of his love for Daphne, who, fleeing from the god's mad pursuit, was metamorphosed into a laurel tree. In a few of the early sonnets the use of the bay wreath crown of poetic fame is obvious and traditional, and nothing more need be said of this particular meaning of the metaphor. Keats is aware, however, of a more significant reason for the ancient linking of laurel and poetry. Like manna, laurel has the power of stimulating the poet to Delphic, imaginative frenzy and thus is another metaphor for

16. *Letters*, II, 126.

poetic inspiration. John Potter's book on the religion and lore of ancient Greece, a book which Keats owned and used for material in his poetry, explains the antique significance of the laurel as a stimulant:

The Person that deliver'd the Oracles of the God [Apollo] was a Woman, whom they call'd Pythia . . . At her first sitting down upon the *Tripus,* she us'd to shake the Laureltree that grew by it, and sometimes to eat the Leaves . . . Nor did the *Pythia* only make use of Laurel in this Manner, but other Prophets also, it being thought to conduce to inspiration; whence it was peculiarly call'd . . . the *prophetic Plant.*[17]

The chewing of laurel leaves induces both poetic and erotic frenzy in which the Pythian priestess spoke her oracles in verse. Often a poet would recast her enigmas into perfect hexameters. Further, the laurel vapors may have been inhaled to inspire the desired trance, and sometimes caused an extreme transport culminating in a death-like swoon.[18]

The special significance of the laurel in Keats's poetry appears in "Sleep and Poetry":

> O Poesy! . . .
>
> . . . .
> Yield from thy sanctuary some clear air,
> Smoothed for intoxication by the breath
> Of flowering bays, that I may die a death
> Of luxury, and my young spirit follow
> The morning sun-beams to the great Apollo
> Like a fresh sacrifice; or, if I can bear
> The o'erwhelming sweets, 'twill bring to me the fair
> Visions of all places. . . .
>
> (53, 56–63)

Keats hopes to re-enact the holy, poetic ritual of Delphi and Tempe. In breathing the intoxicating fumes of laurel, which sweeten the "air" of poesy, he may fall into a Delphian swoon ("die a death of luxury") and take imaginative flight to Apollo, the granter of "fair visions." In these lines Keats is fully aware of the original function of the laurel as the

17. *Archaeologia Graeca: Antiquities of Greece* (London, 1775), I, 276, 278. Douglas Bush, "Notes on Keats's Reading," *PMLA*, L (1935), 785–806, shows in detail the extent of Keats's borrowings from this book.

18. Potter, p. 278, and Robert Graves, *The White Goddess* (New York, 1960), pp. 434–435, 492. There were a number of inspiration-inducing agents. The laurel vapors may have mingled with the mysterious, intoxicating fumes rising from the Delphic cavern mouth, which Potter describes on p. 275.

agent of inspiration. The laurel has a similar signification throughout his poetry.

The linkage of the laurel with other established metaphors for poetic inspiration recurs in several poems. The sonnet, "To the Ladies Who Saw Me Crown'd," compares the beauty of the moon's halo, women's lips and eyes, and the "dewy birth / Of morning Roses" (all of which induce inspiration) with "a wreath from the bay tree." By this kind of association we understand the laurel to have a metaphorical value beyond its ordinary signification of poetic achievement and fame. A further and more interesting demonstration of Keats's linked analogies, by which he describes poetic inspiration, occurs in "I stood tip-toe." At the rare moments of imagination,

> The soul is lost in pleasant smotherings:
> Fair dewy roses brush against our faces,
> And flowering laurels spring from diamond vases. . . .
> (132–134)

The significance of flower-dew we have already examined; its touch, conjoined with the sweet aroma of laurel and the brilliance of diamond vases, is an attempt to characterize in metaphor the moments of poetic inspiration. We may conclude that the metaphorical function of laurel is no different from that of flower-dew. And in yet another linkage, found in the epistle "To My Brother George," the laurel excites the poet to frenzy (i.e., the "sudden glow" of passion) and flight:

> . . . there are times, when those that love the bay,
> Fly from all sorrowing far, far away;
> A sudden glow comes on them. . . .
> (19–21)

Further, the laurel has the power to induce dreams. We discover in *The Fall of Hyperion* that although fanatics "bare of laurel . . . live, dream and die," the poet, not bare (i.e., "deprived" in this context) can dream in fruitful reverie; for only the laurel can induce a "fine spell of words" which fix and make eternal what the imagination has conceived:

> . . . Poesy alone can tell her dreams,
> With the fine spell of words alone can save
> Imagination from the sable chain
> And dumb enchantment. . . .
> (I, 8–11)

Two other stimulants that, like the laurel, manna, and flower-dew, have the power to increase imaginative activity are oak leaves and acorns.[19] Keats is aware of the inspirational properties of the oak, properties which originally made its leaves a traditional part of the poet's wreathed crown. In several instances he uses the tree with other metaphors for poetry to signify the first stages of the putting on of divine poetic knowledge. For example, "To George Felton Mathew" gives the conditions under which the poetic faculties are stimulated into full play. The first of these conditions is, characteristically, moonlight and "dew by fairy feet swept"; then appears "the coy muse," alternately called "the fine-eyed maid," whom we have seen as the chief agent of inspiration. In these circumstances Keats and Mathew

> . . . often must have seen a poet frantic:
> Where oaks, that erst the Druid knew, are growing. . . .
>
> (38–39)

The reason that the oak woods form the background for the fine frenzy is explained by Potter:

Near the Temple there was a sacred Grove full of Oaks or Beeches, in which the *Dryades, Fauni,* and *Satyri* were thought to inhabit. . . . These Oaks or Beeches were endued with an human Voice and Prophetical Spirit, for which Reason they were call'd . . . *speaking and prophesying Oaks.* . . . The Prophets, when they gave Answers, placed themselves in one of these Trees, (for some will only allow this vocal Faculty to one of them) and so the Oracle was thought to be utter'd by the Oak. . . . And some are of Opinion that the oracles were deliver'd from the Branches of the Tree.[20]

By a very subtle process of association, therefore, Keats identifies the

---

19. Graves has listed the various agents which induce imaginative frenzy in the classical poets. His explanation of how they achieved poetic inspiration is directly relevant to the discussion above. He says, " 'Inspiration' may be the breathing-in by the poet of intoxicating fumes from an intoxicating cauldron . . . containing probably a mash of barley, acorns, honey, bull's blood and such sacred herbs as ivy, hellebore, and laurel. . . . These fumes induce the paranoic trance in which time is suspended, though the mind remains active and can relate this proleptic or analeptic apprehensions in verse" (p. 492).

20. Potter, I, 270–271. Graves remarks along the same lines: " 'Inspiration' may also refer to the inducement of the same poetic condition by the act of listening to the wind . . . in a sacred grove. At Dodona poetic oracles were listened for in the oak-grove, and the prophetic trance was perhaps induced in the black-dove priestesses who first controlled the oracle by the chewing of acorns" (p. 492).

frantic state of the poet in "To George Felton Mathew" with the age-old inspirational properties of oak trees, considered as esteemed oracles by the Greeks.²¹ In sacred groves, the bay oak put forth its leaves in honor of Jove, whose divine word was imagined to have come from the trees.

If the oak in "To George Felton Mathew" is justifiably one of the poet's backdrops to scenes of Delphic, poetic frenzy for reasons rooted in myth, we shall easily be able to account for other instances in the poetry where significant moments of vision and inspiration have oak trees as a part of the landscape. At the end of the ode to sorrow in Book IV of *Endymion*, to cite a first example, the Indian Maid, who is really Cynthia, teaches Endymion a basic truth about human life, leading directly to his becoming immortal. He learns that sorrow and pain are inextricably mixed with joy,²² and that he, as a true poet, must know both. Endymion receives her words of truth as if they are uttered by a divinity speaking through the tops of sacred oaks:

> Endymion could not speak, but gazed on her;
> And listened to the wind that now did stir
> About the crisped oaks full drearily. . . .
>
> (293–295)

In *Hyperion*, we again find the oak associated with the words of the gods. In a long speech Thea reveals that Saturn has fallen, and in a long epic simile following, her words of truth are compared with a lone gust of wind through oaks:

> As when, upon a tranced summer-night,
> Those green-rob'd senators of mighty woods,
> Tall oaks, branch-charmed by the earnest stars
> Dream, and so dream all night without a stir,

21. See Virgil, "Georgics," Book II:

> que aesculus quae frondet Jovi, maxima nemorum,
> atque quercus habitae oracula Graiis.

(and the bay oak which put forth leaves in honor to Jove, the greatest tree of the groves, and oaks esteemed oracles by the Greeks). *The Works of P. Virgilius Maro,* ed. Levi Hart and V. R. Osborn (New York, 1952), p. 64. At the age of fourteen, Keats acquired a firsthand knowledge of Virgil by translating in full the *Aeneid* and was, most likely, fully aware of the magical properties of the laurel as Virgil describes them. See Lowell, I, 50.

22. See Glen O. Allen, "The Fall of Endymion: A Study in Keats's Intellectual Growth," *Keats-Shelley Journal,* VI (1957), 48, for this interpretation.

Save from one gradual solitary gust
Which comes upon the silence, and dies off,
As if the ebbing air had but one wave;
So came these words and went. . . .

(I, 72–79)

Clustered here are some of Keats's favorite recurrent metaphors: trance, charm, and dream all point to some kind of revealed truth as the imagination perceives it. The gust of wind through the oaks apparently corresponds to divinely inspired utterance, the reward of dreaming. Our understanding of the passage depends on the identification of wind and the oak as related metaphors expressive of inspiration and divine knowledge. Their coherence indicates the density and richness of Keats's language.

Wine

One of Keats's avowed indulgences, the drinking of wine, is also a metaphor for poetry in a number of places throughout his poems.[23] It is not difficult to see why. The intoxicating effect of wine allows man's fancy a temporary release; it "makes him a Hermes," [24] as Keats says, for the god of eloquence appears when the poet is sufficiently primed with alcohol. The longing for "a draught of vintage" in "Ode to a Nightingale" expresses a desire for a state of impassioned, unpremeditated utterance like that of the nightingale "pouring forth [his] soul abroad in such an ecstasy." Because it stimulates the poetic flow, wine is quite justifiably called "the blushful Hippocrene," a dense epithet not merely denoting the red color of the wine, but suggesting the flush of intense excitement inspired by Helicon, the famed fountain of the muses. Wine is further associated with poetry since it animates man to "Dance and Provençal song" as they were performed in a great age of poetry by the

23. Perkins has noted correctly that wine is "explicitly" associated with poetry "at one time or another" (p. 249). However, there is much implicit in Keats's use of this particular metaphor which demands closer explication than Perkins has given. Moreover, there are several significant linkages of wine with other metaphors for poetry which demonstrate just how closely this metaphor is associated with poetry.
24. *Letters*, II, 64.

poet-troubadours of France. What is more, wine allows the poet to take flight, to "fade far away." It, like other true poetic stimulants such as the laurel, manna, and the oak, has the power to awaken to imagination the "dull brain," which ordinarily "perplexes and retards." Keats would prefer the direct intoxication and attendant poetic frenzy from the "true" wine of Helicon—that is, poetry—rather than from the vulgar wine of Bacchus, which merely casts the poet into a stupor.[25]

In the poem "Fancy" we note that wine is one of the gifts of the maiden, Fancy, which allows for imaginative release and heightened perception:

> She will mix these pleasures up
> Like three fit wines in a cup,
> And thou shalt quaff it:—thou shalt hear
> Distant harvest-carols clear. . . .
>
> (37–40)

The imaginative joy which the wine allows is repeated in "Ode on Melancholy," but in this poem the sensation of bursting "Joy's grape against his palate fine" involves the pain as well as the pleasure of imagination. It is not accidental that Keats here chose the grape as one of the extreme sensory delights. The waning of imaginative sensation, a waning which is painful and pleasurable at the same time, is put in terms of the metaphor of the grape being crushed by the "strenuous tongue." It has been noted elsewhere that the palate and the tongue are not only the organs of taste but also the shapers of utterance—poetic and musical; wine therefore is to be identified with the vital origins of poetry and sensory experience, which are inextricably bound together.

If wine provides sensory experience in "Ode on Melancholy" and poetic frenzy in "Ode to a Nightingale," Keats also invests his metaphor with eucharistic powers that bring the poet to a kind of holy communion with divine truth. Like manna, wine appears to be used as a submerged metaphor for the sacrament whereby the poet achieves "fellowship (i.e., communion) with essence." A critical passage in *Hyperion* uses the wine

25. We should be aware of Keats's consistent distinction between these two kinds of wine throughout his poetry. In "Song," he spurns earthly wines: "Hence Burgundy, Claret, and Port, / . . . Too earthly ye are for my sport." He chooses instead the wine of poetry: "There's a beverage brighter and clearer. . . . / My wine overbrims a whole summer; / My bowl is the sky, / And I drink at my eye, / Till I feel in the brain / A Delphian pain."

metaphor in its eucharistic role of providing Apollo with divine knowledge:

> 'Knowledge enormous makes a God of me.
> 'Names, deeds, grey legends, dire events, rebellions,
> 'Majesties, sovran voices, agonies,
> 'Creations and destroyings, all at once
> 'Pour into the wide hollows of my brain,
> 'And deify me, as if some blithe wine
> 'Or bright elixir peerless I had drunk,
> 'And so become immortal.' . . .
>
> (III, 113–120)

Apollo's "blithe wine" is the "blushful Hippocrene;" both are holy elixirs in the sense that they can excite the poet's dull and mortal brain to unknown intensities of divine, imaginative knowledge. The earth-bound poet in "Ode to a Nightingale" has, unfortunately, no such "peerless elixir" to make him immortal like the nightingale, the Queen-Moon, or Apollo. Nor can the "viewless wings of Poesy" alone alchemize him. Here Keats is talking about the failure of wine to transport the poet from his mortal self to his imaginative apotheosis. The ode speaks of the failure of the poet to stimulate his dull imagination because the wine-elixir that is poetry is not available to him.

Very frequently wine appears with other metaphors for poetry in significant linkages, showing how persistent a role it plays as the *elixir vitae* of the poetic imagination. Endymion's long glorification of the moon clusters metaphors of light, the woman-muse, and the steed around the wine metaphor in an attempt to show the intoxicating and inspiring influence of moonlight, feminine beauty, and flight:

> . . . thou wast my steed—
> My goblet full of wine—my topmost deed:—
> Thou wast the charm of women, lovely Moon!
> O what a wild and harmonized tune
> My spirit struck from all the beautiful!
> On some bright essence could I lean, and lull
> Myself to immortality. . . .
>
> (III, 167–173)

As Endymion's "goblet full of wine," the moon-goddess provides the brilliant elixir or "bright essence" of frenzied (i.e., "wild") imaginative life by which he might "lull" himself "to immortality." Light, love, flight, and wine, as equivalent metaphors for inspiration, have their alchemizing effect on the mortal poet.

The wine-light-woman-muse cluster again appears in the epistle "To My Brother George," where the entranced poet sees "heaven's revels":

> Their ladies fair, that in the distance seem
> Fit for the silv'ring of a seraph's dream;
> Their rich brimm'd goblets, that incessant run
> Like the bright spots that move about the sun;
> And when upheld, the wine from each bright jar
> Pours with the lustre of a falling star. . . .
>
> (37–42)

The feminine libation-bearers provide the same kind of fiercely brilliant intoxicant which Cynthia bestows. It is the "bright elixir" drunk by Apollo at the moment he becomes deified, and, like the fountain of Helicon, forever replenishes the visionary poet with inspiration. We are reminded also of Lamia as a perpetual cup of beauty from which the intoxicated Lycius drinks:

> And soon his eyes had drunk her beauty up,
> Leaving no drop in the bewildering cup,
> And still the cup was full. . . .
>
> (I, 251–253)

Similarly, the holy and radiant vessel of wine which the "venerable priest" swings in worship of Apollo at the opening of *Endymion*,

> From his right hand there swung a vase, milk-white,
> Of mingled wine, out-sparkling generous light. . . .
>
> (I, 153–154)

so entrances Endymion that

> . . . he seem'd
> To common lookers-on, like one who dream'd
> Of idleness in groves Elysian. . . .
>
> (175–177)

In this particular passage the linkage of wine and light to dream further suggests the inspirational capability assigned to all three metaphors.

And finally, Keats ties poetic vision with wine and manna (both of which are invested with light) in the Adonis episode of Book II of *Endymion*. By providing Endymion with these two foods of imagination, attending Cupids allow him to see Adonis being apotheosized by Venus. One of the "feathered lyricists" (Cupids) assures Endymion,

> . . . Though . . .
> . . . thy presence here
> Might seem unholy, be of happy cheer!
> For 'tis the nicest touch of human honour,
> When some ethereal and high-favouring donor
> Presents immortal bowers to mortal sense;
> As now 'tis done to thee, Endymion. . . .
> . . . So recline
> Upon these living flowers. Here is wine,
> Alive with sparkles . . .
>
> . . . .
> And here is manna pick'd from Syrian trees,
> In starlight. . . .
>
> (433–442, 452–453)

All of these metaphors for poetic frenzy reveal the range of Keats's search for the apt analogue and his ability to draw together a wide array of sources. He uses myth, Plato, the Bible, Shakespeare, in fact, the whole lore of the poetic past as sources for his metaphors by which to account for his own poetic experience. If Douglas Bush is correct in concluding, "Into myth Keats put his deepest questionings of himself, [and] of art . . . ," [26] then the same can be said for all other sources of his metaphors for poetry, metaphors that are not merely decorative, as I have attempted to demonstrate, but indeed structural to the poetry and highly integral to his special theme: poetry. They demonstrate in their allusiveness and richness his definition of poetry: it "should surprise by a fine excess and not by Singularity." [27] Further, since these

26. Douglas Bush, *Mythology and the Romantic Tradition* (New York, 1957), p. 527.
27. *Letters*, I, 238.

related metaphors are the product of a poet who had thought long and deeply on his subject, and had assimilated them from several different sources, they quite naturally recur in his poetry as "almost a Remembrance." [28]

28. *Ibid.*

Chapter five

The labyrinth ~ The grot ~ The fountain and stream

The recurrent metaphors of the labyrinth, the grot, and the fountain and stream give the poetic process a local habitation and a name. They are related to one another in that they all figure the channels and well-springs of the active mind, rising in a perplexing and mazy route from the subterranean depths of the unconscious, creative imagination. These metaphors also relate to man's sexual anatomy and activity; for the act of sexual love has already been established as symbolic of, and related to, the poetic process.

We have already noted Keats's attempts to describe the labyrinthine ways of dreams as spontaneous, complex, and protean issuings of the slumbering, imaginative mind. But as an analogue to the active imagination, dreams proved too abstract for his poetic sensibility. In an attempt to depict more satisfactorily the realm of the imaginative mind, he links dreams with the labyrinth, the grot, and the fountain:

> O magic sleep . . .
>
> . . . .
>   . . . O unconfin'd
> Restraint! Imprison'd liberty . . . !
>
> . . . .
> Fountains grotesque . . . bespangled caves,
> Echoing grottos, full of tumbling waves

And moonlight; aye to all the mazy world
Of silvery enchantment! . . .

        (*Endymion*, I, 453 ff.)

The fountain rising spontaneously out of the wellsprings of the earth, the devious hollows of caves and grottos, and the "mazy" world of moonlight all suggest the flux, wonder, and mystery of the active, imaginative mind. The passage further suggests that from within these depths issues a visionary light. Endymion's caves, "bespangled" with diamond points of light, and the luminescent fountains both recurrently signify the imagination.

Like Endymion, Keats is bent on exploring the unfathomable depths of mind back to their source in order to arrive at some kind of knowledge of the creative force. We have already seen how the poet figures the search in terms of flying, swimming, and voyaging. Like the gods and goddesses in *Endymion*, he would also "watch the abysm birth of elements" (III, 28), that is, view the inner process of imagination, shaping in fire and light as does the supreme Maker in Genesis. Once again Keats is concerned with the poetic process as a supreme adventure and vivid experience. Not only does he portray the poet as a soaring, frightened Icarus moving toward Cynthia's visionary light; he also sees him as a Theseus groping his way uncertainly to vision in the labyrinthine depths of the earth. We should regard the poetic descent as no different from the imaginative flight, for to Keats, as to Heraclitus, the path to vision is both up and down, one and the same.

The labyrinth

In the image of the labyrinth, Keats conceives the poetic imagination as an extremely complicated network of passageways, niches, and rooms, perplexing all but the most skilful of poets. He would master its Daedalian mazes. In the early stage of his poetic career, Keats felt that the "lovely" labyrinth of imagination would not entrammel him:

    . . . All hail delightful hopes!
As she was wont, th' imagination
Into most lovely labyrinths will be gone. . . .

        ("Sleep and Poetry," 264–266)

And again, in the sonnet to Georgiana Wylie, the muse appears most lovely when practicing her mazy art of song and dance:

> Nymph of the downward smile, and sidelong glance,
>   In what diviner moments of the day
>   Art thou most lovely? When gone far astray
> Into the labyrinths of sweet utterance?
>
> . . . .
>   . . . or when starting away
>   With careless robe, to meet the morning ray,
> Thou spar'st the flowers in thy mazy dance? . . .

To George Felton Mathew, Keats attributes Daedalian knowledge of the poetic maze:

> Thou hast never told thy travels strange
> And all the wonders of the mazy range. . . .
>
> (90–91)

These early uses of the metaphor do little more than suggest the fairly intricate maze of pathways taken by the imagination on its way to poetic expression.

Keats seldom thought of himself as a Theseus figure able to master the difficult mazes of imagination; for the bewildering path to poetic beauty proves, at best, a chancy as well as perplexing endeavor for the mortal poet. He frequently felt that the infinite number of possible routes to perfect poetic expression would at last cheat him into a blind alley. A letter to Haydon expresses this fear:

I have ever been too sensible of the labyrinthian path to eminence in Art (judging from Poetry) ever to think I understood the emphasis of Painting. The innumerable compositions and decompositions which take place between the intellect and its thousand materials before it arrives at that trembling delicate and snail-horn perception of Beauty . . . I hope [naught] you [achieve] is lost upon me.[1]

The "labyrinthian path" to artistic perfection describes a tenuous and confusing route. In that uncertain process of imagination, the artist frequently becomes maddened by the infinite latitude of choice in the

1. *Letters*, I, 264–265.

materials and ideas which he might use. Between the poet's vague conception of what he wants to say and what he manages to achieve in finished form falls the shadow of possible failure. This attitude seems not unlike Eliot's, for

> . . . Words strain,
> Crack and sometimes break, under the burden,
> Under the tension, slip, slide, perish,
> Decay with imprecision, will not stay in place,
> Will not stay still. . . .
>
> ("Burnt Norton," V)

The labyrinthine ways of the creative process guarantee no "trembling delicate and snail-horn perception of beauty"; rather the poet more often knows the anguish and bewilderment between the initial dim conception and the creation of poetry:

> Such dim conceived glories of the brain
> Bring round the heart an indescribable feud;
> So do these wonders a most dizzy pain. . . .
>
> ("On Seeing the Elgin Marbles")

The sentiments on art, expressed in "On Seeing the Elgin Marbles," inform us of one of Keats's special ideas on his own poetic imagination: the creation of poetry follows the mazy road of chance. Likewise, the sonnet "When I have fears" suggests that in tracing the shadows "of a high romance" the poet creates "with the magic hand of chance." Every poetic attempt seems, therefore, to create its own peculiar maze of possible word choices, image combinations, figures, meters, and themes. Poetry is indeed a labyrinth, for it involves an endless number of possible combinations of its elements, which the working, threading imagination finally resolves into significant form.

Moreover, the labyrinthine poetic process in the most responsible and dedicated poets is, like any serious intellectual searching, painful. The burden of making the best possible word choices, for example, brings on "an indescribable feud" in the poet. A letter to a fellow poet, Reynolds, employs the labyrinth and its "branchings" as metaphors for intense, and in this context, painful thinking:

You say "I fear there is little chance of any thing else in this life." You seem by that to have been going through with a more painful and acute zest the same labyrinth that I have—I have come to the same conclusion thus far. My Branchings out therefrom have been numerous.[2]

The beginning of any creative thinking requires a premise, or at least a fairly solid idea from which issue new "branchings." The labyrinth here figures the associative, imaginative mind at work. Its mazy course leads from the main corridor to a thousand possible exits or departures of thought. It shall be seen that both of the figures used in this letter recur, slightly disguised, in "Ode to Psyche," a poem whose special meaning is tied to our discussion here.

Keats undoubtedly felt the painful burden not only of ordering his material but also of thinking deeply. He remarks in the same letter to Reynolds that the poet, like the master craftsman Daedalus, needs an abundant knowledge in order to channel and control his imagination: "An extensive knowledge is needful to thinking people—it takes away the heat and fever; and helps, by widening speculation, to ease the Burden of the Mystery." "The Burden of the Mystery," a direct quotation from "Tintern Abbey," refers to the perplexing, chaotic world which only the associative imagination, stirred to life in sleep, can fathom and give order to. The quotation is significant, when read in the context of the poem, for it provides us with a further understanding of Keats's metaphor of the labyrinth. Wordsworth describes in a manner similar to Keats's the mazy channels that the imagination takes as it achieves vision:

> . . . that blessed mood,
> In which the burden of the mystery
>
> . . . .
> Is lightened:—that serene and blessed mood,
> In which the affections gently lead us on,—
> Until, the breath of this corporeal frame
> And even the motion of our human blood
> Almost suspended, we are laid asleep
> In body, and become a living soul:
> While with an eye made quiet by the power
> Of harmony, and the deep power of joy,

2. *Ibid.*, p. 278.

We see into the life of things. . . .

(37-38, 41-49)

In this description of the sleeping mind that gently leads the poet on, Keats no doubt saw the same kind of "branchings" of thought in his own imagination. We should note, however, that knowledge plays an important part in guiding the poet through the labyrinth.

If the maze of imaginative thought seems difficult to Keats in his letters to Reynolds and Haydon, at other times it strikes him as a happy ramble. One notes the labyrinth metaphor once again underlying his description of the wandering, creative mind:

let [a man] on any certain day read a certain Page of full Poesy or distilled Prose and let him wander with it, and muse upon it, and reflect from it, and bring home to it, and prophesy upon it, and dream upon it. . . . When Man has arrived at a certain ripeness in intellect any one grand and spiritual passage serves him as a starting post towards all "the two-and thirty Pallaces" How happy is such a "voyage of conception." [3]

Further, a "tapestry empyrean," that is, a well-knit poem, woven by the imaginative mind, provides "space for the Minds of Mortals to wander in." Keats invests his metaphor of the labyrinth with two particular meanings in this letter. He describes the poetic process as a sequence of thought, starting from a principal "passage" [4] and leading into various rooms of delight, and as a finished work of art, an intricate, ingeniously conceived product of imagination provoking speculation in its beholders.

The poet repeatedly attempts to puzzle out the maze of possible avenues in his search for perfect form. Only in those moments of inspired imaginative vision can he swiftly perceive order in the apparently chaotic labyrinth; for the intuitive imagination alone has the power to resolve, accommodate, and shape the stubborn materials of the poet's art. Lamia's "sciential brain," for example, is supremely imaginative, for it can

. . . unperplex bliss from its neighbour pain;
Define their pettish limits, and estrange
Their points of contact, and swift counterchange;

3. *Ibid.*, p. 231.
4. Meaning, of course, both a group of lines in a literary work and a main hallway.

Intrigue with the specious chaos, and dispart
Its most ambiguous atoms with sure art. . . .
                                        (I, 192–196)

Each word she speaks to the possessed Lycius "disparts" and defines
the "pettish limits" of the perplexing and seemingly chaotic maze of
imaginative thought. She is his guide:

. . . every word she spake entic'd him on
To unperplex'd delight and pleasure known. . . .
                                        (326–327)

But he wrongly presumes that he can stay his beautiful, protean imagination forever, a presumption that eventually leads to his disaster. He
tells Lamia that he should like

. . . to entangle, trammel up and snare
Your soul in mine, and labyrinth you there
Like the hid scent in an unbudded rose. . . .
                                        (II, 52–53)

The imagination cannot be entrammeled, just as a labyrinth cannot
be traversed a second time along the same paths; for the imagination
knows only process and change as does the organic life of the rose.

If Lycius knows briefly the labyrinth of imagination, Glaucus does
also. Circe gives him temporary Daedalian powers; he delights in his
imaginative capacity to thread the labyrinths of nature with the same
kind of freedom as the poet in flight:

And I was free of haunts umbrageous;
Could wander in the mazy forest-house
Of squirrels, foxes shy, and antler'd deer;
And birds from coverts innermost and drear
Warbling for very joy mellifluous sorrow—
To me new-born delights! . . .
                              (*Endymion*, III, 467–472)

Keats had previously expressed the desire to trace out and render into
poetry the labyrinthine alleys of nature. In "I stood tip-toe" he would like

To picture out the quaint, and curious bending
Of a fresh woodland alley, never ending. . . .
                                        (19–20)

However temporary Lycius' and Glaucus' mastery of the labyrinth of imagination is, Keats frequently cannot even find entrance to it. The sonnet, "On Receiving a Laurel Crown from Leigh Hunt," records the failure of the poet to "catch an immortal thought" and run with it through the labyrinth of his creative soul:

> Minutes are flying swiftly, and as yet
> Nothing unearthly has enticed my brain
> Into a delphic Labyrinth—I would fain
> Catch an unmortal thought to pay the debt
> I owe to the kind Poet who has set
> Upon my ambitious head a glorious gain.
> Two bending laurel Sprigs—'tis nearly pain
> To be conscious of such a Coronet.
> Still time is fleeting, and no dream arises
> Gorgeous as I would have it—only I see
> A Trampling down of what the world most prizes,
> Turbans and Crowns, and blank regality;
> And then I run into most wild surmises
> Of all the many glories that may be.

The poem suggests that the intuitive, spontaneous mind weaves "gorgeous" poetry in the labyrinths of dreams. The association of the labyrinth with dream, the laurel, and the Delphic frenzy suggests that the imagination's mazy process cannot exist without some kind of spontaneous mental release. The intoxication from laurel, the madness in poetic frenzy, and unearthly dreaming all provide such release. Keats, however, remains too conscious of his coronet and of his "debt" to Leigh Hunt [5] to be able to fly into a "delphic Labyrinth" of imaginative activity. He is, no doubt, more pained that the extent of his poetic efforts on this occasion leaves him with nothing more than the "most wild surmises of all the many" poetic "glories" that his imagination might conceive. The labyrinthine imagination, like the holy caves of Delphi, holds these glories only for the Apollonian poet-priest, the true visionary who is able to resolve its perplexing and devious paths.

5. Colvin, p. 55, reports that Hunt and Keats crowned each other with laurel leaves "and each while sitting so adorned wrote a pair of sonnets expressive of his feelings." Walter J. Bate, *John Keats* (Cambridge, Mass., 1963), p. 138, explains in more detail the seriousness with which Keats entered the contest.

The grot

If the labyrinth signifies the uncertainties and difficulties of the imaginative process, the grot suggests the reachless depths of the mind. The recurrence of the grotto, the cave, the cell, and the mine invariably suggests the darkness and mystery in the unconscious, creative process of imagination as it attempts to strike upon the visionary light of truth. Quite naturally we think of Plato's cave, an elaborately conceived metaphor for the unknowing human mind which sees illusory shadows and takes them for truth.[6] Yet within this cave of the imaginative mind burns the light of truth and beauty, a light which ignorant man may see, as Plato remarks, "only with an effort." [7]

We may attribute to other sources Keats's recurrent association of the grotto with poetry and imagination. The haunts of the Olympian gods and goddesses of poetry and inspiration were well known to him through Lemprière, who reports that Olympus "is covered with pleasant woods, caves and grottos. On the top of the mountain, according to one of the notions of the poets, there was no wind, no rain, no clouds but an eternal spring." [8] On the hillsides of this sacred mountain the gods would charm the groves and caves with music and reward a favored mortal with inspired vision or perhaps even immortality, as the shepherd, Endymion, was so honored by an enamored Cynthia.

In addition to Plato and classical lore, Christian myth and the literary past prove equally important to our understanding of Keats's metaphor of the cave. The grotto was always considered a retreat for holy worship and religious conjuration in the early Judeo-Christian world. Through mystical incantations, prophet-priests filled their grottos with religious visions; indeed, one historian reports

The cave of Machpelah, purchased of Ephron the Hittite, was the sepulchre of Sarah (Gn 23[19]), and afterwards of Abraham (Gn 25[9]), Isaac (35[27-29]), and Jacob (50[13]). There can be no doubt but that the mosque of Hebron covers the last resting place of the patriarchs; it is a spot considered of the highest sanctity by the Arab tribes.[9]

6. Neville Rogers makes this observation in *Shelley at Work: A Critical Inquiry* (Oxford, 1956), p. 148.
7. "Republic," VII, Jowett, II, 776.
8. Lemprière, see "Olympus."
9. *A Dictionary of the Bible*, ed. James Hastings (New York, 1898), I, 364.

Further, in *Paradise Lost* and *The Tempest*, two works that greatly influenced Keats, by his own admission, we find the cave "within the mount of God, fast by his throne," [10] as the sanctum of God's light and as the dwelling place of the artful conjuror, Prospero. Prospero's cell is alive with magical secrets, which he uses to order nature to his will. Nor should we overlook the wondrous caves of the *Arabian Nights*, a work admired by Keats for its supreme fancy,[11] as a source for his metaphor. Aladdin's marvelous journey into the earth's caverns in many ways reminds us of Endymion's repeated descents into grottos and caves, where visions of dazzling beauty await him. And finally, the poetry of Keats's day retained the metaphorical values which the past attached to the cave. *The Prelude*, for example, figures the cave as the retreat of the dormant imagination:

> *Caverns* there were within my mind which sun
> Could never penetrate. . . .
>
> (III, 243–244)

Keats's use of caves and grottos as a metaphor for the haunt of the poetic imagination retains all of these traditional associations. In the simplest examples, the agents of poetic inspiration—the muses, naiads, and elves of poetry—live in grottos. England's own muses, long quiet to insensitive ears of poets, seem to be displaced Olympians:

> Muse of my native land! loftiest Muse!
> O first-born on the mountains! by the hues
> Of heaven on the spiritual air begot:
> Long didst thou sit alone in northern grot. . . .
>
> (*Endymion*, IV, 1–4)

In the second of his two sonnets "On Fame," Keats suggests that poets, like naiads, should content themselves with keeping their enchanted grottos pure. The poet despoils his art and his mind by vexing "all the leaves of his life's book" by actively pursuing fame. Such pursuit seems as foolishly destructive to the poet's imagination as a muse defiling her own grotto:

> As if a Naiad, like a meddling elf,
> Should darken her pure grot with muddy gloom. . . .

10. *Paradise Lost*, VI, l. 5.
11. See Colvin, pp. 175, 184, 190–191, 195.

The forces of reason and natural philosophy can be even more destructive of the fairy land which the fancy conceives. In *Lamia* gnomes of folk-belief live freely in their enchanted hollows only so long as they remain free of the withering effect of cold philosophy:

> Philosophy will clip an Angel's wings,
> Conquer all mysteries by rule and line,
> Empty the haunted air, and gnomed mine. . . .
> (II, 234–236)

The emptying of the gnomed mine signifies the passing of a way of thinking rooted in folklore, fancy, and mythmaking, a passing lamented in "Ode to Psyche."

Not only do the muses and elves live in the enchanted caves of imagination, but so does Morpheus, the arch-feigner of forms. Within his cavern he creates protean visions for dreaming mortals. We recall that in Book IV of *Endymion* he comes forth from his cave and creates a prefigurative dream for Endymion. Here, once again, Keats suggests that the cave represents the hollows of the artful, visionary mind. In the moment of apotheosis in *Hyperion*, Apollo describes his assumption of supreme imaginative knowledge in terms of the cave metaphor:

> 'Knowledge enormous makes a God of me.
> 'Names, deeds, gray legends, dire events, rebellions,
>
> .   .   .   .
>
> 'Creations and destroyings, all at once
> 'Pour into the wide hollows of my brain. . . .
> (III, 113–114, 116–117)

Like the natural caves of the earth, glutted by the sea's untold secrets, Apollo's cavernous imaginative mind is filled with complete knowledge:

> . . . Throughout all the isle
> There was no covert, no retired cave
> Unhaunted by the murmurous noise of waves.
>
> .   .   .   .
>
> He listened and he wept. . . .
> (38–40, 42)

The grotto as the seat of the poetic powers provides the resting place not only for the elves, naiads, and muses of poetry, but for the great poets of the past as well:

> Souls of Poets dead and gone,
> What Elysium have ye known,
> Happy field or mossy cavern
> Choicer than the Mermaid Tavern? . . .
>
> ("Lines on the Mermaid Tavern")

Shakespeare perhaps dwells in a "mossy cavern," because he provides the same kind of inspiration to Keats as do the muses. Grottos and caves are repeatedly inhabited by these various immortal creative beings in an attempt to objectify that inward, mysterious, and vital force of imagination.

Light and music radiating from within the cave figure the active, generative psyche. The recurrent linkage of music and light with the cave appears most graphically in the paean to sleep:

> O magic sleep!
>
> . . . .
>   . . . O unconfin'd
> Restraint! . . .
>   . . . strange minstrelsy,
>   . . . bespangled caves,
> Echoing grottos, full of tumbling waves
> And moonlight. . . .
>
> (*Endymion*, I, 453, 455–460)

Endymion's perception of music and light in a mazy, sounding grotto, where he is blessed with vision, further suggests the radiant power of mind:

> A chamber, myrtle wall'd, embowered high,
> Full of light, incense, tender minstrelsy. . . .
>
> (II, 389–390)

These sounds, echoing in the air, invite the impassioned poet to follow them to their source within the grotto; but he must first be in a highly receptive mood, that is to say, he must be on the threshold of the fine poetic frenzy in order to hear and trace the tender minstrelsy echoing within the cave. In a highly significant passage Keats advises the would-be poet just how he might hear these beautiful airs playing from within the grottos of the earth, grottos which we clearly understand to be the recesses of the poetic mind:

> Ye who have yearn'd
> With too much passion, will here stay and pity,
> For the mere sake of truth; as 'tis a ditty
> Not of these days, but long ago 'twas told
> By a cavern wind unto a forest old;
> And then the forest told it in a dream
> To a sleeping lake, whose cool and level gleam
> A poet caught as he was journeying
> To Phoebus' shrine; and in it he did fling
> His weary limbs, bathing an hour's space,
> And, after straight, in that inspired place
> He sang the story up into the air,
> Giving it universal freedom. There
> Has it been ever sounding for those ears
> Whose tips are glowing hot. . . .
>
> (827–841)

The eternal poetic truths, "sounding" from the cavern, serve as the poet's wind of inspiration, and only the frenzied, Apollonian poet whose ears "are glowing hot" may catch that music and sing it "up into the air." As the residence of poetic power and truth, the grotto invites all aspiring poets to fathom its depths. Endymion proves to be the most serious and intrepid of its explorers.

The fountain and stream

If the grotto signifies the recesses of the poetic mind, the fountain issuing from the cavernous depths figures the powerful overflow of imagination. As a metaphor, the fountain must be considered the common property of all the Romantic poets. Certainly Keats did not coin this analogue, although his use of it, it seems to me, demonstrates an inventive genius superior to all the other poets. In their greatest poems, Wordsworth and Coleridge continually relied on the fountain as an apt metaphor for the projecting, imaginative mind. *The Prelude* describes the imagination as "the river of my mind . . . from yon fountain" (II, 209–210) and, with equal singularity, as

. . . the stream

From the blind cavern whence is faintly heard

Its natal murmur. . . .[12]

(XIV, 194–196)

"Dejection: an Ode" identifies the fountain as the source of spontaneous feeling and therefore of the poet's "genial spirits" of imagination. Sadly, "The passion and the life, whose fountains are within," fail to gush forth in poetic utterance. We are reminded, too, of the power and fertility of Kubla Khan's "mighty fountain" of imagination. As it issues "from caverns measureless to man" and travels its "mazy motion," it fertilizes the landscape of the pleasure dome.

One might cite numerous other examples of this metaphor in all the Romantic poets, especially Shelley, whose creative Witch of Atlas lives "Within a cavern, by a secret fountain." The four examples used here tend to bear out M. H. Abrams' original and highly useful observation that Wordsworth and Coleridge "revert . . . to metaphors of mind which had largely fallen into disuse in the eighteenth century." Both poets "usually agree in picturing the mind in perception as active rather than inertly receptive, and as contributing to the world in the very process of perceiving the world." [13] The new romantic epistemology therefore dictated new metaphors for the mind. No longer regarded as a mirror of nature, but rather as a creative power, the mind was figured as an overflowing fountain by Keats and the Romantics.[14]

12. In the figures of the fountain and stream, Wordsworth in fact summarizes the entire theme and purpose of *The Prelude*, to trace the growth of his imagination. In fourteen books he has

. . . traced the stream

. . . .

. . . followed it to light

And open day; accompanied its course

Among the ways of Nature, for a time

Lost sight of it bewildered and engulphed;

Then given it greeting as it rose once more

In strength, reflecting from its placid breast

The works of man and face of human life;

And lastly, from its progress have we drawn

Faith in life endless, the sustaining thought

Of human Being, Eternity, and God.   (XIV, 194, 196–205)

13. *The Mirror and the Lamp*, p. 58.

14. Although Abrams says nothing of Keats's use of this metaphor, he has provided the early spadework for subsequent critics.

Keats's working of this metaphor is as subtle and skilful as the others we have already investigated, and is perhaps best exemplified in Endymion's account of his first dream-vision, which pictures his teeming imagination as a cavern fountain:

> And then I fell asleep. Ah, can I tell
> The enchantment that afterwards befel?
> Yet it was but a dream: yet such a dream
> That never tongue, although it overteem
> With mellow utterance, like a cavern spring,
> Could figure out and to conception bring
> All I beheld and felt. . . .
>
> (I, 572–578)

Although Endymion feels that no metaphors seem adequate to describe the ineffable vision he has seen, he has indeed "figured out" the poetic process as an overflowing cavern spring. His imagination would "overteem" with words to describe the vision that he has not only beheld, but also felt; for poetry, as Keats asserted repeatedly in his letters, issues in passion, and he would agree with Wordsworth that poetry "is the spontaneous overflow of powerful feelings." We should therefore recognize that fountains and streams figure these spontaneous overflowings of impassioned, poetic utterance. The prologue to *Endymion*, for example, states:

> All lovely tales that we have heard or read [are]
> An endless fountain of immortal drink
> Pouring unto us from the heaven's brink. . . .
>
> (I, 22–24)

Opening a book of his own poetry recalls in Keats the fountain of past emotions projected into poetry:

> Thus I remember all the pleasant flow
> Of words at opening a portfolio. . . .
>
> ("Sleep and Poetry," 337–338)

In yet another poem, he describes this "pleasant flow" as a buoyant "stream of rhyme" ("To Charles Cowden Clarke," 16). The poet "whose head is pregnant with poetic lore" ("To My Brother George," 54) finds the proper occasion for imaginative release in the company of the muses. Their gifts of love and inspiration allow for a gush of poetic feeling:

> With you, kindest friends, in idea I muse;
> Mark the clear tumbling crystal, its passionate gushes.[15]
>
> ("To Some Ladies," 7–8)

These guardians of the Heliconian fountain of inspiration stand ready to raise the deserving poet to poetic passion by granting him "the blushful Hippocrene."

The poet, more often, knows periods of imaginative drought. Weary and unimpassioned, he finds himself, appropriately, in a museless land of "dull rivers" ("What can I do to drive away"). At one point Endymion attempts to relieve his thirst by artificial means. Retiring to a deep grotto behind the temple dedicated to Apollo's mother, he would force up water from a deep well and give life to his imagination.

> Beyond the matron-temple of Latona
>
> . . . .
> Lies a deep hollow, . . .
>
> . . . .
> Some moulder'd steps lead into this cool cell,
> Far as the slabbed margin of a well,
> Whose patient level peeps its crystal eye
> Right upward. . . . .
>
> . . . .
> And there in strife no burning thoughts to heed,
> I'd bubble up the water through a reed.
>
> (I, 862 ff.)

We may consider the "patient level" of this well as the inert fountain of imagination, which Endymion must draw up by contrivance. Once he has set the well flowing, though not spontaneously, he has an inspired vision of Cynthia.

In Endymion's moments of extreme poetic activity, the moon goddess appears at the overflowing "streams of song" to inspire him even further.

---

15. The overflowing fountain and the gush of poetic feeling may also relate to sexual activity. It has already been suggested that poetic activity can be identified with sexual experience. Appropriately, then, the reference to the fountain's "passionate gushes" is suggestive of the seminal overflow.

Even George Felton Mathew has fed from Cynthia's oasis, which has empowered him with poetic vision:

> For thou wast once a flowret blooming wild,
> Close to the source, bright, pure, and undefil'd
> Whence gush the streams of song: in happy hour
> Came chaste Diana from her shady bower. . . .
>
> ("To George Felton Mathew," 76–79)

Keats often characterizes the muses as the mere guardians of the springs of imagination. However, when he wants to suggest the poet's moment of supreme imaginative fulfilment in sexual union, he identifies the impassioned muse as a fountain from which the poet drinks and thereby receives his visionary life. This significant conjoining of two metaphors—the muse and her poet in the fertile act of love, and the nurturing fountain—appears in Endymion's account of his meeting with Cynthia:

> . . . madly did I kiss
> The wooing arms which held me . . .
> . . . 'twas to live,
> To take in draughts of life from the gold fount
> Of kind and passionate looks.
>
> (I, 653–657)

As Endymion's fountain and source of light, Cynthia signifies the fertile, projecting, and sustaining force of imagination. We may now find greater meaning in Keats's enigmatic apostrophe to the moon in Book III of *Endymion*:

> thou wast the deep glen
>
> . . . .
> Thou wast the river . . .
>
> . . . .
> Felicity's abyss. . . .
>
> (163, 166, 176)

These are recurrent and linked metaphors for the unfathomable hollows of the supernal, creative mind from which spout the fountains and streams of poetry and imagination. Endymion's previous address to Cynthia takes on added significance:

> No tumbling water ever spake romance,
> But when my eyes with thine thereon could dance. . . .
> (149–150)

If the fountain emanating from the muses analogizes creative, poetic power, the metaphor of the radiant, overflowing fountain figures the divine overflow of truth. This significant linkage of the metaphors of light and the fountain can be found in Lycius' description of Lamia, who, like Cynthia, excites the poet to powerful exercise of imagination and provides him with a vision of truth:

> 'Stay! though a Naiad of the rivers, stay!
> 'To thy far wishes will thy stream obey.
>
> . . . .
>
> 'Though a descended Pleiad, will not one
> 'Of thine harmonious sisters keep in tune
> 'Thy spheres, and as thy silver proxy shine? . . .
> (I, 261–262, 265–267)

Lamia represents, at the same time, the perpetually flowing stream of imagination and the perpetually shining star of poetic truth. No wonder, then, that Lycius, engulfed in her streams of song and dazzled by her "brighter eyes" (293), pleads for this supreme embodiment of poetry to "stay."

Keats's repeated attempts to "figure out" both the poetic imagination and its visions have been our main concern. But by "figure out" he also means to trace his imagination backward to its source. The labyrinth of imagination presents a challenge to his poet-explorers just as the sea and the airy heights invite his mariners, swimmers, and eagle-poets to search out their "love's far dwelling" (*Endymion*, II, 179). If the mysteries of the imaginative process often teased Keats out of thought, the process never quite frustrated him to the point of giving up entirely the search for some kind of understanding of its mazes. For the imagination, as he reminds us repeatedly, manifests the divinity lodged within him. "Figuring out" that divine power seems a holy occupation to Keats and therefore remains the dominant theme of his poetry. Like Wordsworth, he resolves to trace the stream of imagination, fathom its depths, and thereby make his poetry a holy act of discovery:

> . . . imaginings will hover
> Round my fire-side, and haply there discover
> Vistas of solemn beauty, where I'd wander
> In happy silence, like the clear Meander
> Through its lone vales; and where I found a spot
> Of awfuller shade, or an enchanted grot,
>
> . . . .
>
> Write on my tablets all that was permitted,
> All that was for our human senses fitted. . . .
>
> ("Sleep and Poetry," 71–76, 79–80)

The winding, intricate route of "the clear meander," like the perplexing paths of the labyrinth and grotto, is an analogy of the imaginative process as it finally leads to poetry.

With the metaphorical significance of the labyrinth, the grotto, and the fountain in mind, one can now see how Keats weaves these three analogues in Book II of *Endymion* to produce one of the most profound and complex narratives on the poetic process in all literature. This claim seems justified if one understands their special figurative values as they unfold throughout the corpus of his work, and most revealingly in image clusters.

The whole of Book II explores the labyrinthine caves of imagination. Endymion's maddening descents picture the uncertain, terrorized poet in search of poetic vision. His reactions to these adventures show a strong similarity to the trembling anxiety he repeatedly feels in imaginative flight. Lost in the unfathomable hollows of the earth, his bewilderment represents the poet who, in the act of creation, is overwhelmed by the most "wild surmises" and "indescribable feuds." He feels uncertain that his path to artistic beauty will ever resolve itself, so infinite are the choices of possible routes that the poet must make.

These descents and brief visionary experiences possess all the characteristics of the epic hero's journey into the underworld. Indeed, the similarities with the classical epic help to define with certainty the visionary nature of Endymion's adventures. He seems the figure of Virgil's Aeneas; both search for truth. While Endymion's quest leads to poetic truth,

Aeneas' ends in a vision of the future of his race and of his own destiny. In making these parallels, Keats suggests that the true epic hero for his own time is the poet who is able to trace the labyrinthine path of imagination:

> . . . th' imagination
> Into most lovely labyrinths will be gone,
> And they shall be accounted poet kings
> Who simply tell the most heart-easing things. . . .
> ("Sleep and Poetry," 265–268)

It is especially noteworthy that in imagery and theme Endymion's descent shows striking similarities to Aeneas'. Virgil[16] describes the vast antrum through which Aeneas passes, the diamond points of light, the confusing corridors and fountains, the astonishment of the hero, and the closeness of his vision in that underworld to dream. Significant, too, is the fact that Endymion knows no Sibyl or Anchises to guide him to vision. Aeneas' awe is not quite the terror which Endymion, alone in the labyrinth of imagination, feels as he chances his way downward either to death and failure or to imaginative life.

Airy voices, music, and humming prompt Endymion to descend into the caves of the earth. We may regard these initial sounds as the echoes of half-formed melodies playing within the poet's own mind, beckoning him to pursue them down the labyrinthine ways of imagination. Significantly, Echo calls from her "cell," or grotto, "Endymion! The cave is secreter / Than the isle of Delos" (I, 965–966), suggesting that it is a retreat more alive with poetic secrets than the famed and sacred island of Apollo. A second voice "from the deep cavern" bids Endymion descend:

> . . . descend where alleys bend
> Into the sparry hollows of the world!

16. Further and more directly substantiating evidence might be cited to bear out my claim of the Virgilian model for Endymion's descent, although Homer should not be ruled out as a possible source. Keats's translation of the entire *Aeneid* when he was a schoolboy appears to be the seedbed for some of the ideas, images, and metaphors he was to use later in his poetry. The influence of Virgil has been almost totally overlooked by critics, who attribute to Homer any epic qualities in *Endymion*. See, e.g., Colvin, p. 217. Bate, *John Keats*, provides no additional commentary.

. . . .
. . . descend! He ne'er is crown'd
With immortality, who fears to follow
Where airy voices lead: so through the hollow,
The silent mysteries of earth, descend! . . .

(II, 203–204, 211–214)

Endymion plunges into the earth in a fit of "madness" not unlike the
Delphic passion which he experiences in other moments of imaginative
vision. His descent takes him along a path of gems and gold:

Through a vast antre; then the metal woof,
Like Vulcan's rainbow, with some monstrous roof
Curves hugely: now, far in the deep abyss,
It seems an angry lightning, and doth hiss
Fancy into belief: anon it leads
Through winding passages, where sameness breeds
Vexing conceptions of some sudden change. . . .

(I, 230–236)

We are once again in the perplexing labyrinth of imagination. The flash-
ing light from the metal woof of the path plays tricks on Endymion's
fancy. He cannot know whether these reflections in the deep abyss are
real or merely deceptions of the groping fancy. Moreover, the extreme
variety and yet "sameness" of the winding passages tease him out of
thought. His puzzlement and vexation suggest the same kind of frustration that the poet knows when several possible routes of expression
are open to him and he can decide on none. This passage, more than any
other, suggests the uncertainties of the poet in the pursuit of imagination
and vision.

Endymion's amazement and terror intensify as he presently comes upon
a brilliant source of light within an area of "A hundred waterfalls." He
has therefore traced the mazy, golden path back to the wellsprings and
light of the creative imagination. The light brings form to the dark abyss
and provides him with his first vision:

. . . he, far away,
Descried an orbed diamond, set to fray
Old darkness from his throne: 'twas like the sun
Uprisen o'er chaos: and with such a stun

Came the amazement, that, absorb'd in it,
He saw not fiercer wonders—past the wit
Of any spirit to tell, but one of those
Who when this planet's sphering time doth close,
Will be its high remembrancers: who they?
The mighty ones who have made eternal day
For Greece and England. . . .

(II, 244–254)

Absorbed in the light of truth, Endymion has a vision that is noetic, "past the wit / Of any spirit to tell," except those classical and Elizabethan poets who achieved perfect artistic form. His moment of illumination therefore involves some kind of perception of supremely artistic beauty that is also truth. This first descent into the underworld may be regarded as a trip into the poetry of the past, poetry which, as we have seen elsewhere, "brings honey-dew" of inspiration "from buried days" (II, 7) and the most "wild surmise[s]" ("On First Looking into Chapman's Homer").

After his "deep-drawn sighs" of astonishment abate, Endymion continues along his mazy, cavernous path in the same uncertainty and awe as before,

Till, weary, he sat down before the maw
Of a wide outlet, fathomless and dim,
To wild uncertainty and shadows grim. . . .

(II, 271–273)

At the exit of the labyrinth, he reflects on the overwhelming imaginative experience now ending. The actively weaving and projecting images darting across his vision, the fabrications of his protean imagination, now cease; his plight seems that of the dreamer returning to consciousness:

There, when new wonders ceas'd to float before,
And thoughts of self came on, how crude and sore
The journey homeward to habitual self! . . .

(274–276)

The "journey homeward" from the dark recesses of the grotto figures the poet's return to consciousness. His "thoughts of self," that is, his conscious awareness of his true identity, destroy his intuitive, unconscious "self." The visionary delights of imagination fade into the light of common day. He now knows the attendant miseries of consciousness:

> What misery most drowningly doth sing
> In lone Endymion's ear, now he has raught
> The goal of consciousness? . . .
>
> (281–283)

Endymion's second trip into the labyrinthine grotto takes him to the bower of Adonis, where he has a prefigurative vision of his own fate. Once again in the throes of "elemental passion," that is, the fine poetic frenzy inspired by "Dew-dropping melody," he dives

> . . . down some swart abysm
> . . . .
> So saw he panting light, and towards it went
> Through winding alleys; and lo, wonderment!
> Upon soft verdure saw, one here, one there,
> Cupids a slumbering on their pinions fair.
>
> After a thousand mazes overgone,
> At last, with sudden step, he came upon
> A chamber, myrtle wall'd, embowered high,
> Full of light, incense, tender minstrelsy,
> And more of beautiful and strange beside. . . .
>
> (376, 383–391)

In his fit of imaginative wandering, Endymion has stumbled upon the sleeping Adonis, whom Venus "fills with visions" (485). We may consider his mazy progress and stunned amazement at this sudden vision of a mortal about to be immortalized by Venus, as he himself hopes to be by Cynthia, as a metaphorical expression of the silent, working imaginative mind unexpectedly striking on truth. Keats had described that progress in a letter to Bailey: "The simple imaginative Mind may have its rewards in the repeti[ti]on of its own silent Working coming continually on the spirit with a fine suddenness."[17] Endymion's "reward" in the labyrinth lies not only in his vision of Adonis' bower of

---

17. *Letters*, I, 185.

sensory delights, but, more important, in Venus' assurances that he, like Adonis, will be blessed with the perpetual luxury of dreams and supreme powers of imagination; in short, he too will be immortalized:

> Endymion! one day thou wilt be blest:
> So still obey the guiding hand that fends
> Thee safely through these wonders for sweet ends. . . .
>
> (II, 573–575)

We should note also that Endymion's labyrinthine wanderings have led him into the midst of "light, incense, tender minstrelsy / And more of beautiful and strange beside." He has known these sensory delights in other moments of imaginative experience, particularly in flight and in sexual union with Cynthia. Endymion's surprise in falling upon Adonis' bower seems in part to stem from his recognition of these past delights, which are a part of the imaginative life of sensation. The same letter to Bailey describing the silent working of imagination comments on the poet's surprise in recognizing past sensory experience. His recollection stirs his fancy to travel that old path of imaginative thought once again:

have you never by being Surprised with an old Melody—in a delicious place—by a delicious voice, felt over again your very speculations and surmises at the time it first operated on your soul—do you not remember forming to yourself the singer's face more beautiful [than] it was possible and yet with the elevation of the Moment you did not think so—even then you were mounting on the Wings of Imagination so high—that the Prototype must be here after—that delicious face you will see.[18]

The "tender minstrelsy" and the delicious bower are instrumental in re-kindling Endymion's imagination "with a fine suddenness." We may therefore interpret his descent, his progress in the labyrinth, and his experience in Adonis' bower as a large figure for the associative, imaginative mind, aided by memory, winding its way to a sudden vision of truth in "the elevation of the Moment." Clearly that descent seems no different from Endymion's "mounting on wings of Imagination" in Book I.

Once assured by Venus of his happy fate, he journeys confidently through caves and chasms to a high "diamond balustrade" spanning

18. *Ibid.*

"Streams subterranean" and a "thousand fountains." When he hurls his spear,

> . . . those spouting columns rose
> Sudden a poplar's height, and 'gan to enclose
> His diamond path with fretwork, streaming round. . . .
>
> (II, 606–608)

From his perch of light, surrounded by music, Endymion has struck the wellsprings of the protean imagination, which now spontaneously weave the most indescribably beautiful forms of art in diamond light. These shaping, lyrical, radiant fountains, a dense analogue for the supremely generative imagination, stun him:

> . . . Long he dwells
> On this delight; for, every minute's space,
> The streams with changed magic interlace:
> Sometimes like delicatest lattices,
> Cover'd with crystal vines; then weeping trees,
> Moving about as in a gentle wind,
> Which, in a wink, to watery gauze refin'd,
> Pour'd into shapes of curtain'd canopies,
> Spangled, and rich with liquid broideries
> Of flowers, peacocks, swans, and naiads fair.
> Swifter than lightning went these wonders rare. . . .
>
> (611–621)

These fountains rising from the abyss suggest not only the powerful overflow of imagination, but also the controlling, fluidly creating character of imagination, artfully imitating nature. The swiftly changing fantasies woven by the fountains seem not unlike the creations of dreams.

Though Endymion seems a mere observer of these wonders, we may assume with some justification that the fountains represent his own inner creative soul, momentarily brought to life. Elsewhere in the same labyrinth he frets, "will all this gush of feeling pass / Away in solitude?" (681–682). We may associate his overflow of feeling, which we have already observed as the necessary condition for imaginative vision, with the gush of the fountains. Yet the search for Cynthia, his true wellspring of imagination and origin of all these wonders, forces him to leave:

> . . . He bade a loth farewel
> To these founts Protean, passing gulph, and dell. . . .
>
> (626–627)

until he once again reaches the upper world. Endymion stumbles unwillingly out of the cavernous, mazy realm of imagination. He can no longer "trace / The diamond path" (651–652).

His third passage down the grottos of the underworld leads him to yet another vision of truth. In overhearing the lamentable frustrations of Alpheus and Arethusa, who by decree of the gods may never love each other, he is for the first time touched with human sympathy, one of the great virtues of the aspiring poet. Previous to his encounter with Alpheus and Arethusa, Endymion appears to be the figure of Narcissus, completely concerned with himself and his poetic quest. In effect he has divorced himself from humanity in his monomania. In the labyrinth, however, his love extends outward to these lovers as he prays to Cynthia "to soothe, to assuage . . . these lovers' pains" (II, 1015–1016). In sum, the "visions of the earth" (1022) instil charity in the poet-lover. With the major theme of Book II in mind, let us now trace the structural figures that give meaning to Endymion's progress inward to his perception of truth, voiced in this episode by two mythic fountain streams.

Endymion brings himself to the verge of poetic frenzy by recalling past moments of imaginative ecstasy. "The lyre of his soul" soon becomes "Eolian tun'd" (866), his aroused mind flashes with "Half seeing visions" and his ears echo with "ravishments more keen / Than Hermes' pipe" (874–876). Keats figures Endymion's aroused imagination, pregnant with light and music, as a

> . . . sounding grotto, vaulted, vast,
> O'er studded with a thousand, thousand pearls,
> And crimson mouthed shells with stubborn curls,
> Of every shape and size. . . .
>
> (878–881)

Sitting in the coolness of imagination's abyss, and uncertain whether to leap farther inward in pursuit of that music, the poet feels "the spur / Of the old bards to mighty deeds" (895–896). These deeds take the form of heroic wandering. Reviewing his own previous plunge into the underworld, Endymion knows that ideally it culminates in passion and deep visionary experience:

> . . . into the earth's deep maw he rush'd:
> Then all its buried magic, till it flush'd
> High with excessive love. . . .
>
> (899–901)

His plunge stands metaphorically for the poet's magical transformation from consciousness to poetic reverie, from mental coldness to imaginative intensity,[19] from passivity to sexual arousal. Indeed, Endymion's vital presence in the cool labyrinth flushes its channels with his own passion.

Within, he hears his own thoughts echoing from the grotto's thousand crimson shells. As he listens anxiously, the grotto music grows louder and louder. Bursting from the floor, a fountain of music surrounds him:

> He kept an anxious ear. The humming tone
> Came louder, and behold, there as he lay,
> On either side outgush'd, with misty spray,
> A copious spring; and both together dash'd
> Swift, mad, fantastic round the rocks, and lash'd
> Among the conchs and shells of the lofty grot,
> Leaving a trickling dew. . . .
>
> (916–922)

Once again Endymion has achieved the music-making power of imagination while he is in the throes of passion. The fountains' overflow now leads him to a vision of Arethusa and Alpheus and a truth about life.

---

19. The description of Apollo's investiture into the life of supreme imagination follows very closely the crimson frenzy of Endymion:

> For lo! 'tis for the Father of all verse.
> Flush every thing that hath a vermeil hue,
> Let the rose glow intense and warm the air,
>
> . . . .
>
> Let the red wine within the goblet boil,
>
> . . . .
> . . . let faint-lipp'd shells,
> On sands, or in great deeps, vermillion turn
> Through all their labyrinths.   (*Hyperion*, III, 13 ff.)

By this color imagery, Keats subtly suggests that the inner channels of imagination flush when the poet is raised to the heights of poetic frenzy.

Along the ground they took a winding course.
Endymion follow'd—for it seem'd that one
Ever pursued, the other strove to shun—
Follow'd their languid mazes, till well nigh
He had left thinking of the mystery,—
And was now rapt in tender hoverings
Over the vanish'd bliss. Ah! what is it sings
His dream away? What melodies are these? . . .

(926–933)

The fountains of imagination not only provide Endymion with the power of fancy but indeed sing their truths melodiously in the voices of Alpheus and Arethusa, god and nymph of streams. From the experience Endymion learns more fully what Cynthia has already told him:

. . . grief [is] contain'd
In the very deeps of pleasure. . . .

(823–824)

and the frustrations of mortal life can eventually lead to a higher good if the poet is able to extend his love and sympathy to all sufferers. This last vision in the labyrinthine grotto proves to be the turning point in Endymion's career as an aspiring poet. Moved by the plight of these lovers, he chooses in Book III to become the redeemer of all suffering mankind and saves not only Glaucus and Scylla but countless others entombed by Circe.

Chapter six

The fane and palace — Weaving — The bower

The fane and palace

In his letter to Shelley, Keats remarks, "My imagination is a monastery and I am its monk. You must explain my metaphors to yourself." [1] Written at the very end of his poetic career, this passage provides an apt epilogue to one of his favorite recurrent metaphors for poetry.

The identification of the imagination as a monastery and of the poet as its monk suggests a religious attitude toward poetry which we have already noted briefly in discussing the metaphors of the fine frenzy, wine, and manna-dew. We recall that the writing of poetry was for Keats a holy, priest-like task leading to divine truth. "I am certain of nothing but of the holiness of the Heart's affections and the truth of Imagination—What the imagination seizes as Beauty must be truth—whether it existed before or not." [2] Upon this poetic conviction he builds a religion, its sole worshipper being the supreme artist. He would live apart from the world as a monk taking solemn vows of a life of contemplation. If the imagination is holy and its visions are truth, then the only proper place of worship would be the fane of poetry, with an inner sanctum of creative light. One notes in "Sleep and Poetry" his hermit-like resolve to withdraw into the temple of poetry:

1. Lionel Trilling, *The Selected Letters of John Keats* (Garden City, 1956), p. 332. Rollins' annotation of the word "metap^{rs}" as "metap^{cs}" seems incorrect; Keats is here talking about his metaphors, not his metaphysics. Cf. *Letters*, II, 323, n. 9.
2. *Ibid.*, I, 184.

If I do hide myself, it sure shall be
In the very fane, the light of Poesy. . . .

(275–276)

In his monastic confines, he visualizes an ideal poetic heaven similar to the dead poets' Elysium in Book II of *Endymion*, an Elysium which Endymion himself hopes to achieve in an afterlife. Through prayer and incantation, Keats feels that he may reach that poetic heaven:

O Poesy! for thee I grasp my pen
That am not yet a glorious denizen
Of thy wide heaven; yet, to my ardent prayer,
Yield from thy sanctuary some clear air,

   . . . .

   . . . that I may die a death
Of luxury, and my spirit follow
The morning sun-beams to the great Apollo
Like a fresh sacrifice.

(53–56, 58–61)

The richness of religious imagery in this and other passages suggests that poetry is a kind of holy communion with eternal beauty. "Lines on Seeing a Lock of Milton's Hair" describes the poem as a "burnt offering" in Milton's own "Live Temple of sweet noise." In *Endymion* the goddess of poetry invests the poet with holy powers of imagination:

O Moon! old boughs lisp forth a holier din

   . . . .

Thou dost bless every where, with silver lip

   . . . .

And yet thy benediction passeth not
One obscure hiding-place. . . .

(III, 54, 56, 61–62)

Nor does Keats's poetic church lack its evangelists: a letter to Haydon concludes, "So now in the Name of Shakespeare, Raphael and all our Saints I commend you to the care of heaven!" [3]

More than a place of poetic worship, the fane, in all its architectural and decorative brilliance, figures ideal and almost ineffable imaginative

---

3. *Ibid.*, p. 145.

vision. As a structure, it represents the poetry that a holy act of creation has built. Keats would construct his own "Live Temple of sweet noise," as Milton did, in the incantations of dreams. Sleep unlocks the outer gates of the fane of poetry:

> O magic sleep! . . .
>
> . . . .
>
> . . . great key
> To golden palaces, strange minstrelsy. . . .
>
> (*Endymion*, I, 453, 456–457)

Keats's vision of the unearthly beauty of the palace of imagination is frequently difficult to put into appropriate words. "To J. H. Reynolds, Esq." attempts to describe his dream of the enchanted palace of poetry:

> You know the Enchanted Castle,—it doth stand
> Upon a Rock, on the Border of a Lake,
> Nested in Trees, which all do seem to shake
> From some old Magic like Urganda's sword.
> O Phoebus that I had thy sacred word
> To shew this Castle in fair dreaming wise
> Unto my friend, while sick and ill he lies. . . .
>
> (26–32)

The "Enchanted Castle" seems at once a holy church, standing "upon a rock" [4] as did the early Christian basilicas and monasteries, and an Apollonian oracle "nested in trees" and haunted by Urganda-like elves and fairies of imagination.

A further description of the castle suggests its magical vitality:

> You know it well enough, where it doth seem
> A mossy place, a Merlin's Hall, a dream.
> You know the clear Lake, and the little Isles,
> The Mountains blue, and cold near neighbour rills—
> All which elsewhere are but half animate;
> Here do they look alive to love and hate,
> To smiles and frowns; they seem a lifted mound
> Above some giant, pulsing underground. . . .
>
> (33–40)

4. Indeed, the rock is a Biblical symbol for the church.

The magic castle of poetry appears surrounded by "animate" springs, fountains and streams gushing from a giant, creative force "pulsing underground." The linkage of the castle with the spontaneously overflowing fountains of imagination suggests that, like the landscape surrounding Kubla Khan's pleasure dome, the realm of imagination comprehends both an imagined structure or design (figured by the castle) and a powerful, spontaneous, and fertile overflow of feeling (figured in the fountain). Further, the overflow and vision exist only in dreaming, a chief analogue for the creative process.

The next stanza of this Epistle specifically describes the enchanted castle as a fane and an apostolic see built by a hermit-priest, a "banished Santon of Chaldee":

> Part of the Building was a chosen See
> Built by a banish'd Santon of Chaldee. . . .
>
> (41–42)

These lines have the same metaphorical significance as the remark in the letter to Shelley, "My imagination is a monastery and I am its monk." Like the monk, the Santon figures the poet cloistered in his imagination; but the Santon is not wholly possessed by a life of contemplation, for a Santon, or Turkish priest, is a hermetic dervish who is frequently seized by uncontrollable religious frenzies. The whirling dervish is yet another analogue for the intoxicated, frenzied poet. Further, this Santon originates from Chaldea, a nation noted for its knowledge of astronomical lore. As the supreme poet of religious, imaginative, and philosophical knowledge, he has the power to resolve all mysteries of the universe. Here then is the figure of Keats's ideal poet, reigning in the holy see of the poetic imagination.

Yet another wing of the "Enchanted Castle" holds tenant-elves and fairies who act as caretakers like the Santon:

> The doors all look as if they opd themselves,
> The windows as if latch'd by fays & elves—
> And from them comes a silver flash of light,
> As from the Westward of a Summer's night;
> Or like a beauteous woman's large blue eyes
> Gone mad through olden songs and Poesies. . . .
>
> (49–54)

These sentinels of fancy have the power to release the silver light of poetic truth, radiating from the inner sanctum of the castle. We are reminded of an earlier description of the poetic edifice as "the very fane, the light of Poesy" ("Sleep and Poetry," 276). That the castle represents the inner creative realm of the mind seems unquestionable in the light of other metaphorical uses of architecture in the letters. One describes the imaginative mind as "a Mansion of Many Apartments"; [5] another, describing the effects of wine on the fancy, remarks,

Wine . . . is as fragrant as the Queen Bee; and the more ethereal Part of it mounts into the brain, not assaulting the cerebral apartments like a bully in a bad house . . . but rather walks like Aladin about his own enchanted palace so gently that you do not feel his step.[6]

Like the elves and fairies in the castle of poetry, Aladdin assumes the role of fancy's curate. We may assume that the fays surrounding the Queen-Moon in "Ode to a Nightingale" provide the winged release of the nightingale's song, which charms not only the castle of poetry but also the whole realm of the poetic fairyland. Its elfin beauty

> . . . oft-times hath
> Charm'd magic casements, opening on the foam
> Of perilous seas, in faery lands forlorn.

The song of the nightingale, having been broadcast throughout the world like a brief flash of light, now returns to its ideal dwelling, almost, as it were, recalled and reclaimed by the caretaker elves in the fairyland of poetry. The song, like the winged imagination in the poem "Fancy," is once again sealed within its castle by the "mind's caged door."

If "To J. H. Reynolds, Esq." presents the finished holy palace of poetry from the point of view of the youthful outsider with limited imagination, wistfully guessing at what beauties lie behind its doors and windows, later poems picture a more confident Keats exploring the interior of the poetic palace. The most complete description of his vision of ideal poetic structure occurs in Part II of *Lamia*, a poem that records the destruction of the visionary Lycius and his beautiful mistress on their wedding day. In the midst of Cornith, a city famed for its luxury,

5. *Letters*, I, 280. This is a biblical allusion, further suggesting the holiness of the dwelling of imagination. Jesus states, "ye believe in God, believe also in me. In my Father's house are many mansions. . . . I go to prepare a place for you" (John 14:1–2).
6. *Ibid.*, II, 64.

license, and vulgarity, Lamia foolishly builds her palace of art in defer-
ence to Lycius, who insists that the Corinthian rabble be present at
their marriage. She rightfully fears that the intrusion of the mob on
the holy confines of imagination may destroy her and Lycius. Neverthe-
less, she submits to his will:

> . . . So being left alone,
> (Lycius was gone to summon all his kin)
> And knowing surely she could never win
> His foolish heart from its mad pompousness,
> She set herself, high-thoughted, how to dress
> The misery in fit magnificence. . . .
>
> (II, 111–116)

Lamia, the "high-thoughted" imagination, builds a gorgeous structure
with the aid of "her subtle servitors," that is, her elfin slaves of fancy:

> About the halls, and to and from the doors,
> There was a noise of wings, till in short space
> The glowing banquet-room shone with wide-arched grace. . . .
>
> (119–121)

Lamia frames her palace as a poet constructs his poem. Music alone
provides the frail buttress to her entire "faery" structure:

> A haunting music, sole perhaps and lone
> Supportress of the faery-roof, made moan
> Throughout, as fearful the whole charm might fade. . . .
>
> (122–124)

In providing the support to the structure, the music suggests the meter
of poetry. The extreme tenuousness of the music and the roof suggests
the insubstantiality of a creative act of imagination. It is indeed "such
stuff as dreams are made on," a "baseless fabric" of Lamia's vision.[7] We

---

7. In describing Lamia's castle building, Keats perhaps had in mind Shakespeare's
description of the evanescent imagination, whose visions abruptly melt "into thin
air." The fading of imagination inevitably destroys its visionary towers and palaces:

> The cloud-capp'd towers, the gorgeous palaces,
> The solemn temples . . .
>   shall dissolve
> And, like this insubstantial pageant faded,
> Leave not a rack behind. We are such stuff
> As dreams are made on.   (*The Tempest*, IV. i. 152–157)

should be aware that the haunting music here is "sole supportress," meaning not only "singular" but also "soul" sustainer, that is, the tenuous, evanescent, and essential upholder of fancy's domain. Music, it would appear, is the mainstay of the soul. Indeed, it might be argued that the word "sole" also modifies "music." (Why, otherwise, would Keats repeat himself by using the word "lone"?) In this reading music is essence or soul, playing on the inner ear in moments of supreme poetic creativity. Only so long as the creative act remains inviolable may the music last. Significantly, it disappears as the "dreadful guests" and Apollonius intrude on the solitude of the palace.

Having framed her fairy dome of music and a banquet room of "widearched grace," Lamia proceeds to order her palace further. Light, incense, and color add to the palace's growing opulence. She makes its aisles symmetrical and adds fine secondary touches. Her art imitates nature, yet goes beyond mere imitation to achieve perfect form:

> Fresh carved cedar, mimicking a glade
> Of palm and plantain, met from either side,
> High in the midst . . .
> Two palms and then two plantains, and so on,
> From either side their stems branch'd one to one
> All down the aisled place; and beneath all
> There ran a stream of lamps straight on from wall to wall.
> So canopied, lay an untasted feast
> Teeming with odours. . . .
>
> (125–133)

Like the entranced laboring poet in the act of creating, Lamia feels both the satisfaction and the strain of such arduous imaginative toil:

> . . . Lamia, regal drest,
> Silently paced about, and as she went,
> In pale contented sort of discontent,
> Mission'd her viewless servants to enrich
> The fretted splendour of each nook and niche.
> Between the tree-stems, marbled plain at first,
> Came jasper pannels; then, anon, there burst
> Forth creeping imagery of slighter trees,
> And with the larger wove in small intricacies.

Approving all, she faded at self-will,
And shut the chamber up, close, hush'd and still. . . .

(133–143)

Here we find one of the most phenomenal metaphorical presentations
of poetic activity. Her palace figures a supreme achievement of imagination, a poem of which she approves as her labors come to completion.
Somewhat like the "brede" and "overwrought" formal designs on the
frieze of the Grecian urn, her creation possesses all the intricate orna-
mentation which the imagination can conceive. Moreover, her palace
has a vital organic life like the urn's. Each nook and niche is shaped
in "fretted splendor," suggesting not only an intricate type of lace work,
but also a difficult and complex achievement of mind fretted over, that
is to say, worried over and teased out with effort; for as in all art, the
creative process proves to be a kind of torment to the artist. Further,
we may interpret Lamia's weaving of "creeping imagery" into the larger
architectural structure as the poetic act of joining the parts, namely,
imagery and figurative detail, to the whole. "The fretted splendor of each
nook and niche," as well as the "creeping imagery" are the "small in-
tricacies" woven into "the larger," artistic whole (i.e., the palace). The
artistic lavishness of the palace indeed represents ideal poetic structure
in its fullness, finish, and intricacy. The structure conforms in every
respect to Keats's own sentiment of what the best kind of poetry should
be. In the same letter that identifies the imagination as a monastery, he
advises Shelley to "be more of an artist, and 'load every rift' of your
subject with ore." [8] The repleteness of fretwork, imagery, and niches in
Lamia's palace, and indeed their balance and order, seem a successful
analogue for the kind of poetic "ore" Keats continually attempts to
"load" into his own poetry.

The intrusion of the vulgar wedding guests on Lamia's and Lycius'
fairy palace of poetry ultimately destroys it. "For all this came a ruin"
(II, 16). Like the prophecy of the collapse of Kubla Khan's pleasure
dome, this prediction at the beginning of Book II of *Lamia* proves
truthful. Indeed, Lycius' own loud "ancestral voices" bring about the
ruin of the pleasure dome built by Lamia. The palace of imagination
proves too confining and demanding for Lycius' mortal spirit:

8. *Letters*, II, 323.

> Love in a palace is perhaps at last
> More grievous torment than a hermit's fast:—
> That is a doubtful tale from faery land
> Hard for the non-elect to understand. . . .
>
> (3–6)

Lycius is not willing to remain a hermit cloistered in artistic splendor. Although he is "elected" by Lamia to share in the holy secrets of the palace of imagination, a tale hard for the vulgar, or non-elect, to understand, he feels that he must return to the real world and show off his palace to his kinfolk. Thus his extended monkish isolation does not offer him the complete fulfilment he had hoped for; his real human need for earthly companionship and fame forces him back to the mortal world of Corinth. A "thrill / Of trumpets," leaving a buzzing in his head, announces his recall from the palace of imagination:

> For the first time, since first he harbour'd in
> That purple-lined palace of sweet sin,
> His spirit pass'd beyond its golden bourn
> Into the noisy world almost forsworn. . . .
>
> (30–33)

His isolated castle-building with Lamia ends as he awakens from his dream in the palace. He walks out and returns in full consciousness with his "dreadful guests for the revels rude" (144–145). Keats pronounces his violation of the fane of poetry immediately:

> O senseless Lycius! Madman! wherefore flout
> The silent-blessing fate, warm cloister'd hours,
> And show to common eyes these secret bowers? . . .
>
> (147–149)

Lycius is clearly out of the holy life of sensations (i.e., "senseless") and immersed in the world of cold reality with its "herd" of critical people. His kin are amazed not only by the beauty of the palace but also by the fact of its existence in their city. Castles and castle-building it would seem have been foreign to their experience:

> The herd approach'd; each guest, with busy brain,
> Arriving at the portal, gaz'd amain,
> And enter'd marveling: for they knew the street,

Remember'd it from childhood all complete
Without a gap, yet ne'er before had seen
That royal porch, that high-built fair demesne;
So in they hurried all, maz'd, curious and keen. . . .

(150–156)

Within the splendid banquet room of perfume, stately music, "lucid pannels," holy "censers fed with myrrh," "wool-woofed carpets," overflowing goblets of wine, and foods of "Ceres horn," these visitors are even more amazed. If their raucous talk and revelry seem a sacrilege, Apollonius' cruel eye and tongue prove to be the final destructive force on the palace. The palace and its creator wither together:

. . . the loud revelry
Grew hush; the stately music no more breathes;
The myrtle sicken'd in a thousand wreaths.
By faint degrees, voice, lute, and pleasure ceased;
A deadly silence step by step increas'd. . . .

(262–266)

until finally "all was blight" (275). The profaned temple of poetry, its goddess, and its monk fade and die under the withering gaze of the rationalist, Apollonius. He does indeed "Conquer all mysteries" of the temple "by rule and line" and "empty" its "haunted air" (II, 235–236).

As the complex architecture of Lamia's palace signifies ideal poetic form, so the "mimic temple" which Endymion stumbles upon in Book II figures the gorgeous, yet mysterious realm of poetry.[9] At the end of his long dream-journey of imagination in the labyrinthine depths, he strikes upon the poetic temple. Exploring its interiors, he is awed and perplexed by its architectural excellence as were Lycius and the revelers in Lamia's palace:

. . . he went
Into a marble gallery, passing through

9. An interesting, tangential, broadly archetypal interpretation of Endymion's adventure is found in Robert Harrison's essay, "Symbolism of the Cyclical Myth in *Endymion*," *Texas Studies in Language and Literature*, I (1960), 538–554. He reads the adventure as a Jungean search for the self in the realm of the collective unconscious, a much too broad exegesis, but not irrelevant, for it recognizes the psychological nature of the journey. Keats's references to art, architecture, and design suggest that this is, more specifically, an aesthetic, imaginative, and poetic experience.

A mimic temple, so complete and true
In sacred custom, that he well nigh fear'd
To search it inwards. . . .

(255–259)

But Endymion does not presume to be its complacent monk as did
Lycius. An awe-struck, unsure apprentice poet attempting to find his
way in the labyrinths of imagination, he holds this sacred temple in
deepest reverence. From afar, he sees a goddess of imagination, "a quiver'd Dian," pacing delicately near the temple shrine in the manner of
Lamia's and Cynthia's cadences:

. . . far off appear'd,
Through a long pillar'd vista, a fair shrine,
And just beyond, on light tiptoe divine,
A quiver'd Dian. . . .

(259–262)

He summons up enough courage to advance hesitatingly into the innumerable recesses of this marvelous fane:

. . . Stepping awfully,
The youth approach'd, oft turning his veil'd eye
Down sidelong aisles, and into niches old. . . .

(262–264)

Like "the fretted splendor of each nook and niche" and "aisled" balance
of Lamia's palace, this subterranean temple of poetry has its own detailed
artwork and symmetry. The ingenious plan of the temple more than
commands Endymion's attention; it mystifies him, for the temple seems
a work of complex yet ordered intricacy, a labyrinth which only the most
astute poet-apprentice can fathom and trace out:

. . . he began to thread
All courts and passages, where silence dead
Rous'd by his whispering footsteps murmured faint:
And long he travers'd to and fro, to acquaint
Himself with every mystery, and awe. . . .

(266–270)

Endymion's attempt to acquaint himself with the entire structure represents the fledgling poet learning his craft from an example of ideal

artistry. Keats appears to be dramatizing another remark he made on the character of ideal poetry:

Do not the Lovers of Poetry like to have a little Region to wander in where they may pick and choose, and in which the images are so numerous that many are forgotten and found new in a second Reading: which may be food for a Week's stroll in the Summer? [10]

Endymion's exploration is certainly more than a "stroll"; rather, it is a concentrated, exhausting attempt to learn the architectonics of poetry. No wonder, then, that he finds himself "weary" and in "wild uncertainty" at the end of his long investigation of every niche and aisle of the temple. Its labyrinthine plan remains "fathomless and dim" (II, 272) at this point in his search for poetic imagination.

Endymion offers other examples of the complex fane and palace of poetry, but only brief mention need be made here. Venus' assurances in the bower of Adonis give Endymion new strength to continue his journey of imagination with more confidence. Richer pleasure domes await his inspection, as for example in

> . . . palaces of mottled ore,
> Gold dome, and crystal wall, and turquois floor,
> Black polish'd porticos of awful shade
> And, at the last, a diamond balustrade. . . .
>
> (II, 594–597)

The particular mineral richness of this palace seems a most fitting analogue for poetry that "load[s] every rift of [its] subject with ore." More than providing structure to the palace, these precious stones and metals fill the palace with a dazzling wealth of light, which we have already identified as a recurrent metaphor for the overflow of imaginative truth (e.g., "A drainless shower of light is Poesy"). Keats seems to be demonstrating in highly metaphorical terms that poetry comprehends imaginative truth and structural form as one and the same; these lucent gems provide both structure and light. At another point in his poetry, he identifies architectural form and the radiant light of imagination as the same:

10. *Letters*, I, 170. Significantly, *Endymion* is the poem toward which this remark is directed.

If I do hide myself, it sure shall be
In the very fane, the light of Poesy. . . .

("Sleep and Poetry," 275–276)

This passage and the description of Endymion's palace suggest that from within the very structure of poetry—from the structural beauty of the walls, floors, columns, and balustrades—emanates the light of truth. What the imagination seizes as structural beauty must therefore be poetic truth.

Overflowing fountains as well as radiant light form an inseparable part of the design of the poetic palace. These protean fountains shape the dome, pillars, and frieze of yet another edifice visited by an amazed Endymion. We may interpret its architecture as the product of the spontaneous imagination which imitates forms as it shapes fluidly:

And then the water, into stubborn streams
Collecting, mimick'd the wrought oaken beams,
Pillars, and frieze, and high fantastic roof,
Of those dusk places in times far aloof
Cathedrals call'd. . . .

(II, 622–626)

The two Hyperion fragments provide the most revealing use of the temple as a central thematic metaphor. The descriptions of Hyperion's palace and Moneta's temple reveal the main ideas of these later poems and the aesthetic thinking which Keats was undergoing near the end of his career. We may identify Hyperion's palace as the immortal counterpart of Lamia's and Endymion's evanescent, fairy temples of poetry; but we may not make the same claim for Moneta's sanctuary in The Fall of Hyperion, for several important descriptive details show how different is her dwelling from all the rest of Keats's castles of poetry.

The architectural differences between Moneta's and Hyperion's temples point up the essential difference between two types of poetry. If Hyperion represents the old order of gods who live in an unthinking, child-like existence—what Keats had called the "realm . . . / Of Flora and old Pan" ("Sleep and Poetry," 101–102) and "the Chamber of Maiden-Thought"—then his palace represents a kind of poetry of unthinking sensation, of warmth and luxury, which, as Keats knew at the writing of both Hyperion poems, was not the highest form of poetry. Hyperion fears that his airy poetic palace is about to crumble; he is unable to accept the new order of gods, led by Apollo, who professes that both joy and pain must be the fit subjects of poetry.

As Clarence Thorpe makes abundantly clear, Keats was applying to the Hyperion poems the ideas of his letter on "The Vale of Soul-making." Thorpe maintains that Apollo receives his gift of divine knowledge through agony and suffering and, therefore, becomes a great poet. He, like other great poets of the stature of Milton and Shakespeare, has experienced "The vale of Soul-making," described as a "necessary . . . World of Pains and troubles . . . to school an Intelligence and make it a soul." [11] The two poems and this letter, taken together, reveal the kind of poetry Keats was striving for: one that fuses both heaven and earth, a poetry half imagined and half real, its reality always anchored in an awareness of the human condition. The isolated, purely visionary poet, therefore, cannot match up to the superior knowledge of Apollo. Thorpe states:

Only an educated, seer-like imagination, ballasted by the wisdom of the earth, can wing its way with steady sureness to the heart of the 'Mystery.' To possess such an imagination is to be strong in a beauty that shall some day rule the earth. It was this power that enabled the Olympians to upset the Titan dynasty, and by virtue of its perfect fruition Apollo was to cast the sun-god from his throne.[12]

At Moneta's throne in the Apollonian palace of poetry, the mortal intruder learns that for the poet of eminence "the miseries of the world / Are misery, and will not let them rest" (*The Fall of Hyperion*, I, 148–149). The poet now can no longer live apart in his luxurious, isolated palace of imagination, for in cutting himself off from the suffering of humanity he rejects his true role of "sage, / A humanist, physician to all men" (I, 189–190).[13] Let us now explore the temples of Moneta and

11. *Ibid.*, II, 102.   12. *The Mind of John Keats*, p. 146.

13. Sperry, pp. 135–137 *et passim*, amplifies Thorpe's observations, identifying Hyperion's dismay and nervousness as a biographical allegory of Keats's unstable imaginative life. Sperry, following Thorpe, views Hyperion as the isolated, self-centered poet whom Keats would reject in favor of the great poet of humanity, Apollo. Where Hyperion remains apart from reality, Apollo indeed thrives in the painful struggle of the real world. The gods therefore represent two kinds of poets; their struggles represent two attitudes toward poetic theory. The two Hyperion fragments record this antithesis not only dramatically (with practically all the critical commentary directed to this element of the poems) but also metaphorically, which is our concern here.

Hyperion, that we may note how Keats figuratively expresses the two different attitudes toward poetry.

The very austerity and dimness of Moneta's temple suggests a way of poetic life that is close to the ascetic. The "eternal domed Monument" (I, 71) possesses no fairy canopy, but rather a "roof august" (62). Its exterior is compared to earth's "grey Cathedrals" and "rent towers" (67). Within her "old sanctuary" hang particularly somber draperies, wholly unlike the dazzling carpets and splendorous draperies of Lamia's palace:

> Upon the marble at my feet there lay
> Store of strange vessels, and large draperies,
> Which needs had been of dyed asbestos wove,
> Or in that place the moth could not corrupt,
> So white the linen; so, in some, distinct
> Ran imageries from a sombre loom. . . .
>
> (I, 72–77)

Moneta's palace affects no wild splendor, for the domain of serious, philosophical poetry does not permit the fantastic excesses found in the fanciful palaces of poetry. The white draperies of asbestos and the "imageries" from a "sombre" poetic loom may not be so scintillating, yet they are the more appropriate and permanent decorative part of poetry. We presume that with these more fitting materials and designs Moneta has revamped Hyperion's more gaudy palace, for

> All in a mingled heap confus'd there lay
> Robes, golden tongs, censer, and chafing dish,
> Girdles, and chains, and holy jewelries. . . .
>
> (78–80)

The serious poet may throw away such ornaments as unnecessary or may use them discreetly in his austere fane.

Other properties of this particular temple distinguish it from Endymion's, Lamia's, and Hyperion's palaces. No music fills its stately naves and dome; no dazzling light radiates from its inner sanctum, only the flicker of a "sacrificial fire." The poet remains in shadows of uncertainty during his colloquy with Moneta. Here poetic truth is, at best, a dim reality, an attitude which conforms to Keats's own growing skepticism of what ultimates the imagination can reveal.[14] Only a faint swirl of incense drifts to the extremities of this vast palace, which the poet, like Endymion, tries to "fathom every way" (I, 82). The pronounced austerity of Moneta's temple seems in keeping with the kind of poetry she professes. Such poetry demands sacrifice and suffering on the part of the poet, who, for the sake of poetic vision, chooses to mount the steps to her throne:

> Prodigious seem'd the toil. . . .
>
> . . . .
> . . . and the hard task proposed. . . .
>
> (121, 120)

The poet in fact risks his life to achieve Moneta's height; he may live to

> '. . . [venom] all his days,
> 'Bearing more woe than all his sins deserve. . . .
>
> (175–176)

because in achieving Moneta's throne, he takes on the burdens of the world as do the most dedicated altruists and prophets. The ordinary poet, on the other hand, never thinks to come to this particularly severe temple of poetry:

> 'They seek no wonder but the human face;
> 'No music but a happy-noted voice—
> 'They come not here, they have no thought to come. . . .
>
> (163–165)

No luxurious pleasure dome, Moneta's gloomy temple appropriately figures serious and responsible poetry.

Hyperion's temple, however, represents a kind of "happy-noted," pleasurable poetry which inevitably failed Lycius and presumably would have collapsed around the hysterical Titan. In his palace, Hyperion knows only a life of sensory indulgences such as Lycius knew in Lamia's palace. He asks if its pleasures could possibly vanish:

> 'Am I to leave this haven of my rest,
> 'This cradle of my glory, this soft clime,
> 'This calm luxuriance of blissful light,

14. Bate, *John Keats*, 550, 585–588.

'These crystalline pavilions, and pure fanes,
'Of all my lucent empire? It is left
'Deserted, void, nor any haunt of mine.
'The blaze, the splendor, and the symmetry,
'I cannot see—but darkness, death and darkness. . . .

(I, 235–242)

The poet in *The Fall of Hyperion* knows no such luxuries in Moneta's palace. And Apollo himself, even as he assumes the ultimate powers of imagination at his investiture, knows the pain as well as the pleasure of his "knowledge enormous" (*Hyperion*, III, 113). But Hyperion's knowledge remains limited to simple, pleasurable sensations; he rules an inferior poetic castle, which must fall before the new poetic order as Apollo presses on with indomitable might. The color, the incense, and the music all betray the woeful inadequacy of Hyperion's palace, where suffering and hardship are unknown. We detect its instability and can foresee its inevitable collapse in the description of its reddening courts, aisles, and domes. The palace seems a mirror to Hyperion's uncertainty and fear as he flares from hall to hall:

. . . His palace bright
Bastion'd with pyramids of glowing gold,
And touch'd with shade of bronzed obelisks,
Glar'd a blood-red through all its thousand courts,
Arches, and domes, and fiery galleries;
And all its curtains of Aurorian clouds
Flush'd angerly. . . .

(I, 176–182)

The references to Egyptian architecture identify Hyperion's realm as an old and extinct order of art and further suggest the reason for its imminent collapse before the new Apollo. Moreover, the once pleasant incense in his palace turns to poison as he strides anxiously "within each aisle and deep recess" (196). Hyperion has no time for "rest divine upon exalted couch / And slumber in the arms of melody" (192–193) as was his habit. The sensuous music alone remains undiminished. Like the "haunting music" supporting Lamia's "faery-roof," are the organ tones in this doomed castle of sensuous poetry:

> . . . solemn tubes,
> Blown by the serious Zephyrs, gave of sweet
> And wandering sounds, slow-breath'd melodies. . . .
> (206–208)

The sumptuous brilliance of the naves, arcades, and dome at the center of the palace reminds us of the diamond work and the overflowing fountains of light at the very center of Endymion's subterranean temple of poetry:

> . . . On he flared,
> From stately nave to nave, from vault to vault,
> Through bowers of fragrant and enwreathed light,
> And diamond-paved lustrous long arcades,
> Until he reach'd the great main cupola. . . .
> (217–221)

Hyperion's castle, in effect, is too splendid. In the two Hyperion fragments, Keats seems to have arrived at the conclusion that the true poet cannot isolate himself in an unreal, wholly sensory, and dazzling palace of poetry, but must inevitably turn to human problems. Hyperion therefore seems juvenile in his inability or unwillingness to bow to Apollo's higher poetic station. He will not quit his lavish pleasure dome; nor is he willing, we assume, to accept a more sober and austere temple of poetry like Moneta's.

The two kinds of poetry figured in the contrasting palaces were equally attractive to Keats. He never made a firm choice between the two for the simple reason that he did not live long enough to estimate fully the virtues of each. His inclination in his later poetry, however, seems to be toward more weighty and philosophical themes. This tendency is confirmed by letters which reveal an increasing admiration for Wordsworth and Milton. Inevitably Keats visited Hyperion's palace once more in *Lamia* and saw how insubstantial it really was, saw indeed its destructive influence on the bemused poet. Yet in *The Eve of St. Agnes*, written in the same months as *Lamia*, we find an almost complete return to sensuous poetry relatively free from weighty philosophical discussion. Apparently the kind of poetry which Moneta's fane represents failed to engage Keats's attention for very long; for, though he saw the need for philosophy and commitment to humanity, his imagination was best equipped to describe sensation. The weighty thoughts and the relatively abstract style of *Hyperion* seem a somewhat unnatural grafting of Milton's epic mode. Keats appears to be more at home finally in the pleasure dome of poetry.

Weaving

In discussing Keats's use of architecture as a metaphor for poetry, we had occasion to speak briefly of the decorative plants, flowers, and trees in Lamia's palace of poetry. After Lamia's "high-thoughted" imagination creates the pleasure dome, it weaves a bower or "glade" down the aisles. The inclusion of organic life, spontaneously weaving a natural structure within a larger, spanning architectural design suggests that in the creative process, as it is conceived by Keats, art and nature complement each other. The metaphors of architecture and the bower attempt to define the poetic process as a highly planned, deliberate, and laborious act of mind, and at the same time, as a spontaneous, organic growth. Taken together, architectural contrivance and vegetable growth figure the supreme act of imagination, which combines "high-thoughted" deliberation and natural, intuitive, spontaneous perception. M. H. Abrams makes a lucid comment on how the creative mind operates in "reflective freedom" and at the same time in "blind necessity."

The inventive genius combines in himself the elements both of art and of nature, both the process of adapting means to freely chosen ends according to knowable rules and a reliance on a blind spontaneity outside his knowledge or control. The productive activity, as Schelling phrases the idea, includes 'what is generally called art . . . that which is practised with consciousness, deliberation, and reflection, and can be taught and learned,' and also that which cannot 'be achieved by application or in any other way, but must be inherited as a free gift of nature.' [15]

This passage on the aesthetics of creation in Romantic poetry provides an almost perfect description of Lamia's travail—her "discontent" and fretting—in the act of creating her pleasure dome, and, at the same time, of the spontaneous ease with which she sets organic nature to

15. *The Mirror and the Lamp*, p. 209.

work. Under her gentle urging, nature weaves its own forms, free of any exterior control: The lines

> . . . there burst
> Forth creeping imagery of slighter trees,
> And with the larger wove in small intricacies. . . .
>
> (II, 139–141)

demonstrate that poetry follows a spontaneous and self-creating, natural process, with Lamia as its prime mover. Indeed, the passage seems to exemplify a remark on the aesthetics of poetry made in a letter to Taylor: "if Poetry comes not as naturally as the Leaves to a tree it had better not come at all." [16] In the organic process of nature, therefore, Keats sees an ideal model to be imitated: "The rise, the progress, the setting of imagery should like the Sun come natural [to] him—shine over him and set soberly although in magnificence leaving him in the Luxury of twilight." [17]

The short passage in *Lamia* on the organic nature of poetic activity introduces us to yet another metaphor for the poetic process, weaving. It also introduces us to a recurrent analogue for the poetic product of such weaving, the bower. Let us first consider in detail the metaphor of weaving.

Keats would be the supremely creative poet by following the example of nature's organic processes. As nature weaves its forms spontaneously, so he would weave his own poetry, using the materials of nature. One of the most remarkable descriptions of this weaving occurs in Endymion's reverent address to Cynthia:

> In sowing time ne'er would I dibble take,
> Or drop a seed, till thou wast wide awake;
> And, in the summer tide of blossoming,
> No one but thee hath heard me blithely sing
> And mesh my dewy flowers all the night. . . .
>
> (III, 153–157)

Under Cynthia's divine influence, which fertilizes all natural life, including the poet's seeds of imagination, Endymion is able to cull and weave imagination's flowers into a finished wreath or garland of poetry. But un-

16. *Letters*, I, 238–239.   17. *Ibid.*, p. 238.

like nature's organic, self-creative weaving, Endymion's imaginative weaving involves human effort:

> "Daily, I pluck sweet flowerets from their bed,
> "And weave them dyingly. . . .[18]

(I, 954-955)

The word "dyingly" suggests the spending of the poet in the difficult act of creating. We have seen a similar spending of the poet's powers in the act of sexual union.

Yet at other times Keats compares poetic weaving to the natural and effortless tracings of the spider, who instinctively gives order and symmetry to her own "airy Citadel": "Man may like the Spider spin from his own inwards his own airy Citadel—the points of leaves and twigs on which the Spider begins her work are few and she fills the Air with a beautiful circuiting." [19] But often the ability to weave spontaneously a "Citadel" or "tapestry empyrean" fails. In states of indolence, the shuttles of the poet's loom of imagination remain almost inert. The epigraph to the "Ode on Indolence"—"They toil not, neither do they spin"—speaks metaphorically of the poet's inability to create poetry. The poem describes the indolent imagination as a dull sleep, "embroidered with dim dreams." Barely two months after his indolent spell, Keats, now in more favorable moments of imaginative zeal, once more compares himself to the eager, spontaneously weaving spider: "I mean I should *do* something for my immediate welfare—Even if I am swept away like a Spider from a drawing room I am determined to spin—home spun any thing for sale." [20]

If his spider-like imagination weaves in dreams where intuitive thought replaces cold reason, one should presume that the return to consciousness would destroy the fabric of unpremeditated weaving. The destruction of Lamia's palace provides the best example of the withering effect of

18. Keats's use of flowers as a figure for poetry, though not the concern of this chapter, needs some qualification here. Keats's first stage of his announced ten-year immersion in "Poesy" ("O for ten years, that I may overwhelm / Myself in Poesy") takes him into the realm of "Flora and old Pan" ("Sleep and Poetry," 102). Keats's occasional identification of "poesy" with "posy" is apparent in even so late a poem as *Hyperion*, where Mnemosyne reminds Apollo of his early and innocent poetic days in the sensuous realm of Flora. At that time and place the young Apollo's "infant hand / Pluck'd witless the weak flowers" (III, 73-74).

19. *Letters*, I, 231-232.   20. *Ibid.*, II, 178.

the dissecting, rational mind. Her sumptuous fabrics disintegrate and fade as Apollonius,

> . . . with eye severe,
> And with calm-planted steps walk'd in austere;
> . . . something too he laugh'd,
> As though some knotty problem, that had daft
> His patient thought, had now begun to thaw,
> And solve, and melt. . . .
>
> (II, 157–162)

The philosopher indeed "unweave[s] the rainbow" (237) and causes the myrtle to "sicken in a thousand wreaths" (264) in his attempt to understand the mysterious process and product of imagination. He would know the mystery of her weaving "by rule and line" (235), an act which appears a sacrilege.

If, on the one hand, Apollonius unweaves the fabric of Lamia's palace, and destroys her as well, Circe, on the other hand, weaves a net of sensory delights that entangles Glaucus and eventually sends him to his ruin:

> With . . . honey-words she wove
> A net whose thraldom was more bliss than all
> The range of flower'd Elysium. . . .²¹
>
> (*Endymion*, III, 426–428)

Circe's woven bower of poetry takes captive Glaucus' "o'er-sweeten'd soul" (445). She practices the same kind of cold calculation as Apollonius, and her effect on the visionary wanderer is equally destructive. She represents the enthralling, perversely weaving, poetic imagination

---

21. Keats's identification of weaving as the creation of poetry follows the classical tradition beginning with Homer. In *The Odyssey*, Circe enchants Odysseus' men by weaving and singing at the same time. Though Circe is merely an enchantress in the epic, Keats sees her as the demonic poetic force, weaving dazzling colors and shapes on her loom and singing men to their destruction. Homer's description of Circe at her loom seems to have had this special meaning for Keats: "Presently they reached the gates of the goddess's house, and as they stood there they could hear Circe within, singing most beautifully as she worked her loom, making a web so fine, so soft, and of such dazzling colors as no one but a goddess could weave" (*The Odyssey*, trans. Samuel Butler [New York, 1944], p. 122). In the Circe episode of *Endymion*, the weapons of the enchantress are, in fact, weaving and singing. What she weaves proves as "fine" and "soft" and splendid (though perniciously so) as anything the supreme poetic imagination could devise.

whose overwrought net of delights proves so irresistible that Glaucus cannot and will not disentangle himself from it.

To this point in our discussion of the metaphor of weaving, the examples given have been restricted to the floral wreathings of Lamia, Circe, and Endymion and to the fine web of the spider-poet. Keats does not identify human poets and divine goddesses as the only workers at the poetic loom. In a highly significant linkage of metaphors, he demonstrates that the weaving process may also be performed by spontaneously welling fountains. One of Endymion's greatest amazements in the labyrinths occurs at the moment that he views the fountains weaving natural patterns in the air. We may take the following passage as a complex analogue for an organically creative act of imagination:

> . . . Long he dwells
> On this delight; for every minute's space,
> The streams with changed magic interlace:
> Sometimes like delicatest lattices,
> Cover'd with crystal vines; then weeping trees,
> Moving about as in a gentle wind,
> Which, in a wink, to watery gauze refin'd,
> Pour'd into shapes of curtain'd canopies,
> Spangled, and rich with liquid broideries
> Of flowers. . . .
> Swifter than lightning went these wonders rare. . . .
>
> (II, 611–621)

The fountains, in effect, create the same kind of "fretted splendor" which we discerned in Lamia's palace. Moreover, as we have already seen, these fountains mimic architectural forms, "Pillars, and frieze, and high fantastic roof" (624). Thus, by combining the metaphors of weaving and the fountain, Keats describes not only the poetic process but also its product—that is, a latticed structure which other poems identify as the bower of poetry.

The bower

The bower is a persistent analogue for achieved poetic form. It stands for structure and space, much like the architectural dome. Indeed, the letter describing a "tapestry empyrean" makes poetry out to be an embowered enclosure, woven "full of Symbols for [man's] spiritual eye, of softness for his spiritual touch, of space for his wandering, of distinctness for his Luxury." [22] Like the palaces and fanes, grots and labyrinths, the bower figures poetry as "a little Region to wander in where [one] may pick and choose, and in which the images are so numerous that many are forgotten and found new in a second Reading." [23] And like the Santons and monks caring for their poetic monasteries, the poet cultivates his bower. He assumes the role of a gardener. "Sleep and Poetry" describes him as the arranger and pruner of organic life, that it may grow, not chaotically, but formally. The artist controls nature to his own aesthetic ends:

> Then let us clear away the choaking thorns
> From round its [the myrtle's] gentle stem. . . .
>
> (255–256)

Keats attributes to his fellow poet, Leigh Hunt, the role of apprentice gardener in Spenser's bower of poetry:

> In Spenser's halls he stray'd, and bowers fair,
>   Culling enchanted flowers. . . .
>
>   ("Written on the Day that Mr. Leigh Hunt Left Prison")

Having tended his poetic bower with care, the poet leaves his "little space" for others to admire. The finished woven poem provides the reader with a sense of compact and intricate organization as found in a trellis:

>   . . . when a tale is beautifully staid,
> We feel the safety of a hawthorn glade. . . .
>
>   ("I stood tip-toe," 129–130)

"A thing of beauty is a joy forever" insofar as it achieves that highly composed steadfastness of a bower:

> Its loveliness increases; it will never
> Pass into nothingness; but still will keep
> A bower quiet for us. . . .
>
>   (*Endymion*, I, 2–4)

22. *Letters*, I, 232.   23. *Ibid.*, p. 170.

In his attempt to achieve ideal poetic structure, the poet is constantly driven to weave:

> Therefore, on every morrow, are we wreathing
> A flowery band to bind us to the earth. . . .
>
> (6–7)

The idea that art manifests a staidness, or perfect fixity, of a bower is repeated in a more subtly objective fashion in "Ode on a Grecian Urn." Note that the urn embowers or encloses its "legend" of human and divine life with a circular "leaf-fring'd" frame. Moreover, Keats attributes a part of the urn's "fair attitude" to the "forest branches" and "happy boughs" which arch and embower the "flowery tale" of human life. Such persistent allusion to the bower seems yet another instance of nature weaving, enclosing, and unifying in a self-organizing process of creation. Art, like a bower, is indeed "staid," permanent, and complex, a mazy "little region to wander in." Appropriately, therefore, poetic art is figured as a labyrinthine bower in "I stood tip-toe":

> There was wide wand'ring for the greediest eye,
> To peer about upon variety;
>
> . . . .
> To picture out the quaint, and curious bending
> Of a fresh woodland alley, never ending. . . .
>
> (15–16, 19–20)

All of the metaphorical values we have ascribed to the bower appear summarized in one of Keats's most interesting sonnets, the one on Chaucer's "The Floure and the Lefe."

> This pleasant tale is like a little copse:
>   The honied lines do freshly interlace
>   To keep the reader in so sweet a place,
> So that he here and there full-hearted stops;
> And oftentimes he feels the dewy drops
>   Come cool and suddenly against his face,
>   And by the wandering melody may trace
> Which way the tender-legged linnet hops. . . .

The last seven lines of this octet clarify the introductory statement of line one; poetry is like a copse in its carefully tended structure, its dome-like unity, and its wreathed intricacy. The woven branches forming the sides and roof are here associated with the spontaneous, "wandering melody" of poetry. Moreover, within the woven intricacy of the poem, the beholder can "trace" and comprehend the direction and nature of the "wandering melody." An underlying pattern, rooted in meter, allows him to trace "which way the tender-legged linnet hops," for just as the meter jumps (perhaps erratically, since Chaucer's verse was generally considered to be metrically irregular [24]) so does the linnet. We are reminded in other poems of a similar use of animal movement as a metaphor for meter. The regular pace of the steed of poetry, for example, figures metrical regularity.

With equal importance, the sonnet suggests that the bower provides Puck's "dewy drops" of poetic inspiration for the beholder within the copse. Achieved poetic form provides one of the main sources of inspiration for Keats; remembrance of poetry of the past "brings honey-dew from buried days," as the opening lines of Book II of *Endymion* attest. "The Floure and the Lefe," as a bower, contains "honied lines" that inspire him by the artistic manner in which they "interlace."

We may therefore consider Keats's bower not only a metaphor for woven poetry, but also the place of poetic inspiration, for two reasons: first, the woven artistry of the bower provides the poet with a concrete example of unity and beauty; second, its fertile organic growth is associated with spontaneous, imaginative activity. Its form represents poetic structure, and its vital growth represents the process of imagination. The bower serves as a kind of holy, natural fane harboring a divine gift of inspiration. "Sleep and Poetry" provides an early example of the poet receiving natural inspiration in its sheltered privacy:

> . . . a bowery nook
> Will be elysium—an eternal book
> Whence I may copy many a lovely saying
> About the leaves, and flowers—about the playing
> Of nymphs in woods, and fountains; and the shade
> Keeping a silence round a sleeping maid;

24. In remarking that Chaucer appears "a rough diamond, and must be polished ere he shines," Dryden initiated a long-standing misconception of Chaucer's meter. Even in Keats's day, Chaucer's verse was considered as metrically irregular. Correct scansion of Middle English poetry did not come until the late nineteenth century.

And many a verse from so strange influence
That we must ever wonder how, and whence
It came. . . .

(63–71)

Further, the scenery within the bower kindles the poet's myth-making
imagination. The story of Narcissus is born out of an inspired vision
which the poet experiences in the sanctity of the bower:

> What first inspired a bard of old to sing
> Narcissus pining o'er the untainted spring?
> In some delicious ramble, he had found
> A little space, with boughs all woven round;
>
> · · · · · · · · · · · ·
>   . . . tendril wreaths fantastically creeping.
> And on the bank a lonely flower he spied,
>
> · · · · · · · · · · · ·
> So while the Poet stood in this sweet spot,
> Some fainter gleamings o'er his fancy shot;
> Nor was it long ere he had told the tale
> Of young Narcissus, and sad Echo's bale. . . .
>
> ("I stood tip-toe," 163–166, 170–171, 177–180)

Keats apparently associates the teeming growth of the bower with imaginative fertility. Just as the bower wreathes its tendrils "fantastically,"
the poet's imaginative mind weaves poetic myth. The superior poet
need only read the messages which nature lays at his feet; for he knows
that it provides both the materials of poetry and the woven verbal form
it would take. The poet in the bower therefore seems the inspired imi-
tator of nature.

At any moment on a journey of imagination, one may achieve immediate poetic vision by chancing upon a bower of poetry built by
great poets of the past. By pulling its trellises aside, the poet allows us to
view visionary wonders within its hidden recesses. Apuleius and other
classical poets not only built eternal bowers, but also provided windows
for our vision inward:

> So did he feel, who pull'd the boughs aside,
> That we might look into a forest wide,

To catch a glimpse of Fawns, and Dryades
Coming with softest rustle through the trees;
And garlands woven of flowers wild, and sweet,

   . . . .

Telling us how fair, trembling Syrinx fled
Arcadian Pan, with such a fearful dread. . . .

          ("I stood tip-toe," 151–155, 157–158)

We, as readers, "feel" both the inspired vision re-created by the poet, and the perfect form which the tale takes. In these lines Keats demonstrates that the flawless order of truly visionary poetry inspires our aesthetic sensibility; for

     . . . when a tale is beautifully staid,
We feel the safety of a hawthorn glade. . . .

          ("I stood tip-toe," 129–130)

The recurrent identification of the bower as the site of poetic inspiration can be found in even so late a poem as *The Fall of Hyperion*. In this poem the sensory delights of the bower are preliminary to the greater inspired vision to come in Moneta's temple. The initial setting describes the embowered realm of "Flora and old Pan," that is, the simple delights of imagination celebrated in "Sleep and Poetry" [25] and "I stood tip-toe." Within the woven

     . . . arbour with a drooping roof
Of trellis vines, and bells, and larger blooms,
Like floral censers swinging light in air. . . .

          (I, 25–27)

the mortal poet falls asleep, having drunk "transparent juice"—that is, manna-dew.[26] In swooning away in his delightful bower and awakening in Moneta's somber sanctuary, the poet symbolically moves from the realm of simple and sensuous poetry of "Arcadian Pan" to the austere realm of philosophical poetry. Keats's shifting of scenery, therefore, has a highly appropriate function in the meaning of the poem. In the bower, the poet's inspirational swoon indeed leads to vision, but not of sportive "Fawns and Dryades." The vision involves a serious, sober, and painful

25. See especially ll. 101–121.   26. See Chapter four above, p. 100.

initiation into the true poetic fraternity. The aspiring poet must inevitably pass through the simple and sensuous bower before he can enter, "in fair dreaming wise," Moneta's temple of high poetry. Reflecting on his short but accomplished poetic career, Keats is apparently conceding that the bower of poetry is important in that it serves as a stage in the poet's developing life of imagination.

Since the bower provides the initial setting for poetic inspiration we should quite naturally expect to find a number of linkages between it and other established, recurrent metaphors for inspiration. We have already seen, for example, how manna-dew is associated with the bower in *The Fall of Hyperion* and in the sonnet on "The Floure and the Lefe." The act of sexual union, a major recurrent metaphor for poetry, often takes place within a trellised bower. Cynthia invests the embowered poet with "power to dream deliciously" (II, 708) as he embraces her. At one point, Endymion addresses her as "the deep glen" (III, 163), for she alone blesses his bowers of poetry with inspiring beauty:

> No woods were green enough, no bower divine,
> Until thou liftedst up thine eyelids fine. . . .
>
> (III, 151–152)

Like Cynthia, the muses bring to the poet

> Shapes from the invisible world, unearthly singing
> From out the middle air, from flowery nests. . . .
>
> ("I stood tip-toe," 186–187)

The muses prove to be "kind" to Keats by granting inspiration in the poetic bower:

> Should e'er the fine-eyed maid to me be kind,
> Ah! surely it must be whene'er I find
> Some flowery spot, sequester'd, wild, romantic,
> That often must have seen a poet frantic. . . .
>
> ("To George Felton Mathew," 35–38)

He describes that "spot" as fertile "clusters" of laburnum and "intertwined . . . Cassia," threading between "pillars of the sylvan roof" (35 *et passim*). All these examples suggest that in the recesses of the bower of poetry the poet knows sexual and imaginative frenzy and achieves the heights of inspired vision.

One of the most significant descriptions of the bower of poetry links Endymion's "jasmine bower" with woven caves, honey-combs, wreathing, floral incenses, and spontaneous music:

> . . . exhaled asphodel,
> And rose, with spicy fannings, interbreath'd,
> Came swelling forth where little caves were wreath'd
> So thick with leaves and mosses, that they seem'd
> Large honey-combs of green, and freshly teem'd
> With airs delicious. . . .
>
> (II, 663–668)

This teeming bower, in effect, raises Endymion to the heights of sensory stimulation, culminating ultimately in his sexual union with Cynthia. Keats's use of weaving and wreathing imagery more than describes the sensory delights of the bower; the music-mingled incenses, the knitted foliage, and windings of fertile caves subtly prefigure the sexual union of Endymion and Cynthia, the union of the poet and imagination. The inclusion of "honey-combs" in the bower in this cluster of metaphors has the force of suggesting not only the bower's structural intricacy, but, indirectly, its manna-laden provisions of imaginative inspiration. The music filling these caves, the manna-dew, and the extreme fertility of this poetic bower of bliss alchemize Endymion into a state of increasing imaginative capability, culminating in union with Cynthia at which point spontaneous poetic utterance flows harmoniously from both their lips.

The bower of Adonis in Book II of *Endymion* provides an equally revealing example of Keats's technique of linking metaphors for poetic inspiration. Adonis' bower appears to Endymion as

> A chamber, myrtle wall'd, embower'd high,
> Full of light, incense, tender minstrelsy. . . .
>
> (389–390)

Once again, music and incense suffuse the woven structure of the bower. In addition, it harbors the light of poetic truth; for we are in the immortal bower of Adonis, who becomes blessed with perpetual imaginative dreaming. The imagery of weaving and wreathing again suggests the supreme fertility of his imaginative dreaming:

> . . . Above his head,
> Four lily stalks did their white honours wed
> To make a coronal; and round him grew
> All tendrils green, of every bloom and hue,
> Together intertwin'd and trammel'd fresh:
> The vine of glossy sprout; the ivy mesh. . . .
>
> (407–412)

Flying through "the woven roof" as if to nurture his organically wreathing imagination, Cupids shake inspiring flower-dew and violets upon Adonis' eyes.

Endymion's visit to this particular bower of poetry ends in a vision of Adonis being immortalized. The bower, like the fane and palace, is a favorite retreat where poetic vision may ultimately be granted. The poet takes the role of the gardener in the bower, or of the monk in his monastery; both attempt repeatedly to achieve poetic vision through their craft and office. In virtually every example of his use of the bower, the fane, and the palace, Keats attempts to re-enact the poetic ritual expressed in "Sleep and Poetry":

> If I do hide myself, it sure shall be
> In the very fane, the light of Poesy. . . .
>
> (275–276)

Chapter seven

Images of reality

Keats's imaginative flights and descents into the realms of poetry follow a semicircular arc, the apex or nadir of which may be considered as the point of poetic release. We have previously noted metaphors describing the poet's journey[1] of ever-increasing imaginative sensations along that arc, which leads by degrees to "the chief intensity," i.e., supreme poetic fulfilment. We have also noted the figurative role of manna-dew, wine, the laurel, and flower-dew,[2] the agents of poetic inspiration, and have seen how the poetry expresses ecstatic poetic fulfilment in the metaphor of sexual union.[3] We now need to see in what ways Keats describes the decline of imagination after its moments of vision.

The world of mutability remains arrested only so long as the poet's dream and lovemaking last; unhappily, he must return to the world of reality as his vision fades, a return described as "the journey homeward to habitual self" (*Endymion*, II, 276). The experience is invariably painful; his dream is vexed to waking nightmare. All of the afflictions of mortal life seem doubly strong as he descends the arc of imagination.

But before considering the recurrent images and metaphors for the sensations of that "journey homeward to habitual self," we should be

1. See the discussions in Chapter three above on flight and the wings of poetry, swimming, the steeds of poetry, and the poetic bark; see also in Chapters five and six the descent into the labyrinth and grot, and the exploration of the fane of poetry.
2. See Chapter four above.   3. See Chapter three above.

aware of the importance of pain in Keats's aesthetic creed. "A life of sensations" involves not only the pleasure and excitement of imaginative release, but also pain, which he believes is an integral part of the poet's experience. Though at times Endymion resents the intrusion of pain on his imaginative dreaming, he later accepts it as an inevitable and even necessary part of a poet's development. At the time just prior to writing his great odes in May, 1819, Keats asserts that the world is a "vale of Soul-making . . . where the heart must feel and suffer in a thousand diverse ways." [4] Moreover, in remarking that the suffering heart "is the Minds Bible, it is the Minds experience," he identifies pain as the chief agent shaping the poetic soul. The lines spoken by Cynthia:

> Endymion: woe! woe! is grief contain'd
> In the very deeps of pleasure. . . .

> (II, 823–824)

pronounce much earlier than the "Ode on Melancholy" the fact that the life of imagination comprehends both pleasure and sorrow. Indeed, the ode makes clear that the fane of poetry enshrines Melancholy as well as Delight:

> Ay, in the very temple of Delight
> Veil'd Melancholy has her sovran shrine. . . .

The life of imagination, thriving in the life of sensation, must inevitably end in a melancholy fit as the poet returns to the real world. He knows physical and mental hurt, the price of reaching the heights of imaginative transport. Acute depression attends that falling off and dying out of poetic power; after bursting "joy's grape against his palate fine,"

> His soul shall taste the sadness of her might,
> And be among her cloudy trophies hung.

The poetic soul, having briefly but joyously tasted the wine of inspiration, returns to "The weariness, the fever, and the fret" of the real world. The continual references in "Ode to a Nightingale" to "fever,"

---

4. *Letters*, II, 102. Perkins justly remarks that the "vale of Soul-making" letter is central to an understanding of the late odes. Keats's "realization of the inevitability of suffering in a world of process" stands behind the themes of these odes (see p. 283).

"palsy," "paleness," and "leaden-eyed despairs" speak metaphorically of the debility and inevitable death of the poetic imagination unable to sustain its vision. No wonder, then, that the nightingale's fading song is described as a "high requiem," soon to be "buried deep"; for the fancy can "cheat" the poet into vision only momentarily and then dies. The ode speaks as much of the death of the poet's own imagination as of the funeral of the nightingale's song. Like Endymion, the speaker takes the "journey homeward to habitual self" as he repeats the word "forlorn," which acts as a funeral bell to his fancy:

> . . . the very word is like a bell
> To toll me back from thee to my sole self! . . .

Thirst, among other symptoms of the poet's mortality, accompanies that journey back to consciousness; for example, Glaucus, awakening from Circe's bower of imaginative delights, suffers "fever'd parchings" and "palsy," and feels "gaunt, wither'd sapless, feeble cramp'd and lame" (*Endymion*, III, 636–638). Likewise, Endymion complains that "A homeward fever parches up my tongue" (II, 319). He would find relief from his pain in sleep, where he might once again drink in Cynthia's inspiring beauty:

> O think how this dry palate would rejoice!
> If in soft slumber thou dost hear my voice. . . .
> (II, 328–329)

Accompanying the fever and painful parching of imaginative drought, the din and uproar of the real world dispel the silent or muted music of imaginative entrancement. We should be aware of Keats's recurrent emphasis on silence as a necessary circumstance of poetic creation. One reason why his poet-monks perform acts of imagination in the isolation of bowers and fanes stems from his notion that only in perfect silence may the poetic rite be performed. The poet cannot contend with distracting noises from the world, a world which he repeatedly attempts to overcome and bring order to. He feels the delight of poetic fulfilment in

> The silence when some rhymes are coming out;
> And when they're come, the very pleasant rout. . . .
> ("Sleep and Poetry," 321–322)

The noiseless process of shaping and ordering his materials ends in a pleasant thronging of verses. Like heaven's "Thousand" creative "powers . . . silent, as a consecrated urn" (*Endymion*, III, 30, 32), Keats's imagination pipes "ditties of no tone," unheard by the "sensual ear" but understood as perfectly realized "silent form" like a Grecian urn. In effect, the poet allows his weaving fancy to run noiselessly through all its labyrinths until "its own silent Working [comes] continually on the spirit with a fine suddenness." [5]

The noises of the real world intruding on the poet's "silent Working" of imagination pain him as he falls out of poetic reverie.[6] Endymion complains, "Upon my ear a noisy nothing rings" (II, 321). Cut off from Cynthia's dew-dropping melody, he painfully passes his time trying to rediscover the upward path of imagination. Unhappily, he cannot hear her harmonious strokes upon her golden lyre, but rather the dull strokes of the woodcutter:

> . . . For many days,
> Has he been wandering in certain ways:
> Through wilderness . . .
> Counting his woe-worn minutes, by the strokes
> Of the lone woodcutter. . . .
>
> (II, 47–51)

The regular noise of the axe suggests not only the monotony of the poet's existence in the real world but also the cutting pain of the despondency he feels. Either music or divinely creative silence can relieve him of his misery and anxiety. Until happier moments of imaginative transcendence befall him, he must bear reality's crude noises.

Where Endymion would forswear the world's noises, Lycius almost wilfully returns to "the hoarse alarm of Corinth's voice" (*Lamia*, II, 61). The piercing snarl of trumpets, ringing in Lycius' ears, dispels the fairy music of Lamia's palace, disrupts their love-dream, and sends Lycius back to vulgar Corinth:

5. *Letters*, I, 185.
6. Pettet, pp. 77–79, notes the contrast between silence and noise in Keats's poetry, a contrast which he considers merely a characteristic stylistic device in many poems. He fails to see the distinction Keats is drawing between the noisy world of reality and the silent world of imagination.

His spirit pass'd beyond its golden bourn
Into the noisy world. . . .

(32–33)

The same shrill trumpets of reality that awaken Lycius prove insufficiently powerful to dispel Porphyro's and Madeline's dream-union in "The Eve of St. Agnes." Porphyro shuts the door against

> The silver, snarling trumpets . . .
>
> .   .   .   .
>
> The boisterous, midnight, festive clarion,
> The kettle-drum, and far-heard clarionet [that]
> Affray his ears. . . .

(31, 258–260)

and thereby protects the consecrated silence of Madeline's monastic chamber of "triple-arch'd" Gothic casement from the uproar of the vulgar world of reality below.

Further, in shutting the door, he rejects the Bacchanalian revelries of the "barbarian hordes" for a far superior intoxication, sexual union with Madeline, which, if perfectly realized, may lift both him and his love to an immortality of passion.[7] Porphyro's avoidance of the vulgar world of pleasure below reminds us of Keats's own rejection of the falsely intoxicating, earthly wine of Bacchus in "Ode to a Nightingale"; he realizes that imaginative flight cannot be achieved by charioting with "Bacchus and his pards," but rather by soaring on the strong and silent wings of "Poesy."

In contrast with Porphyro's prudent insurance of utmost silence in Madeline's chamber, Lycius commits one of the gravest profanations in the sacred and silent palace of poetry. He opens its doors to the noisy herd, who, after drinking Bacchus' earthly wine, soon fill the halls with the direst uproar:

> . . . the happy vintage touch'd their brains,
> Louder they talk, and louder come the strains
> Of powerful instruments . . .
>
> .   .   .   .
>
> Soon was God Bacchus at meridian height.

(*Lamia*, II, 203–205, 213)

7. See Wasserman, *The Finer Tone*, pp. 84–137, for a full explication of this theme.

In effect, the noise of these worldlings, flushed with the wine of Bacchus, tumbles the palace of poetry. Of all the crude noises of the real world, Keats most frequently associates the clamor of the Bacchanalian rites with the painful waning and collapse of imagination.

We are now able to understand the metaphorical meaning of the ravenous Bacchanalian festival in the "Ode to Sorrow" in Book IV of *Endymion*. At the time when the Indian Maid sings her ode, Endymion has fallen into deep despondency, Cynthia having just deserted him. Alone and unable to revive his feeble imagination, he begs for the inspiring grace of love:

> 'Is no one near to help me? No fair dawn
> Of life from charitable voice? No sweet saying
> To set my dull and sadden'd spirit playing?
> No hand to toy with mine? No lips so sweet
> That I may worship them. . . .
>
> .   .   .   .
> . . . I am sad and lost.' . . .
>
> (44–48, 51)

He questions whether his visions with Cynthia have all been airy nothings, the cheatings of a deceptive fancy. Disillusioned, he finds in the Indian Maid a more earthly, substantial love,[8] and, what is more, finds appealing her remedy for dispelling the sorrows and pains of imagination's struggles. She sings in praise of the Bacchic rites, whose wine, uproar, and license promise to erase all mental anguish. Endymion almost forswears his monkish role of poet to join the noisy world of reality. Hearing the "merry din" of "Bacchus and his crew" with

> . . . earnest trumpet . . . and silver thrills
> From kissing cymbals . . .
>
> (196–198)

he asks the Indian Maid to destroy his imaginative soul and nurture only his earthly soul:

8. I am indebted to Allen for his observation that the "Ode to Sorrow" provides the clue to a main theme that Keats was attempting to carry out in Book IV of *Endymion*: that pleasure and pain, joy and sorrow must be accepted by Endymion as a fact of human and imaginative existence. In contrast with the passage in Book I on "fellowship with essence," which celebrates the idea that imaginative joy is a pure and etherealized happiness in heaven, the "Ode to Sorrow" in the last book of *Endymion* suggests that "joys as they are to be found in the earthly realm [are] inextricably mixed with the dross of sorrow" (p. 48).

Do gently murder half my soul, and I
Shall feel the other half so utterly! . . .

(309–310)

The Bacchanalian revels seem a distracting force not only on Endymion's life of imagination, but also on the Muses of poetry. In her ode,
the Indian Maid asks the Muses,

Why have you left your bowers desolate,
    Your lutes, and gentler fate? . . .

(220–221)

Like Endymion, they have found the wild revelry of Bacchus appealing,
for it provides a momentary stay of their arduous poetic task. By intro-
ducing the muses into the ode, Keats clearly suggests that the noisy,
vulgar rites of Bacchus are at odds with the silent and holy poetic rites
of the muses. The identification of the Bacchanalians as the element
destructive of the imagination is not arbitrary or private, but rather
makes brilliant and appropriate use of the materials of the myth. Traditionally, the Bacchic rites were initiated to allow everyone to put
aside hard work for unlicensed pleasure. Ovid, whom Keats read and
admired through Sandys, wrote:

[Bacchus'] Priest proclaims a solemn Feast;
That Dames and Maids from usuall labour rest; . . .
Their Webs, their un-spun Wooll, aside they lay. . . .[9]

The "Ode to Sorrow" presents Ovid's weaving damsels as the muses
who lay aside their poetic weaving and their lutes, leaving their "bowers
desolate." We must be aware that Keats continually uses his sources for
his own particular poetic ends. He interprets the task of Ovid's women
at their weaving, like the role of Homer's Circe singing at her loom, as
poetic creation.

An even more significant aspect of the Bacchus myth accounts for
Keats's choice of the wine-god as the figure of the anti-poetic force. Like
Milton, he identifies the dissolute Bacchanalians not only as the seducers
of poets, but also as their defilers. Keats read with care the invocation

9. Sandys, p. 65. Finney identifies Ovid as the source of Keats's damsels (I, 286);
however, his source hunting does not lead to any critical insight into the meaning
of Keats's passage.

to Urania in Book VII of *Paradise Lost*.[10] Milton asks his muse, who
visits his "slumbers nightly," to

> . . . drive far off the barbarous dissonance
> Of Bacchus and his revelers, the race
> Of that wild rout that tore the Thracian bard
> In Rhodope, where woods and rocks had ears
> To rapture, till the savage clamor drowned
> Both harp and voice; nor could the muse defend
> Her son. . . .
>
> (32–38)

These lines allude to the legend of Orpheus, the supreme lyric poet
whose music enchanted all nature, being torn to pieces by Thracian
Bacchanalians. In the light of this source, it seems apparent that Keats
associated the Bacchic rites with the cruel and indomitable forces of
reality, destructive of the poetic imagination. Appropriately, the god of
the Indian Maid's heaven winces at the earthly rout of Bacchus; even

> Great Brahma from his mystic heaven groans,
> And all his priesthood moans. . . .
>
> (*Endymion*, IV, 265–266)

Keats's lengthy description of the animals bearing Bacchus and his
train of revelers through the earth leads us to yet another recurrent
group of images associated with the non-poetic world of reality. If the
elephants, leopards, and crocodiles bearing Bacchus seem an ironic contrast to the winged horses drawing Apollo's chariot, we may say the same
for the altogether ponderous lions drawing Cybele's chariot in Book II
of *Endymion*. Coming at the time when Endymion has just lost sight of
"founts Protean," Cybele (or mother earth) represents mythically the
poet's "journey homeward to habitual self," a journey back to consciousness and pain. Keats is here describing the internal withering of imagination which Endymion feels:

> The solitary felt a hurried change
> Working within him into something dreary. . . .
>
> (633–634)

10. The care and sensitivity with which Keats read Milton can be seen in his
essay, "Notes on Milton's *Paradise Lost*," in *Works*, ed. Forman, III, 19–33.

Whereas Apollo's golden chariot and nimble steeds soar upward in poetic flight, Cybele's sombre chariot and sluggish lions seem the perfect analogue for the vexing, slow, and inevitable decline of imagination felt by the poet:

> . . . in the dusk below,
> Came mother Cybele! alone—alone—
> In sombre chariot; dark foldings thrown
> About her majesty, and front death-pale,
> With turrets crown'd. Four maned lions hale
> The sluggish wheels; solemn their toothed maws
> Their surly eyes brow-hidden, heavy paws
> Uplifted drowsily, and nervy tails
> Cowering their tawny brushes. Silent sails
> The shadowy queen athwart, and faints away
> In another gloomy arch. . . .
>
> (639–649)

The highly suggestive diction—"death-pale," "sluggish," "heavy," "drowsily," and "nervy"—describes Endymion's "hurried change" from the world of imaginative vision to the fretful world of reality. Endymion's experience, like the speaker's in "Ode to a Nightingale," is akin to dying. Cybele, known also in myth as the mother of sorrows,[11] ushers in the deathly world of fever, fret, and palsy as the poet's vision fades.

In yet another context, the despised noises of the fierce world of reality are described in the same animal imagery. Thrust back to consciousness after sexual union with Cynthia, Endymion moans like a pained, caged lion:

> . . . Love's madness he had known:
> Often with more than tortured lion's groan
> Moanings had burst from him; . . .
>
> (II, 860–862)

The ugly discord of Endymion's mortal voice contrasts directly with his "lispings empyrean" granted by Cynthia at moments of poetic fulfilment

11. Lemprière makes this identification and gives a full description of her chariot. In addition, he describes her festival as a din of "dreadful shrieks and howlings mixed with the confused noise of drums, tabrets, bucklers and spears . . . in commemoration of the sorrow of Cybele for the loss of her favorite Atys." Thus by alluding to yet another myth, which he perhaps read in Lemprière, Keats suggests the destructive force of the noisy, vulgar world on the imagination.

when "the sounds / Of [their] close voices marry at their birth" (II, 815–816). In his embrace of Cynthia, he assumes a "honied tongue," but with her departure normal "roughness of mortal speech" returns to him (818). Understandably then, his despondency over losing his muse and therefore his poetic voice leaves him "with . . . tortured lion's groan." He becomes a part of the crude animal world of reality; indeed he contributes to that world's ugly noises.

The pains attending the decline of imagination are figured in other animal imagery. Endymion's love-dream ends, not with the fading song of a nightingale, but with the painful croaking of the "ouzel" which sings "A heavy ditty" to "the sullen day" (I, 684). Another of Keats's favorite birds heralding poetic failure, the vulture, preys on forlorn poets in the world of reality. Thus, Circe is described as a "vulture witch" (III, 620). In Book II of *Endymion*, these birds of prey cannot intrude on the finely woven, sacred bower of poetry [12] to destroy the poet's imaginative dreaming. In sum, the poet's protective sanctuary excludes the rapacious world of reality which the vulture represents:

> Bushes and trees do lean all round athwart,
> And meet so nearly, that with wings outraught,
> And spreaded tail, a vulture could not glide
> Past them. . . .
>
> (I, 865–868)

Infrequently the poet is able to conquer the animal world of reality, not by withdrawing into his poetic bower, but by playing on his Delphic reed so beautifully as to lull them to sleep. In the sonnet, "As Hermes once took to his feathers light," Keats's "idle sprite" of imagination conquers the "dragon-world of all its hundred eyes" in the same manner that Hermes lulled Argus, the hundred-eyed monster who guarded Io. The "dragon-world" represents ugly reality, which is transcended by music and dream. As we have already noted, the successful poetic act culminates in ecstatic vision; in this sonnet Keats knows the joy of flight and sexual union with Francesca, but only after the "dragon-world" has been conquered, that is, only after poetry has tamed crude reality.

Yet inevitably the predatory animal world triumphs over the poet,

12. Appropriately situated near the "Matron-temple of Latona," who was mother of Apollo and Cynthia.

bringing him pains that he has only temporarily avoided. After reaching the heights of imaginative ecstasy with Cynthia, Endymion descends to the inevitable world of pain, sharp-toothed and clinging like the sloth:

> . . . the fair form had gone again.
> Pleasure is oft a visitant; but pain
> Clings cruelly to us, like the gnawing sloth
> On the deer's tender haunches. . . .
>
> . . . .
> How sickening, how dark the dreadful leisure
> Of weary days. . . .
>
> (I, 905–908, 910–911)

The collapse of imaginative vision leaves Endymion, like the plaintive speaker in "Ode to a Nightingale," forlorn. Abandoned in a world "Where but to think is to be full of sorrow," he experiences the most frightful waking nightmare offered by the dragon world of reality. In the epistle "To J. H. Reynolds, Esq.," Keats, after having explored the enchanted castle of imagination, returns to a consciousness which leaves him with thoughts that seem to border on total despair:

> Still do I that most fierce destruction see,
> The Shark at savage prey,—the hawk at pounce,
> The gentle Robin, like a pard or ounce,
> Ravening a worm—Away ye horrid moods,
> Moods of one's mind! You know I hate them well,
> You know I'd sooner be a clapping bell
> To some Kamschatkan missionary church,
> Than with these horrid moods be left in lurch.
>
> (102–109)

Not only is the poet vexed by the noises and sights of the real world intruding on and dispelling the silent working of his imagination; he is also stung by the briars of reality. In *Endymion*, the poet complains that his elfin fancy has deceitfully led him through painful briar thickets and into a swamp. He describes the journey of imagination as

> A mad-pursuing of the fog-born elf,
> Whose flitting lantern, through rude nettle-briar,

Cheats us into a swamp . . .
Into the bosom of a hated thing. . . .[13]

(II, 277–280)

Endymion and Glaucus prove to be the continual victims of the deceiving fancy, which teasingly leads them back to the painful, thorny brake
of reality. Endymion's uncertain wanderings, for example, leave him

Holding his forehead, to keep off the burr
Of smothering fancies, . . .

(138–139)

or striving

. . . by fancies vain and crude to clear
His briar'd path to some tranquility. . . .

(IV, 722–723)

His struggle along the briar path of the everyday world is in direct contrast to his effortless glide along the "diamond path" (II, 608, 652) of
imagination in happier moments of his journeys.

Glaucus shares with Endymion the vexations of the cheating, Ariel-
like fancy. Upon awakening from his bower he complains that

. . . barbed shafts
Of disappointment stuck in me so sore. . . .

(III, 480–481)

He feels terror as Circe cruelly promises him pleasure which her other
victims in their confining "thorny brake" (493) already know to be an
eternal "serpent-skin of woe" (240). More than a deceptive elf, Circe
seems a positively destructive force of fancy in committing Glaucus to
one thousand years of suffering a life-in-death existence in the scum and
briars of Ariel's swamp. He laments to Endymion that his

13. Once again we must look to Shakespeare for the source and for the special
significance Keats attached to the swamp, the nettle, and the briar, all of which
are images of reality. In reading *The Tempest*, Keats interpreted Ariel as the cheating
fancy leading mortals into briars and swamp, only to abandon them (see pp.
75–77). Ariel reports how he charmed Trinculo, Stefano, and Caliban:

. . . so I charm'd their ears
That calf-like they my lowing follow'd through
Tooth'd briars, sharp furzes, pricking goss and thorns
Which enter'd their frail shins. At last I left them
I' the filthy-mantled pool beyond your cell,
There dancing up to the chins, that the foul lake
O'erstunk their feet.   (IV. i. 178–184)

> . . . long captivity and moanings all
> Are but a slime, a thin-pervading scum. . . .
>
> (335–336)

Only the life of imagination can remove that foul film of reality, as Endymion remarks in the "pleasure thermometer" section of Book I. The poet, interknit with the light of imaginative truth,

> . . . wipe[s] away all slime
> Left by men-slugs and human serpentry. . . .
>
> (820–821)

The association of the briar with the non-imaginative world of pain recurs in Lamia. When Apollonius intrudes into the palace of poetry, bringing pain and death to the poet and his imagination, he comes crowned with "spear-grass and the spiteful thistle." Like Urizen, who subdues the perfectly integrated soul of man, the rationalist represents the cold and painful world of reality and must therefore wear its common, prickly flora that "wage / War on his temples" (II, 228–229). He would have no place in Keats's vision of a truly great world of inspired men, tall and proud like oak trees, rather than squat and scrubby like tangled briars. Once again Keats associates the ignoble briar with the non-poetic, unheroic, uninspired world of reality:

Man should not dispute or assert but whisper results to his neighbour, and thus by every germ of Spirit sucking the Sap from mould ethereal every human might become great, and Humanity instead of being a wide heath of Furse and Briars . . . would become a grand democracy of Forest Trees.[14]

Apollonius' "garland," therefore, seems an ironic contrast to the poet's distinctive laurel crown, a contrast that is highly appropriate when we consider that he rejects as worthless the visions and creations of imagination. Equally contrasting is Lycius' crown of thyrsus, "that his watching eyes may swim / Into forgetfulness" (II, 226–227). The thyrsus refers not so much to the poet's crown, as might be claimed, but to its direct opposite, the staff of ivy and grapes carried by Bacchus. Keats suggests that Lycius now be identified with the Bacchanalian revelers, whom he has joined against the pleading of Lamia. His crown associates him with

14. *Letters*, I, 232.

their visionless, noisy, chaotic world.[15] He suffers an Orpheus-like death as much from their destructiveness as Lamia's.

One of the images describing the death of Lycius, of his imagination and of the "wealthy lustre" of the palace of poetry leads us to a final consideration of Keats's language describing reality. The dying out of color and light both in Lamia's features and in her palace figures the blighting of the imagination. The same destructive power by which he "unweave[s] a rainbow" melts Lamia "into a shade" (II, 238). Lamia's light-giving powers of imagination also fade as a consequence; she is unable "to illume / The deep-recessed vision," which inspires Lycius' own life of imagination. We may say that this fading of light and color figures the inevitable decline of the poetic fancy, a decline which Shelley describes by the same imagery as Keats: "the mind in creation is as a fading coal." [16] Similarly, Endymion's dreaming is as a coal illumined to transitory brilliance and then faded to ash:

> . . . like a spark
> That needs must die . . .
> . . . my sweet dream
> Fell into nothing. . . .
>
> (I, 675–678)

We may explain the imagery of death and light in "Ode to a Nightingale" as also expressive of the waning of imaginative vision. The "fast fading violets" seem closely related, metaphorically, to the spark of imagination "that needs must die"; and the statement, "But here there is no light," speaks of "the dull brain" unable to envision the Queen-Moon and all her radiant realm. Keats's weak vision in the ode is already on the wane even as the poem begins. He can only guess in "embalmed darkness" at the vision that is soon to be buried in total eclipse.

The fading coal of imagination eventually turns to ashes, darkening the surroundings it once illuminated. Endymion knows the frightful

15. Further, the thyrsis also symbolizes Lycius' intoxication, or mental stupefaction, which serves to dramatize the baleful effect of the war between reason and imagination, or science and poetry. His intoxication has two other purposes: First, it saves him from the painful shock of learning the real nature of Lamia, as Apollonius sees her and reveals her. Second, it protects him from the pain of the "heavy body wound" left by Lamia and the warring Apollonius.

16. "A Defence of Poetry," Works, VII, 135.

gloom and blackness once the adamantine still point of light fades. Uncertainly he passes

> . . . through deepest gloom, and griesly gapes,
> Blackening on every side, . . .
>
> . . . .
>
> Vex'd like a morning eagle, lost and weary,
> And purblind amid foggy, midnight wolds. . . .
>
> (II, 629–630, 635–636)

Placing the poet in mist and fog is yet another figurative way by which Keats describes the loss of poetic vision. Like the dusk enveloping Cybele's "sombre chariot," shadowy landscape suggests the poet's "hurried change" of imagination. Amid "foggy, midnight wolds" Endymion finds himself cheated by his "mad pursuing of the fog-born elf." Apparently the elf of fancy leads men not only into swamps and briars but also into the most obscuring mists. Yet at other times Keats regards himself as his own deceiving, "poor witless elf"; blind in mist on top of Ben Nevis, he complains

> . . . that all my eye doth meet
> Is mist and crag, not only on this height,
> But in the world of thought and mental might!
>
> ("Read me a lesson, Muse")

Once again fog shrouds the pure and radiant light of poetic truth.

Just as the light of imagination is obscured, the clear streams of imagination grow cloudy and contaminated as the gush of poetic feeling wanes and dies. The compressed metaphor of the darkening stream suggests the contamination and fading of the poet's creative power as he returns to the real world. Apollo's chariot, the dancing and singing muses, the bright wings and steeds having fallen from sight:

> The visions all are fled—the car is fled
> Into the light of heaven, and in their stead
> A sense of real things comes doubly strong,
> And, like a muddy stream, would bear along
> My soul to nothingness. . . .
>
> ("Sleep and Poetry," 155–159)

By an even denser cluster of images, he describes the blighting of the domain of poetry. The defilement of the bower, the stream, the flower, and their pure light and color analogizes the noxious and painful decline of imagination within the poet. Endymion describes the scenery to which he has just unwillingly returned after an imaginative flight:

> . . . heaths and sunny glades
> Were full of pestilent light; our taintless rills
> Seem'd sooty, and o'er-spread with upturn'd gills
> Of dying fish; the vermeil rose had blown
> In frightful scarlet, and its thorns out-grown
> Like spiked aloe. . . .
>
> (I, 693–698)

Just as the once beautiful rose turns a deathly scarlet, then bare and thorny, the imaginative process has its own short spring, summer, and fall. The rose, a common symbol for love, seems appropriately sick here, for it suggests the dying out of Endymion's imagination, which (as we have noted repeatedly) thrives in passion. Further, the thorns growing from the withering rose suggest the painful and ugly world of reality, of which Endymion is all too conscious in these frightful moments of awakening. Once more the elfin imagination has cheated the poet and brought him back to the briars and furzes of reality. His pains come doubly strong upon seeing the pestilent-ridden, corrupted bower and stream of poetry.

In one of his most remarkable uses of practically all these recurrent images and figures which we have been tracing—i.e., pain, thirst, palsy, noise, Bacchanalian revelry, darkness, animals, the briar, and fog—Keats estimates the worth of contemporary poets, those who have never made an inspired flight of imagination but remain perpetually grounded in the noisy world of reality. I speak of the totally misread introduction to Book III of *Endymion*, an introduction that declaims on poets and poetry, not on the political situation in England and Europe, as critics have believed. Keeping in mind the imagery and metaphors for reality, the careful reader will recognize Keats's drift:

> There are who lord it o'er their fellow-men
> With most prevailing tinsel: who unpen
> Their baaing vanities, to browse away

The comfortable green and juicy hay
From human pastures; or, O torturing fact!
Who, through an idiot blink, will see unpack'd
Fire-brand foxes to sear up and singe
Our gold and ripe-ear'd hopes. With not one tinge
Of sanctuary splendor, not a sight
Able to face an owl's, they are still dight
By the blear-eyed nations in empurpled vests,
And crowns, and turbans. With unladen breasts,
Save of blown self-applause, they proudly mount
To their spirit's perch, their being's high account,
Their tip-top nothings, their dull skies, their thrones—
Amid the fierce intoxicating tones
Of trumpets, shoutings, and belabour'd drums,
And sudden cannon. Ah! how all this hums,
In wakeful ears, like uproar past and gone—

. . . .
Are then regalities all gilded masks?

(1–19, 21)

We find in this passage the kind of highly indirect, satiric thrusting which Keats was to perfect much later in *The Cap and Bells*.[17] Who might these "regalities" "who lord it o'er their fellow-men" be? None but those poets who have achieved either the laureateship or a degree of fame from the "blear-eyed," myopic nations. They dress with crowns and turbans those whom they consider their most esteemed poets; yet these poets seem failures in Keats's estimation, for they live not in the world of imagination but in the world of reality.

An analysis of the imagery in this passage bears out this reading. Keats compares some poets to sheep, which "unpen / Their baaing vanities" on the rest of humanity. Punning on the word "unpen," he suggests that these poets write (i.e., "pen") freely without restraint; they create only animal noises. These straying maverick-poets neglect their common bond with humanity by merely browsing in the fields of nature. Other equally

17. The compounding ironies of *The Eve of St. Agnes* involve a satire on religion and romance. Satire, then, is not foreign to Keats's poetry, although its subtleties have only recently been recognized. See Jack Stillinger, "The Hoodwinking of Madeline: Skepticism in *The Eve of St. Agnes*," *Keats: A Collection of Critical Essays*, ed. Walter J. Bate (Englewood Cliffs, 1964), pp. 71–90.

worthless poets are compared to "fire-brand foxes" burning up the landscape of poetry and thereby destroying Keats's fond hopes of a golden
age of a mature, national poetry which the ancient Greeks once achieved.
Keats may be indicting the excesses of Wordsworth in this particular
context, for not only did he consider that poet of nature as undisciplined
in his works, but also as an arrogant, self-appointed emperor over the
entire English domain of poetry. He speaks of Wordsworth's and of
Hunt's inflated egos and their "self-applause" in a highly significant
letter to Reynolds:

but for the sake of a few fine imaginative or domestic passages, are we to
be bullied into a certain Philosophy engendered in the whims of an
Egotist—Every man has his speculations, but every man does not brood
and peacock over them till he makes a false coinage and deceives himself. . . . We hate poetry that has a palpable design upon us. . . . Each
of the moderns [i.e., poets] like an Elector of Hanover governs his petty
state . . . the antients were Emperors of vast Provinces.[18]

Wordsworth and Hunt, as baaing lambs and yelping foxes, do more
than create animal noises in their poetry. They and their followers produce that same kind of chaotic din which grates on the ears of Endymion
and Lycius. Their "fierce . . . tones / Of trumpets, shoutings, and be-
labor'd drums," and what is more, their "sudden cannon" firings suggest
a poetry of "uproar" crashing on Keats's sensitive and altogether "wakeful ears." Their noise adds to the general din of the non-imaginative
world of reality that Endymion hears in failing poetic vision.

We may further identify these Wordsworthians as members of
Bacchus' noisy party, possessed not by the fine poetic frenzy, but rather
by a vulgar, wholly earthly drunkenness that produces "fierce intoxicating tones." Rooted to the earth, their attempts at proud poetic flight
are actually short-winged mountings to a bird's perch. From their lowly
height, they weave a cheap and deceiving "tinsel," [19] which only artifi-
cially reflects rather than generates the light of poetic beauty. In using
the word "tinsel" to describe their poetry, Keats suggests not only the
deceptive brilliance of their poetic fabric, but also the inherent worth-
lessness of its falsely sparkling appearance, got at small expense. By com-

18. *Letters*, I, 223–224.
19. Keats perhaps means tinsel cloth, a fabric of interwoven, metallic threads,
and, at the same time, the separate strands used in decoration.

parison we recall the richness of the weaving in Lamia's and Moneta's palaces; in Wordsworth's and Hunt's poetry, however, "not one tinge / Of sanctuary splendor" is generated from their gaudy weave. Thus they have failed as poets on two accounts: first, by using false materials, and, second, by constructing a valueless fane of poetry. Immersed in the uproar that they themselves have created, these would-be poets cannot hide themselves, as Keats did, "in the very fane, the light of Poesy." Having failed to radiate the light of poetic truth, they must live in a dim and drab world. The poets themselves are responsible for "their dull skies" and, as a consequence, the aggravations of "blear-eyed nations." And ironically, the nations, lacking the splendor and brilliance of true poetry, honor these poets with royal crowns and dress.

Chapter eight

"La Belle Dame sans Merci" ～ "Ode to Psyche"

"La Belle Dame sans Merci"

"La Belle Dame sans Merci" describes perfectly the poet's semicircular arc of imaginative ascent, fulfilment, and decline into the world of reality. Within the poem we find almost all of Keats's recurrent metaphors describing the poetic process, metaphors used so economically, because of the strict limitations of the ballad form, and so subtly that the meaning of the poem is not readily apparent. More than in any other single poem, one needs the whole corpus of Keats's figures behind him to understand "La Belle Dame sans Merci" as a poem about poetry and imagination; for without that background (which has been our concern in previous chapters), the reader would most likely regard the poem as a mere excursion into balladry on Keats's part, rather than as a symbolic narrative about poetic experience. One of the most private of all of his poems, "La Belle Dame sans Merci" could only have been written at a point in his poetic career when all of the figures he had been habitually using recur as "almost a Remembrance," albeit woven into new combinations.

The poet begins and ends with a stark picture of a dying season. The sedge, a common grass of marshes and swamps, has withered; no birds sing. We are thrust at once into the mutable world which the poet must recurrently endure after falling out of his imaginative trance. The wretched knight is presently experiencing the same pain felt by Endymion after his "mad pursuing of the fog-born elf." Both are lured into the desolate, thorny mire of reality, a purgatory whose landscape mirrors the desolation within Keats's disillusioned poets.[1] Like the sedge, the knight is withered; like the speaker in "Ode to a Nightingale," forlorn; and like Lycius, anguished and deathly pale. If these other victimized mortals represent the poet, agonized by the world of reality, we may identify the knight-at-arms as a poet also.

And now the question: why a knight-at-arms?[2] We should remember that all of Keats's heroes in search of poetic insight are characterized as royal, Apollonian in feature and manner, visionary wanderers, and lovers. Endymion, for example, is not only a shepherd and pastoral poet, but also a "prince" (II, 227). Lycius, too, springs from royal lineage. Both he and Endymion are charioteers and, therefore, identified as Apollo figures. As lovers, both dedicate themselves to poetry, represented as a woman. The knight-at-arms is like Endymion and Lycius. We may regard him as a latter-day Calidore in Keats's poetry, a youthful wayfarer on a quest; an altruist who hopes to serve humanity but, unhappily, seems to have forsworn his duty as he falls under the strange power of the beautiful lady without pity; a courtier who in the courtly fashion of his age dedicates his love to this lady without the slightest hope that she will requite it. We should also bear in mind that, as a rule, the medieval knight in France played the important role of the troubadour.[3] As artist he achieved excellence in his poetry through the inspiration of love. Thus his lady's beauty finds its mirror in the troubadour's poem.[4]

Further, we must pay special attention to the pastoral setting of the poem, for it contributes significantly to our identification of the knight

1. Ll. 7–8 appear in ironic contrast to the desolation of the knight. The fact that "the squirrel's granary is full, / And the harvest's done" suggests that for everything else (animal and man) fruition has come. The rewards for one's efforts are gathered in by all except the knight.

2. In using the original version of the poem, I rely on Bate for the basis of my preference. I agree with his good judgment that the revision of "knight-at-arms" to "wretched wight" is jarring and needless. Keats made this change when he was "far too ill to have any confidence in his own judgment" (*John Keats*, p. 479).

3. Of the medieval troubadour Maurice Valency, *In Praise of Love* (New York, 1958), pp. 41–42, 48, states that knights were regarded as a "petty nobility" which "constituted the bulk of the European upper class.... The greater part of the noble troubadours and trouveres were drawn from this lesser nobility." These knightly poets valued creative talent and the sensibilities of the "gentle heart" over riches and formed a poetry based on these values. The notion seems to conform with Keats's attitude of the superior status of the poet, as seen in Endymion and Lycius.

4. *Ibid.*, p. 109.

as a poet and to our reading of the poem as a symbolic statement of the knight's initiation into poetic experience. The youthful, questing poet-knight meets his beautiful lady in the isolation of the meads. If we may assume that Keats's choice of character has a wider significance than has been recognized, we may say the same for his choice of setting. Traditionally, the first poetry written by novice troubadours are pastorals set in meadows and fields. These poets often sing plaintively of their ill-fortuned love of an indifferent mistress. We may with some justification, therefore, identify the knight as a pastoral poet, an Endymion figure, who ascends to the heights of imaginative vision under the inspiration of La Belle Dame sans Merci. Keats's subtle characterization of the knight as the poet demonstrates once more the ingenuity with which his poetry " 'load[s] every rift' of [its] subject with ore." Critics have failed to see the weighty implications in Keats's choice of a knight-at-arms as a character. Earl R. Wasserman, for example, provides a much too simple explanation of Keats's choice of a knight as his hero. He claims correctly that "all mortals who engaged in 'Imagination's struggles' are knights-at-arms," but fails to see the several other reasons, noted herein, for the appropriateness of a knight as the character of the poet.

In stanza four, the knight-at-arms begins his narrative account of how he has arrived at the mental and physical state described in the first three stanzas. Quite by chance he has met a lady whose beauty and singing enthral him almost immediately. Like Lamia, she is born "a faery's child" and sings "A faery's song." We associate her with the light and winged elfin, poetic imagination. In calling attention to her "wild eyes" and long hair, Keats refers to two particular physical characteristics of his other women-muses which repeatedly fascinate and charm the admiring poet. For example, the beauty of Cynthia's abundant "golden tresses" inspires him to poetic frenzy and leads him to enthralment:

> . . . she had,
> Indeed, locks bright enough to make me mad;
> And they were simply gordian'd up and braided. . . .
>   (I, 612–614)

A part of the loveliness of Keats's poetic vision in "Sleep and Poetry" involves the muses, "Parting luxuriant curls" (334), "Dancing their sleek hair into tangled curls" (150), and "sing[ing] out and sooth[ing] their wavy hair" (180). Indeed, sleep itself is described as the "Silent entangler of a beauty's tresses" (15). These examples demonstrate that a woman's tresses are recurrently associated with imaginative inspiration and imaginative vision. La Belle Dame's long hair very subtly identifies her as a companion to Cynthia and the muses.

But this subtle linkage of image (wavy hair) and idea (poetic experience) does not end here. The connection is rooted in Keats's Apollo-worship. On many occasions he tends to identify himself as that ideal poet he was striving to become,[5] as for example, in the writing of the two *Hyperion* fragments and in "Sleep and Poetry," where he might die and follow the "great Apollo / Like a fresh sacrifice" (59–60). One of the most prominent features of the god's beauty, as Lemprière points out, lies in his "long hair," a detail which seems to have continually fascinated Keats. *Hyperion*, for example, mentions Apollo's "golden tresses famed / Kept undulation round his eager neck" (III, 131–132). By a process of association in Keats's mind, this particular feature of the god finds its way into other poems describing poetry and imagination. Apollo's wavy hair and chariot figure prominently in the short poem, "On Leaving Some Friends at an Early Hour," which recounts Keats's initial imaginative visions dancing before his eyes as he begins to write. The images of "wavy hair" and "pearly car," which allude to Apollo and his chariot, are clearly linked with inspiration. Passing across Keats's inward eye, they excite him to "write down a line of glorious tone." Apollo's curly hair, associated with the controlling idea of poetry and imagination, and carrying secondary connotations of beauty, fertility, youth, and vigor,[6] is transferred to La Belle Dame. She becomes in this poem the female presider of poetry.

5. On at least one occasion, Baily attributed to Keats the appearance and form of Apollo: "His hair was beautiful . . . the silken curls felt like the rich plumage of a bird. . . . Indeed the form of his head was like that of a fine Greek statue:—and he realized to my mind the youthful Apollo, more than any head of a living man I have known" (Colvin, p. 143).

6. Appropriately, the anti-imaginative villain, Apollonius, is "bald" (I, 364; II, 245), as well as "lashless," "wrinkled," "grey-bearded," and "cold." All these characteristics suggest the essential sterility of reason destructive of the Apollonian poet, Lycius. That baldness suggests the passionless, the sterile, and the anti-poetic is evident in "Song" ("Hush, hush! tread softly . . .") of two fleeing lovers. They are types modeled on Endymion and Cynthia, Lycius and Lamia, successfully eluding their enemy, "the jealous old bald-pate," who would, like Apollonius, destroy the noiseless, fairy-like love-flight. The flight represents the swift, silent, and impassioned release of the fertile imagination as it deceives the intellect, figured as "old bald-pate."

The beautiful lady's "wild" eyes also prove to be a significant detail. They suggest not only the Maenad-like frenzy of the Apollonian priestesses, but also the untamed energy of imagination which the knight is attempting to subdue. Her wildness seems closely associated with the frantic and violent nature of Lamia in the process of metamorphosing from serpent to woman:

> . . . her elfin blood in madness ran,
>
> . . . .
> Her eyes in torture fix'd, and anguish drear,
> Hot, glaz'd, and wide, with lid-lashes all sear,
> Flash'd phosphor and sharp sparks, without one cooling tear.
>
> (I, 147, 150–152)

Such virulence and yet beauty in the same woman suggest the ambiguous nature of the imagination as it inspires and at the same time destroys the poet. Like Lycius, the knight attempts to tame this wildness in his beautiful lady, with the direst results.

If stanza four describes the initial confrontation of knight and lady and suggests her bewitching physical appearance, stanza five pictures the knight being progressively drawn to her by her beauty and singing. Significantly, the lady begins to sing her "faery's song" only after the knight places her on his "pacing steed." With the perfect fixity of the poet in trance, his eyes are trained on the regularly moving, singing lady "all day long." This first of two deeds which the knight performs for the lady, placing her on his steed, appears to lead directly to his trance and to her singing. One notes the use of the conjunction "for," suggesting this cause and effect relationship. Stanza four, in effect, speaks metaphorically of the poet's curbing his wild imagination by meter. Keats here revives one of his recurrent metaphors for poetry, the steed, whose regular pace in other poems served as a figure for metrical regularity.[7] Note that the lady is "set," not "put" or "placed," on the steed. Keats's diction is extremely precise here, for the word used denotes that which is regulated or put in order. Having been "set" or regularized temporally by the poet, the imagination, in consequence,

7. See Chapter three above, pp. 85–86.

sings.⁸ And while she sings, the poet becomes charmed by what he has put in order and set into motion.

The poet-knight takes an active part in the process that is enthralling him. He weaves a garland in honor of her, just as Endymion weaves his flowers "dyingly" to Cynthia. We may interpret the garland as either the woven poem or the poetic coronal. In either reading, his act seems to parallel Endymion's worshipful indulgence to his imagination. The poet states to Cynthia:

> No one but thee hath heard me blithely sing
> And mesh my dewy flowers all the night.
> No melody was like a passing spright
> If it went not to solemnize thy reign. . . .
>
> (III, 156–159)

With equal devotion, the transfixed knight-at-arms offers to his lady "bracelets" and "fragrant zone," as well as his woven garland. One may question the appropriateness of the first two of these gifts to the overall theme of the poem. They subtly suggest that the knight would bind and hold forever his evanescent imagination; for, like Lycius and Endymion, he hopes for a permanent intensity of poetic passion in the arms of La Belle Dame. Sadly, the knight's attempt fails, as the first three stanzas indicate. His suffering and haggardness may be attributed to the loss of his passion as his beautiful lady fades and disappears.

La Belle Dame takes his gifts and returns the knight's fixed glance "as she did love," while at the same time making "sweet moan." Her plaintive yet paradoxically beautiful utterances suggest that in the very temple of the poet-knight's imaginative delights, melancholy has her sovereign

8. Wasserman's comment on the knight's act—"the lady is set up as an ideal"— fails to specify what ideal is involved here. "Essence" seems much too nebulous, and his steadfast application of the "pleasure thermometer" theme appears an inadequate, though not irrelevant, approach to the poem. In using the "pleasure thermometer" principle in "La Belle Dame sans Merci," Keats is talking about the various degrees of poetic intensity within the poet. But in this and other stanzas, he is concerned essentially with the poetic process. As I have suggested earlier, the meaning of the poem seems dependent on a full understanding of Keats's metaphors for poetry. Wasserman's explication of the poem appears strongest when he refers to sections in *Endymion* that describe the poet's return to reality. But he fails to perceive and use Keats's past metaphors for poetry and imagination to explicate this particular poem (*The Finer Tone*, p. 79).

shrine; for the beautiful lady of imagination provides not only the transcendent pleasures of poetic experience but also its inevitable pains, both suggested in the word "moan." Before she vanishes, the knight knows an ever-ascending series of delights in love, that is, imaginative feeling. Its inevitable decline, thrusting the knight back into the world of reality, seems anticipated in La Belle Dame's making "sweet moan." We should recall a like utterance from Lamia, who fills her palace of poetry with moans "as fearful the whole charm might fade" (II, 124). And yet the grammatical structure of stanza five suggests that the beautiful lady, like Circe, is wilfully deceiving the knight. The line, "She look'd at me as she did love" expresses the conditional and should read, "She look'd at me as *if* she did love"; [9] she seems to be practicing a feminine wile that leads to his enthralment.

The exchange of gifts in stanzas five and seven further suggests the perfect interaction of poet and imagination. The beautiful lady gives her knight the manna-dew of inspiration, thereby preparing him for the greater sensory pleasures soon to come in her "elfin grot." In addition to the honey of imagination, the lady finds him "roots of relish sweet." On the literal level of meaning, this act seems just another of the delights provided by the beautiful lady. But on a metaphorical level of meaning, her gift, like her bestowal of manna-dew of inspiration, seems to plant within the poet roots of music. Keats's use of the words "roots" and "relish" [10] refers not only to gustatory pleasure in some fairy-like, unnamed tuber, but also to the fundamental chords (i.e., "roots") being struck within the fertile depths of the poet-knight's own soul of imagination.[11] For in making "sweet moan," in speaking "language strange," and in singing "a faery's song," La Belle Dame is nurturing the musical and verbal roots of the imagination, which in the organicism of creation will grow and develop into poetry. Thus, Keats seems to be saying, "she provided me with the basic and most pleasurable roots of

9. Perkins, p. 261.

10. We should also note that the word "relish," in an archaic sense, denotes "a grace or embellishment in old music," according to Webster.

11. Perkins' reading of stanza seven seems inadequate for its assumption that La Belle Dame provides literal nourishment to the knight. He remarks, "One need only point out that roots, honey, and manna might be appropriate for a 'faery's child,' but they would not provide much nourishment to a knight at arms" (p. 262). Metaphorically, the knight acquires poetic inspiration by these agents. Perkins' remark is representative of the critical tack taken by many scholars.

melody and words," roots granted in a similar manner by Cynthia, who strings and plucks the "lyre of [Endymion's] soul" until it is "Aeolian tun'd" (II, 866). The knight's deeply seated, divinely activated musical power seems to be what Keats calls the "relish," or the extreme pleasure of quickening imaginative feeling in a life of sensations.

Intoxicated by manna-dew, honey, and her fairy song, the knight hears the first protestations of La Belle Dame's love for him "in language strange." Her language is "strange" because any supreme visitation of the poetic imagination, in Keats's estimation, proves extraordinary, un-familiar, and inexplicable. The entranced poet cannot account for the mysterious music playing on his inner ear, nor for the wild visions dancing before his eyes. Imaginative frenzy opens up an unfathomable world of new sensory experience in the poet. We recall, in this regard, Endymion's perception of "strange minstrelsy" (I, 457) while he is locked in "magic sleep" (I, 453), of Cynthia's "strange voice" singing to him in a sexual-imaginative embrace (II, 849), of the unannounced and inexplicable "strange influence" of bowers, nymphs, and intoxicating bays, all of which induce the frenzied creation of verse within the poet. To Keats, the gratuitous visitation of intense poetic feeling seems so strange and mysterious

> That we must ever wonder how, and whence
> It came. . . .
>
> ("Sleep and Poetry," 70–71)

Raised to the heights of passionate and therefore imaginative intensity by the beautiful lady's confession of love ("I love thee true"), the knight gains entrance to her "elfin grot," which we have already identified as a recurrent metaphor for the sanctuary of poetry and imagination, a place alive with the spontaneous music of animistic nature, as we have seen elsewhere. In the haunts of her labyrinthine "gnomed mine," he finds complete imaginative fulfilment in sexual union with her. And yet in the very act of lovemaking, she sighs "full sore," knowing well that all fertile, impassioned acts of imagination must perforce come to an end. Their perfect seizure subsequently leads to visionary dreaming as poet and imagination slumber, much like the lovers entwined in each other's arms in "Ode to Psyche."

If stanza seven sets the knight's dream in the "elfin grot," stanza eight

abruptly places him "on the cold hill side." We must consider this
swift transition as characteristic of the ballad form; we must also presume that some time has lapsed between the initial stages of the knight's
warm and impassioned love-dream in the grot and its final stages on the
cold hill side, where he had a vision of his complete enthralment. We
are told only of the knight's "latest dream," that is, his most recent
vision, which presumably follows all the others in the elfin grot. That
final, waking dream of troubled visions on the cold hill side announces
the death of imagination and the ensuing pains of the poet's return to
the numbing world of reality.

He hears "pale kings and princes," the former victims of the beautiful
lady's charms, crying that the knight, like themselves, has been enthralled by a beautiful but deceiving fancy. Whereas she once nourished
the poet with manna-dew of inspiration and fulfilled his hunger for
poetic vision by offering him a long love-dream, she pitilessly withdraws
her favors, starving, enfeebling, and destroying all those who dedicate
themselves to the strenuous pursuit of poetry and imagination.

We may identify these starving, enslaved kings and princes as poets
who, like the knight-at-arms, have journeyed the path of poetry and have
destroyed themselves in searching for its visions. In "Sleep and Poetry"
Keats remarks:

> And they shall be accounted poet kings
> Who simply tell the most heart-easing things. . . .
>
> (267–268)

In this poem, however, his poet-kings painfully tell the most heart-
breaking things. In identifying kings and princes as the most fanciful of
mortals, Keats is not being arbitrary or even private in his association,
but rather is relying on classical myth for the source of his analogy. From
Ovid he learned that Morpheus' son, Phantasus, provides the power of
fancy solely to kings and princes:

> . . . *Phantasus*
> Of different facultie, indues a tree,
> Earth, water, stone the severall shapes of things
> That life enjoy not. these appeare to Kings

And Princes in deepe night: The rest among
The vulgar stray.[12]

The knight as well as the kings and princes has been unable to realize
the risks and dangers involved in attempting to capture and bind the
wily imagination, which thrives and breeds only for the moment and then,
with elfin fickleness, vanishes. The poet's quest involves the greatest
hazards even to poet-kings; for as Keats warns in *Endymion,*

There never liv'd a mortal man, who bent
His appetite beyond his natural sphere,
But starv'd and died. . . .[13]

(IV, 646–648)

Awakening from his "latest dream," the knight appears to possess all
the symptoms of pain found in other poet-heroes who have fallen out
of poetic frenzy. The inevitable waning of imaginative ecstasy leaves him
sapped of strength and vitality. We may regard the knight's "anguish
moist and fever dew" as the painful, consumptive effects of a short, but
intense, life of imaginative sensation. Indeed, does not the knight's experience describe the inevitable fever that Keats himself suffers after a
day of writing poetry? He remarks that the "artificial excitement" induced by his imagination "goes off more severely from the fever I am
left in." We have already commented on his own awareness of the
pernicious effect of poetry on his mind and body; and yet that enthralling
love affair with poetry seems never to have estranged itself. For Keats
knew that with the passage of time his painful fever would vanish, and
hopefully, would be followed by another visitation of the poetic imagination. Although the knight-at-arms suffers, he "sojourns" on the cold hill
side, "alone and palely loitering," without muse or music and significantly
too, without his steed. Horseless at this point in his career, the knight
remains immobile, directionless, and wholly out of the world symbolized
in his most cherished personal possession, the elemental gift of rhythm
and music. His loitering denotes aimless and idle stops and pauses that

12. Sandys, p. 232. Colvin's comment, "that Keats, more than from any other
source, made himself familiar with the details of classic fable" (p. 171), seems
helpful in further establishing the source of Keats's analogue of the poet as king.
13. I am indebted to Perkins for noting this important parallel (see p. 264).

stand in direct contrast to the regularity of movement and the intensity
of purpose of La Belle Dame as she sits and sings on his pacing steed.
His sojourning and loitering are with hopes that he may again fall upon
his beautiful lady of poetry and have another exalted, though temporary,
love-dream. What is more likely, he will die in enthralment, as rapidly
as the color of the fading rose. For in describing the end of a season, the
withering of organic life, and the end of a dream, Keats suggests that
the imagination, too, has its inevitable and natural decline, forcing the
poet back to the fever, the palsy, and the fret of the real world. That
inevitable process returns him not to the warm and blossoming meads of
springtide, but to the flowerless, songless, cold, and profitless world of
late autumn.

"Ode to Psyche"

The "Ode to Psyche" [14] may be considered Keats's prayer in worship
of the imagination. Psyche, the winged soul of imagination, serves as the
central symbol around which cluster thirteen distinct metaphors for
poetry and the imaginative process. Love, dream, flight, the fountain
stream, light, architecture, the bower, music, the labyrinth, wind, flowers,
weaving, and pain form a network of linkages to describe that process and
product of imagination. They recur in this poem almost spontaneously,
like a melody recalled from the past. Indeed, they seem like familiar
chimes pealing out a theme played over and over throughout the poetry;
and Psyche seems the keynote from which all the chimes logically follow.
As Keats himself described the associative, poetic process, "by merely
pulling an apron string we set a pretty peal of Chimes at work." [15]

The poem begins with an invocation to Psyche to hear his "tuneless
numbers, wrung," that is, shaped and compressed into form by his

14. Some recent critics of this poem generally understand its theme to be involved with a celebration of the human mind, or psyche. However, the direction
the poem takes and the figurative language used have been given to wide, varied,
and—from my understanding of the ode—inadequate interpretation. The most
useful commentaries are: Leonidas M. Jones, "The 'Ode to Psyche': an Allegorical
Introduction to Keats's Great Odes," *Keats-Shelley Memorial Bulletin*, IX (1958),
22–26; Harold Bloom, *The Visionary Company* (Garden City, 1961), pp. 389–397;
Max F. Schulz, "Keats's Timeless Order of Things," *Criticism*, II (1960), 55–65.

15. *Letters*, I, 280.

straining imagination. Keats's imaginative act is a pleasant labor (sweet enforcement") and a "dear" remembrance of a theme that he returned to repeatedly and almost compulsively in his poetry. That theme is, of course, the poetic imagination, which at this late point in his poetic career, he viewed as habitual and therefore treated as almost a recollection, though not in tranquility. In describing his "tuneless numbers" as a "remembrance dear," he suggests that metaphors born and used in the past habitually recur, yet linked in new combinations when they reappear. The fusion of image and idea, while the poet is in the act of creation, comes "continually on the spirit with a fine suddenness"; for as Keats said elsewhere, poetry "should ... appear almost a Remembrance."

The short invocation ends as the poet asks pardon that he should whisper the "secrets" of imagination in Psyche's labyrinthine ear, for he well realizes that the secrets are so sacred that they should not be voiced even to the one who has just communicated them:

> And pardon that thy secrets should be sung
> Even into thine own soft-conched ear. . . .

Moreover, he implies that the omniscient poetic imagination knows no mysteries.

Lines five to twenty-three recall the vision of the poet. He cannot be certain whether what he saw was a dream or a waking vision, just as the speaker in "Ode to a Nightingale" cannot estimate whether his was a true vision or a deception of the cheating fancy:

> Surely I dreamt to-day, or did I see
> The winged Psyche with awaken'd eyes? . . .

Once again Keats is not willing to say whether he was dreaming or awake; however, he feels that he has seen the winged imagination in reverie, that indefinable state between sleep and consciousness, when the mind is most active. He comes upon his vision of Psyche and Cupid with a fine suddenness after having "wander'd in a forest thoughtlessly." We should interpret the "forest" here as the tangled confusion of the poet's own mind before his dream-reverie provides him with unexpected vision, a mind wandering without conception (i.e., "thoughtless") like an elfin forester weaving his way through dense woods. His reverie at this point seems not unlike the labyrinthine confusion dreaded in the sonnet "On Sitting Down to Read King Lear Once Again":

> When through the old oak Forest I am gone,
>   Let me not wander in a barren dream,
> But, when I am consumed in the fire
> Give me new Phoenix wings to fly at my desire. . . .

The sight of Cupid and Psyche lying in perfect withdrawal in their bower of bliss kindles, as it were, Keats's dormant, aimless imagination, consuming him "in the fire" of fanciful speculation.

> And, on the sudden, fainting with surprise,
> Saw two fair creatures, couched side by side
>   In deepest grass, beneath the whisp'ring roof
>   Of leaves and trembled blossoms, where there ran
>   A brooklet, scarce espied. . . .

In this fountained sanctuary, Cupid and Psyche have known perfect moments of sexual fulfilment. They seem suspended between sleep and waking in an immortality of passion; each awakening promises new love that is perpetually "aurorean" or light-giving:

> Their arms embraced, and their pinions too;
> Their lips touch'd not, but had not bid adieu,
>   As if disjoined by soft-handed slumber,
>   And ready still past kisses to outnumber
>   At tender eye-dawn of aurorean love. . . .

The recurrent metaphors of sexual passion, sleep, the bower, the fountain stream, and generative light clustering in the introductory stanzas should suggest the meaning of this initial vision; for they figure ideal, unending, imaginative fulfilment. Withdrawn into their bower, so often identified in other poems as the place of poetic inspiration, these lovers have lapsed into that twilight area between sleep and waking where the fancy is most active; close by gushes the fountain of imagination, which is a counterpart perhaps of that internal surge of feeling within the two lovers as they dream in close embrace. Furthermore, their passion and visions in reverie seem to be reborn at each "aurorean" or light-giving awakening.

If Psyche represents the soul of imagination, and her union with Cupid figures supreme poetic fulfilment, we now come to the critical question: what does Cupid represent? Keats cryptically identifies him as "the winged boy I knew." Without understanding his role the meaning of the poem remains blurred.[16] Cupid must be identified as the embodiment of love or passion, without which the imagination as woman cannot exist. The sexual union of Cupid and Psyche figures the perfect, because divine, synthesis of emotion and imagination, of heart and head, of sense and soul, a union whose issue is poetry. In the same letter containing "Ode to Psyche," Keats wrote, "the Heart . . . is the Minds Bible, it is the Minds experience, it is the teat from which the Mind or intelligence sucks its identity." In the ode, Psyche, the imaginative mind, receives her identity from Cupid, the embodiment of passion. Their perfect marriage stands for fulfilment that Keats wished for himself in his poetic life. The myth of Cupid and Psyche, therefore, attempts to explain the psychological and emotional sources of poetry.

We have already met "the winged boy" in the character of Endymion and other mortal poets, who, in inconstant and imperfect seizures of love, search for their beloved goddesses of imagination with less than the ideal fulfilment expressed in "Ode to Psyche." Endymion knows such fulfilment only briefly. In fact, Book II of *Endymion* provides an almost identical description of the poetic consummation which we find in the ode:

> . . . long time they lay
> Fondling and kissing every doubt away;
> Long time ere soft caressing sobs began
> To mellow into words, and then there ran
> Two bubbling springs of talk from their sweet lips.
> 'O known Unknown! from whom my being sips

16. An example of this blurring, as it seems to me, can be found in Schulz, pp. 55–60. The failure to account for the symbolic role of Cupid obscures the very quality of imagination, the very vitalizing power which makes it creative: passion, or feeling. Cupid fertilizes the imagination. He therefore cannot be ignored or discounted; the meaning of the poem depends upon our understanding of his mythic, figurative role.

> Such darling essence, wherefore may I not
> Be ever in these arms? in this sweet spot
> Pillow my chin for ever? ever press
> These toying hands and kiss their smooth excess?
> Why not for ever and for ever feel
> That breath about my eyes?' . . .
>
> (734–745)

Endymion needs Cynthia's "essence" or imaginative inspiration as much as she needs his passion. But unlike Cupid and Psyche, they are in constant fear of separation. Endymion frets,

> . . . Ah, thou wilt steal
> Away from me again, indeed, indeed—
> Thou wilt be gone away, and wilt not heed
> My lonely madness. . . .
>
> (745–748)

After her departure, he foresees his own madness, the result of thwarted passion that is not released by the controlling imagination. In this same scene, the goddess too, feels the pain of his imminent departure. She speaks as the imagination lacking its fulfilment in passion:

> Revive, dear youth, or I shall faint and die;
> Revive, or these soft hours will hurry by
> In tranced dulness. . . .
>
> (766–768)

Their love, unfortunately, promises no perpetual kisses "at tender eye-dawn of aurorean love." For Endymion is not Cupid, the perfect embodiment of passion, but mortal; inevitably the demise of feeling tolls him back to his sole self, a fate unknown to the eternally inspired gods. The ecstasies of union between the imaginative mind and the passionate heart, mythically represented in the sexual embrace of Psyche and Cupid, cannot fade, and the ode commemorates that supreme union. Since Psyche represents the imagination—his "known Unknown" (*Endymion*, II, 739)—that he worships as a goddess, his ode appears almost as an offertory.

Stanzas three and four of the ode deplore not only the loss of mythology, which has fallen on evil days, and the disbelief in animistic nature, but also the modern poet's inability to worship his imagination as the poet-priests worshipped their gods in the days of the "fond believing lyre." Keats therefore resolves to act as the celebrant priest and prophet of Psyche by dedicating his verse to her. The vision he has just described in the first stanza ("O latest-born and loveliest vision far") proves to be a powerful and true experience, one that demands his worship. Indeed, the deified Psyche appears

> Fairer than Phoebe's sapphire-region'd star,
> Or Vesper, amorous glow-worm of the sky. . . .

This comparison suggests that his vision of the imagination is more beautiful, more gracious, and more radiant (that is, "fairer,") than the other two goddesses of imagination in "Olympus' faded hierarchy" into which Psyche now enters. For Phoebe's light remains inconstant and dimmed, and Venus' starlight cannot match the brilliance of Psyche. Here again, Keats identifies the imagination as the source of spontaneous, generative light inspiring the poet with vision. Appropriately then, Keats addresses Psyche, his own creative mind, as "O brightest!"; her "lucent fans, / Fluttering among the faint Olympians," shower light upon Keats so that he can "see, and sing, by my own eyes inspired." Psyche, like the Queen-Moon in "Ode to a Nightingale," symbolizes the dazzling wings of poetry and imagination, capable of transporting to vision the poet graced with inspiration.

Since Psyche proves to be a true and lovely presence in unbelieving days "too late for antique vows, / Too, too late for the fond believing lyre," Keats would like to assume the role of the classical poet-priest taking vows of belief in "this latest born" divinity of Apollo's realm. In days when nature was alive with goddesses like Psyche—

> When holy were the haunted forest boughs,
> Holy the air, the water, and the fire. . . .

the poet and priest were one and the same person; his imaginative visions were regarded as not only real, but at once holy and beautiful. That is to say, in the days of antique vows and "the fond believing lyre," the devotee saw no distinction between religious truth and artistic truth. Indeed, these ancient vows of religious faith were uttered in poetic form;

the frenzied, incanting priestesses and prophets at Delphi, for example, voiced their oracles in hexameters. The poet's divinely inspired imagination was the gift of Apollo and of lesser gods and goddesses in "Olympus' faded hierarchy," as Keats suggests throughout his poetry. His firm belief in "the holiness of the Heart's affections and the truth of Imagination" leads him to worship Psyche, the embodiment of imagination. He therefore will be her

> . . . choir, and make a moan
>   Upon the midnight hours;
> Thy voice, thy lute, thy pipe, thy incense sweet
>   From swinged censer teeming;
> Thy shrine, thy grove, thy oracle, thy heat
>   Of pale-mouth'd prophet dreaming. . . .

As poet-oracle, Keats himself will take the place of the priests of Delos and Delphi and create poetry in the frenzy of inspiration (i.e., "make a moan"). Psyche's voice becomes Keats's voice, just as Cynthia's honeyed whisperings blend with Endymion's mortal speech to produce a burst of spontaneous poetry. That mortal "heat" within the dreaming, incanting, poet-prophet must be interpreted as the frenzied, powerful overflow of poetic feeling.

The vow to solemnize Psyche's reign "upon the midnight hours" reminds us of Endymion's similar intent to consecrate through poetry Cynthia's royal sway:

> No one but thee hath heard me blithely sing
> And mesh my dewy flowers all the night.
> No melody was like a passing spright
> If it went not to solemnize thy reign. . . .
>
> (III, 156–159)

As Keats assumes the role of celebrant to Psyche, he vows to be not only her voice and instrument but also her grove, i.e., her holy ground. We are reminded of Endymion's identification of Cynthia, his counterpart, as his "deep glen." Both glen and grove identify the enclosing bower-like retreat where the poet experiences his inspirations and imaginative frenzies.

In the magnificent last stanza of the ode, Keats resolves just how he will serve as Psyche's "voice," "lute," "shrine," and "oracle." A poem of homage to her would be the highest form of worship to her fame and power. He expresses this intention in the recurrent metaphor of the fane, which, as we have already seen, signifies the sacred structure of poetry: "Yes, I will be thy priest, and build a fane." Once again we are reminded of a similar use of the metaphor of the fane in a letter expressing Keats's own worship of his imagination: "My imagination is a monastery and I am its monk." What is more, as priest-architect, he will construct his fane of poetry

> In some untrodden region of my mind,
> Where branched thoughts, new grown with pleasant pain,
> Instead of pines shall murmur in the wind. . . .

Here, the shaping process of the creative mind is figured by yet another recurrent metaphor, the labyrinth. Creating his fane of poetry will be as original and inventive as an adventurous flight down the passageways of the Daedalian maze. In the "untrodden" labyrinth of his mind, new "branched thoughts" [17] will lead the poet through its perplexing alleys to final form. The labyrinthine searching of imagination seems a "pleasant pain," an epithet that recalls Keats's earlier description of his "tuneless numbers wrung / By sweet enforcement." Keats suggests that the perplexity of the poet, while in the labyrinth of creation, is painful, although his vision of final achievement of form holds the poet in pleasant anticipation. Moreover, the words "pleasant pain" suggest that the imaginative process within the confident poet-Theseus involves a struggle in overcoming the perplexities of choice, and yet at the same time implies the pleasure of an arduous sport; for exertion and delight seem the handmaidens of imagination, as Keats reminds his reader so well in "Ode on Melancholy" and *Endymion*.

17. An investigation of medical texts in Keats's day reveals that the cerebellum was in fact described as a branching tree. See Charles W. Hagelman, Jr., "Keats's Medical Training and the Last Stanza of the 'Ode to Psyche,' " *Keats-Shelley Journal*, XI (1962), 74–75. There are, however, many sources of the tree and plant life as metaphoric of the organicism of creation in the mind. See Abrams, *The Mirror and the Lamp*, pp. 201–225, and also *The Complete Works of William Hazlitt*, ed. P. P. Howe (London, 1930–34), VI, 109; XVI, 209–210.

"Branched thoughts," like dreamwork, describe the spontaneous, associative poetic process; for the poet under the spell of imagination
facilely—indeed quite intuitively—associates image and idea. Under
favorable psychological conditions, his imaginative thoughts branch
smoothly and easily like the organic growth of deciduous trees rather
than like the spiny branchings of the pine tree, which Keats apparently
identifies with the pricking thorns and briars of reality.

This seemingly arbitrary association demands interpretation, and
when fathomed provides a prime example of a wholly private use of
metaphor. We may only understand the figurative significance of the
pine tree as an inhibiting influence on the imagination by knowing its
source in Shakespeare. Once again we turn to *The Tempest* which Keats
read as a play about the poet and his elfin imagination.[18] Prospero represents the poet-conjuror in masterful control of his sprightly fancy, Ariel.
Through his magic, Prospero releases Ariel from painful imprisonment
in a cloven pine, an imprisonment made by the ugly, "earthy . . . foul
witch," Sycorax. Prospero's account of the sprite's past had special significance for Keats, who interpreted the glutinous pine as the prison house
of imagination:

> . . . Thou, my slave,
> As thou report'st thyself, wast then her servant;
> And, for thou wast a spirit too delicate
> To act her earthy and abhorr'd commands,
> Refusing her grand hests, she did confine thee,
> By help of her more potent ministers
> And in her most unmitigable rage,
> Into a cloven pine; within which rift
> Imprison'd thou didst painfully remain
> A dozen years. . . .
>
> . . . .
> . . . It was mine art,
> When I arrived and heard thee, that made gape
> The pine and let thee out. . . .
>
> (I. ii. 270–279, 291–293)

In the light of this source, therefore, the lines

18. See Chapter three above, "The elf."

> Yes, I will be thy priest, and build a fane
>   In some untrodden region of my mind,
> Where branched thoughts, new grown with pleasant pain,
>   Instead of pines shall murmur in the wind. . . .

celebrate Keats's own Ariel-like imagination that cannot be confined to the pine of reality, earth, and frustration.

Alien to the soft, bowery realm of poetry, the pines therefore remain on the peripheries of the domain of imagination, circling, fledging, and defining the bowery fane of poetry:

> Far, far around shall those dark-cluster'd trees
> Fledge the wild-ridged mountains steep by steep. . . .

For Keats intends to weave in silence his own bower of poetry, to order wild nature into form, to clear a space flanked on its outer limits by the dark pines of reality:

> And in the midst of this wide quietness
> A rosy sanctuary will I dress
> With the wreath'd trellis of a working brain. . . .

Keats's intention of dressing and weaving his poetic structure in the tangled forest of his mind repeats his resolution of line 50:

> Yes, I will be thy priest, and build a fane
>   In some untrodden region of my mind. . . .

Keats's "working," shaping "brain," like a "wreath'd trellis," describes the labyrinthine process of the creative imagination. The "rosy sanctuary," or fane, figures the shaped product of imagination, the poem itself, a woven matrix of words in a spanning structure.

In the final lines of the poem, Keats describes these creative acts of his weaving brain in pronouncedly sexual imagery. The fancy, like a skilful "gardener . . . who breeding flowers, will never breed the same," weaves and dresses a rosy, fretted sanctuary of poetry. The fancy and the "working brain" are one and the same; supremely productive and inventive, they never repeat themselves, for in the organic process of creation, no two poems can ever be identical. The teeming fancy can never "breed the same," just as the poet in the labyrinth of imagination cannot follow the same route twice; for the imagination knows only change, variety, and uniqueness. Every new poetic attempt transports the poet to "untrodden regions" in the infinite labyrinth of the creative mind.

We may now see a clear relationship between the sexual imagery dominating Keats's vision of Cupid and Psyche at the beginning of the ode and the similar sexual imagery at its close. If the eternal embrace of Cupid and Psyche figures the perfect union of passion and imagination, the fertility of Keats's own aroused, impassioned fancy breeds the same sort of sensuous, "soft delight" within the poem. His "shadowy [19] thought" parallels the "dim-conceived glories of the brain" ("Elgin Marbles") before and during the arduous, uncertain process of sculpting words into form. Certainly thoughts are vague (another sense of shadowy") even while the imagination conceives and works on them in order to body them forth. Only then do they become the "soft delight" of all the senses, i.e., the concrete language of the image and metaphor. Fixed eternally in perfect poetic form, the winnings of "shadowy thought" seem to Keats the radiant beacon of imaginative truth, an open-casemented, elfin palace of poetry:

> And there shall be for thee all soft delight
>   That shadowy thought can win,
> A bright torch, and a casement ope at night,
>   To let the warm Love in!

More than a monument to her fame, Keats's poem seems to be Psyche's dwelling place, a shrine housing her just as the Parthenon housed at its center the colossal statue of the reigning Athena, a castle of sensory delights with an open window to allow her "warm Love" (i.e., Cupid) to fly in. Working the narrative of the myth brilliantly, Keats may be suggesting that not only Psyche, the imagination, belongs in his palace, but also Cupid, who represents poetic passion; for both passion and imagination play their parts in the creation of poetry. He is suggesting that the palace of poetry itself provides the trysting place for new and repeated acts of imagination, that is, of "shadowy thought" performed in

---

19. Meaning "imitative," "reflective of an image," as well as "phantom" and "insubstantial." See the NED. One is reminded of the shadows representing truth in Plato's cave, a classical symbol for the mind. Keats's "shadowy thought," like Plato's, can mirror eternal truths, and in poetic form, as the context of the poem suggests.

the half darkness of the love chamber by the mythic gods. By using several recurrent metaphors for poetry and inspiration, he has described just how the imaginative process unfolds from the initial dim conception to the finished representation of that vision. He represents the process of imagination within himself by the mythic conjoining of Psyche and Cupid, that is, the perfect union of mind and feeling, fancy and love. That fertile act of imagination within the poet releases the most delightful "shadowy thought[s]"; builds the structure of his fane, or poem, "In some untrodden region of [his] mind"; and organically weaves and decorates within its structure "a rosy sanctuary" and a "wreath'd trellis," intricate with local imagery of buds and bells. Keats's "working brain," like Psyche's and Cupid's love-dream, creates all manners of "soft delight" and visions of truth as beauty and beauty as truth which perfectly realized poetry embodies. The poem celebrates in poetic form the very kinetic process of imagination which created it, and thus reconciles the paradox of stasis within process that "Ode on a Grecian Urn" encompasses in defining art.

The theme of "Ode to Psyche" concerns the power and the visionary capabilities of the poetic imagination.[20] By successfully rendering his vision of the imagination into poetic form, Keats has finally achieved what repeatedly frustrates the inexperienced poet, the inability to objectify the dreams that he sees and feels. In "Ode to Psyche," he would no longer identify himself as an apprentice poet, an Endymion despairing of insufficient craft to embody perfectly his vision:

> . . . Ah, can I tell
> The enchantment that afterwards befel?
> Yet it was but a dream: yet such a dream

20. My claim for the capability of the imagination here and elsewhere in the chapter stands in contrast to Robert D. Wagner, " 'Ode to Psyche' and the Second 'Hyperion,' " *Keats-Shelley Journal,* XIII (1964), 32–34, which interprets the poem to be about "a disillusioned or limited imagination." I cannot agree. The metaphors picture the imagination as possessive of divine properties, and as creative of essential beauty in artistic form, specifically poetry, which is the product of "shadowy thought." Keats is not rejecting the infinite possibilities of the Romantic imagination. Critics of the ode fail to appreciate that the passion being infused into the imagination is perpetual and divine. The supreme union of the god Cupid and the apotheosized Psyche analogizes the perfectly fulfilled, unlimited visionary imagination. Nor is Keats so much interested in developing a neat, codified, philosophic theory of imagination as he is in figuring the astonishing, shadowy process which he experienced unfolding magically within him. He is, in short, the poet ever.

That never tongue, although it overteem
With mellow utterance, like a cavern spring,
Could figure out and to conception bring
All I beheld and felt. . . .

(I, 572–578)

Between the conception and the creation of poetry, the shadow of imperfection has not fallen on Keats. The ode records one of his supremely
confident moments as a poet. Its attempt to account for the poetic process
through recurrent, referential, and almost private metaphorical language
makes it one of the most unusual and significant poems that he ever wrote.
No other poem says so much about the poetic imagination as does "Ode
to Psyche," and certainly none clusters together so many iterative metaphors for poetry and the imaginative process in so small a space, metaphors that provide a basis of structure and meaning to the poem.

Chapter nine

Conclusion

A major aim of this study has been to point out the integrity of Keats's metaphors and images throughout his work, an integrity which, when once perceived, can contribute significantly to our understanding of his complex later poems. The last chapter has attempted to demonstrate the value of a close examination of the recurrent figures. Based on the accumulated evidence of the figurative and imagistic language used by Keats, the readings of "La Belle Dame sans Merci" and "Ode to Psyche" reveal a level of meaning hitherto unexplored. The "Ode to Psyche," especially, has long baffled its readers, including Earl R. Wasserman, one of the most astute of Keats scholars. He has remarked: "My only regret is that I have not learned to read the 'Ode to Psyche,' for I believe it is a major poem and is still to be understood." [1] My purpose has been, in part, to meet the challenge voiced by Wasserman.

An understanding of the metaphors allows us to explore and find meaning in other poems as well. The meaning of "When I have fears that I may cease to be," the sonnet "Written . . . at the end of Chaucer's tale 'The Floure and the Lefe,' " "On Receiving a Laurel Crown from Leigh Hunt," as well as central passages from the longer poems—for example, the Hyperions and the introductions to the four books of *Endymion*—is dependent upon our comprehension of many of the recurrent figures.

1. Wasserman, *The Finer Tone*, p. 9.

By tracing and comparing the metaphors within his entire work, we have arrived at an understanding of Keats's subtlety and method as a poet. Furthermore, significant variations in his figures have provided us with clues to his shifts in aesthetic, critical, or intellectual thinking. For example, in recasting the metaphor of flight, which suggests the spontaneous soaring of the imagination in the early poetry through *Endymion*, as an uphill struggle afoot, Keats is making a broad revision in his concept of the role and task of the poet; for if flight suggests the spontaneous soaring of imagination, the trudge to the lofty poetic eminence of *The Fall of Hyperion* suggests the hardships and pain assumed by the responsible poet. The shift in metaphors provides an understanding of Keats's new tacks in critical and intellectual attitude toward the poet and his poetry, marked, for example, by Moneta's fane.

If we may claim that the metaphors are at the center of Keats's intellectual thought and development, the same may be said for his aesthetics and metaphysics. His use of the bower and of weaving makes graphic his Romantic concept of the organicism of creation. As well, his use of the fane and palace of poetry reveals his aesthetics: structural order, balance, and planned intricacy seem main attributes to his idea of poetic beauty. Through these metaphors, therefore, we find ourselves at the heart of Romantic aesthetics and metaphysics. Lamia's spontaneous weaving of organic life within her more deliberately constructed palace is a profound analogue for the nature of the creative process.

Keats was vitally concerned with the sublime mystery of creation and fascinated with the adventure inherent in each new act of imagination. The sexual encounters of the poet-hero and his entrances into each new labyrinth occasion a sense of risk and awe, as both these metaphors fully imply in the poetry. These figures, along with the related metaphor of enthralment, are, in my estimation, Keats's most interesting and significant in evoking the complexity and the mystery of the imaginative process.

Keats's mind worked in coherent patterns, and his recurrent figurative language is the graphic evidence of that wholeness in thought and expression. Poetry to Keats involved an act of faith in the potentialities of the mind, a theme which he expresses through most of his poetry. When a poet's deepest thoughts and feelings root themselves early in the vivid language of metaphor and image, he has habitual recourse to that ingrained language. The recurrence of these metaphors, always in new contexts and combinations, reveals not only Keats's abiding felt-thoughts about his craft and his imagination, but also the unity of the corpus of his work, letters as well as poems. In short, they are an element of the design and order of his work.

In probing the creative process and Keats's aesthetic and metaphysical thought, this study ranges into the rationale and purposes of Romanticism, a term that defies adequate summary or definition but nonetheless defines itself repeatedly in the language of its poetry. If the common aim of the Romantic poets is to make external the internal soul, then the study of the Romantics' chief tool of expression—analogical language —stands at the heart of our understanding of the movement. The allegory of Keats's deepest life, the inner life of imagination and poetry, expresses itself through figurative language:

A Man's life of any worth is a continual allegory—and very few eyes can see the Mystery of his life—a life like the scriptures, figurative—which such people can no more make out than they can the hebrew Bible. Lord Byron cuts a figure—but he is not figurative—Shakespeare led a life of Allegory; his works are the comments on it.[2]

Keats's continuing allegory (taken in its widest sense to mean "figurative of something") is the life of poetry and the state of excitement that creates it, of which he said: "that is all I care for, all I live for." [3] These passages therefore suggest that the life of supreme worth, the creative life, is the constant parable which he is writing in his poetry.[4] The recurring, analogical language of the poems "are the comments on" that inner life of imagination—thought, feeling, inspiration, vision, the whole verbal process from conception to final, formal embodiment.

This study has attempted to make out that inner life which Keats guarded so well and yet revealed time and again in his poetry. Like Apuleius, "who pull'd the boughs aside, / That we might look into a forest wide," Keats, through metaphor, allows us a deep vision of the

2. *Letters*, II, 67.   3. *Ibid.*, p. 147.
4. Cf. John Bayley, "Keats and Reality," *Proceedings of the British Academy*, XLVIII (1962), 96. This essay denies the role of the imagination as the allegorizer of the inner life, and surprisingly, in fact, rejects as glibness what Keats is saying in all seriousness in this passage. Shakespeare's plays are the allegories of the inner, imaginative life, at least as Keats saw them. But what is more important is the fact that Keats's poems are indeed figurative statements of the visionary imaginative life.

geography of his Romantic imagination. When the metaphors are properly understood, the mirror of Keats's poetry becomes a glass allowing the reader, when his angle of view is correct, to penetrate in and through the surface of the poems to that inner world of imagination. The figures form the weave of the allegorical life referred to by Keats in his letter.

If René Wellek is correct in characterizing Romanticism by three criteria: imagination for the view of poetry; myth and metaphor as its vehicle; and nature for the view of the world,[5] then this study in embracing and indeed amplifying his criteria, thereby provides a continuous commentary on the essential nature and concerns of the Romantic movement. For this study deals with the tenors of imagination and poetry; it investigates the vehicles by which these two themes are expressed; and, to a lesser degree, it examines the concept of animistic nature as revealed in several metaphors for inspiration and in the use of myth in the poetry.

The poetry is therefore profoundly revealing of the character and function of art. This study repeatedly suggests that Keats's own critical attitudes need not be the exclusive property of his prose writing, as critics have believed. Literary students, scholars, and critics wanting to find out the nature of the organic process of creation and of Keats's concept of formal beauty, in short, the poet's real and extended ideas of poetry, can profitably view the poetry as criticism. It is my conviction that through a knowledge of Keats's figurative and imagistic language one can arrive at the fullness of his special meaning.

5. René Wellek, "The Concept of 'Romanticism' in Literary History," *Romanticism: Points of View*, eds. Robert F. Gleckner and Gerald E. Enscoe (Englewood Cliffs, 1962), pp. 201–205.

Bibliography

Abrams, M. H. *English Romantic Poets: Modern Essays in Criticism.* New York, 1960.
———. *The Mirror and the Lamp.* New York, 1960.
Allen, Glen O. "The Fall of Endymion: A Study in Keats's Intellectual Growth," *Keats-Shelley Journal,* VI (1957), 37–57.
Armstrong, Edward A. *Shakespeare's Imagination.* London, 1946.
Bate, Walter Jackson. *John Keats.* Cambridge, Mass., 1963.
———. (ed.). *Keats: A Collection of Critical Essays.* Englewood Cliffs, 1964.
Bateson, F. W. *English Poetry: A Critical Introduction.* London, 1950.
Bayley, John. "Keats and Reality," *Proceedings of the British Academy,* XLVIII (1962), 91–125.
Berger, Harry, Jr. "Spenser's Gardens of Adonis: Force and Form in the Renaissance Imagination," *University of Toronto Quarterly,* XXX (1960), 128–149.
Blake, William. *Poetry and Prose of William Blake,* ed. Geoffrey Keynes. New York, 1956.
Bloom, Harold. *The Visionary Company.* Garden City, 1961.
Bodkin, Maud. *Archetypal Patterns in Poetry.* New York, 1961.
Boswell, James. *Journal of a Tour to the Hebrides,* ed. H. B. Cotterill. London, 1926.
Brooks, Cleanth. "The Poem as Organism: Modern Critical Procedure," *English Institute Annual, 1940.* New York, 1941.
Bush, Douglas. *Mythology and the Romantic Tradition.* New York, 1957.
———. "Notes on Keats's Reading," *PMLA,* L (March 1935), 785–806.
———. *Science and English Poetry.* New York, 1950.
Byron, Lord George Gordon. *The Works of Lord Byron: Letters and Journals,* III, ed. R. E. Prothero. London, 1899.
Caldwell, James Ralson. *John Keats' Fancy.* Ithaca, 1945.
Coleridge, Samuel Taylor. *Biographia Literaria.* Everyman Edition. London, 1910.
———. *Coleridge's Miscellaneous Criticism,* ed. Thomas Raysor. London, 1936.

———. *The Complete Works of Samuel Taylor Coleridge*, IV, ed. William G. T. Shedd. New York, 1854.

———. *Unpublished Letters of Samuel Taylor Coleridge*, II, ed. Earl Leslie Griggs. New Haven, 1933.

Colvin, Sir Sidney. *John Keats: His Life and Poetry, His Friends, Critics and After Fame*. New York, 1917.

Dryden, John. *Selected Works of John Dryden*. New York, 1953.

Dubos, René and Jean. *The White Plague: Tuberculosis, Man and Society*. Boston, 1952.

Eliot, Thomas Stearns. *Selected Prose* (Penguin), ed. John Hayward. Harmondsworth, 1953.

Finney, Claude L. *The Evolution of Keats's Poetry*. 2 vols. Cambridge, Mass., 1936.

Foakes, R. A. *The Romantic Assertion*. New Haven, 1958.

Fogle, Richard Harter. *The Imagery of Keats and Shelley: A Comparative Study*. Chapel Hill, 1949.

Ford, Newell F. "Keats's Romantic Seas: 'Ruthless' or 'Keelless'?" *Keats-Shelley Journal*, I (1952), 11–22.

Freud, Sigmund. *A General Introduction to Psychoanalysis*. New York, 1949.

Gittings, Robert. *The Mask of Keats*. London, 1956.

Gleckner, Robert F. and Enscoe, Gerald E. (eds.). *Romanticism: Points of View*. Englewood Cliffs, 1962.

Graves, Robert. *The White Goddess*. New York, 1960.

Haber, Tom Burns. "The Unifying Influence of Love in Keats's Poetry," *PQ*, XVI (1937), 192–209.

Hagelman, Charles W., Jr. "Keats's Medical Training and the Last Stanza of the 'Ode to Psyche,'" *Keats-Shelley Journal*, XI (1962), 73–82.

Hale-White, Sir William. *Keats as Doctor and Patient*. London, 1938.

Harrison, Robert. "Symbolism of the Cyclical Myth in *Endymion*," *Texas Studies in Language and Literature*, I (1960), 538–554.

Hartley, David. *Observations on Man*. London, 1749.

Hastings, James. *A Dictionary of the Bible*. New York, 1898.

Hazlitt, William. *The Complete Works of William Hazlitt*, V, VI, XVI, ed. P. P. Howe. London, 1930.

Hogue, Caroline. "Dickinson's 'I Heard a Fly Buzz When I Died,'" *The Explicator*, XX, 3 (November 1961), Article 26.

Homer. *The Odyssey*, trans. Samuel Butler. New York, 1944.

Jack, Ian. "'The Realm of Flora' in Keats and Poussin," *Times Literary Supplement*, April 10, 1959, p. 212.

Johnson, Samuel. *The History of Rasselas*, ed. R. W. Chapman. Oxford, 1927.

————. "Lives of the Poets: Cowley," *The Works of Samuel Johnson*, VI. London, 1818.

Jones, Leonidas M. "The 'Ode to Psyche': an Allegorical Introduction to Keats's Great Odes," *Keats-Shelley Memorial Bulletin*, IX (1958), 22–26.

Keats, John. *The Letters of John Keats*, ed. Hyder Rollins. 2 vols. Cambridge, Mass., 1958.

————. *The Poetical Works and Other Writings of John Keats*, III, ed. Harry Buxton Forman. London, 1883.

————. *The Poetical Works of John Keats*, ed. H. W. Garrod. Oxford, 1958.

————. *The Selected Letters of John Keats*, ed. Lionel Trilling. Garden City, 1956.

Knight, G. Wilson. *The Starlit Dome*. London, 1959.

Lemprière, J. *Bibliotheca Classica*. Dublin, 1792.

Lowell, Amy. *John Keats*. 2 vols. Cambridge, Mass., 1925.

Lowes, John Livingston. *The Road to Xanadu: A Study in the Ways of the Imagination*. Cambridge, Mass., 1927.

Muir, Kenneth. *John Keats: A Reassessment*. Liverpool, 1958.

Murry, J. Middleton. *Studies in Keats, New and Old*. London, 1939.

————. *Keats*. Oxford, 1955.

Partridge, Eric. *Shakespeare's Bawdy*. New York, 1960.

Peckham, Morse. "Toward a Theory of Romanticism," *PMLA*, LXVI (March, 1951), 5–23.

Perkins, David. *The Quest for Permanence*. Cambridge, Mass., 1959.

Pettet, E. C. *On the Poetry of Keats*. Cambridge, 1957.

Plato. *The Dialogues of Plato*, ed. Benjamin Jowett. 2 vols. New York, 1937.

Potter, John. *Archaeologia Graeca: Antiquities of Greece*. 2 vols. London, 1775.

Roberts, John H. "Poetry of Sensation or of Thought?" *PMLA*, LXV (December, 1930), 1124–1139.

Rogers, Neville. *Shelley at Work: A Critical Inquiry*. Oxford, 1956.

Rollins, Hyder. *The Keats Circle*. 2 vols. Cambridge, Mass., 1948.

Sandys, George. *Ovid's Metamorphoses Englished*. London, 1626.

Schneider, Elizabeth. *Coleridge, Opium and Kubla Khan*. Chicago, 1953.

Schorer, Mark. *William Blake: The Politics of Vision*. New York, 1959.

Schulz, Max F. "Keats's Timeless Order of Things," *Criticism*, II (1960), 55–60.

Shakespeare, William. *A New Variorum Edition of Shakespeare*, IX, ed. H. H. Furness *et al.* Philadelphia, 1892.

Shelley, Percy Bysshe. *The Complete Works of Percy Bysshe Shelley*, VII, ed. Roger Ingpen and Walter E. Peck. London, 1930.

Slote, Bernice. "La Belle Dame as Naiad," *Journal of English and Germanic Philology*, LX (1961), 22–30.

Spence, Joseph. *Polymetis*. London, 1747.

Sperry, Stuart M. "The Concept of the Imagination in Keats's Narrative Poems." Unpublished Ph.D. dissertation, Harvard, February, 1960.

———. "The Allegory of 'Endymion,'" *Studies in Romanticism*, II (1962), 38–53.

Spurgeon, Caroline. *Keats's Shakespeare*. London, 1928.

Stevens, Wallace. *Opus Posthumous: Poems, Plays, Prose by Wallace Stevens*, ed. Samuel French Morse. New York, 1957.

Thorpe, Clarence D. *The Mind of John Keats*. New York, 1926.

——— et al. *The Major English Romantic Poets*. Carbondale, Ill., 1957.

Valency, Maurice. *In Praise of Love*. New York, 1958.

Virgil. *The Works of P. Virgilius Maro*, ed. Levi Hart and V. R. Osborn. New York, 1952.

Wagner, Robert D. " 'Ode to Psyche' and the Second 'Hyperion,' " *Keats-Shelley Journal*, XIII (1964), 29–41.

Ward, Aileen. *John Keats: the Making of a Poet*. New York, 1963.

Wasserman, Earl R. *The Finer Tone*. Baltimore, 1953.

———. "Keats and Benjamin Bailey on the Imagination," *MLN*, LXVIII (1953), 361–365.

Wellek, René. *A History of Modern Criticism: 1750–1950*, II. New Haven, 1955.

———. "The Concept of 'Romanticism' in Literary History," *Romanticism: Points of View*, ed. Robert F. Gleckner and Gerald E. Enscoe. Englewood Cliffs, 1962, 201–205.

Wordsworth, William. *Letters of William Wordsworth*, ed. Philip Wayne. London, 1954.

———. *The Poetical Works of William Wordsworth*, II, ed. E. de Selincourt. Oxford, 1944.

———. *The Prelude*, ed. Carlos Baker. New York, 1948.

Index

Metaphors, individual (*cont.*)
    swimming, 89–91; poet as fish, 89; stream of song, 89; and moon, 90
    tresses; *see* hair
    underworld, 132–141
    weaving, 160–164; clustered with other metaphors, 171; and enthralment,
        163; and fountains, 164; in "La Belle Dame sans Merci," 197; Lamia's
        artistry, 148–149, 160–161; in "Ode to Psyche," 211, 213; spider,
        162, 164; spontaneous creativity, 161; mentioned, 179, 191
    wildness, 196
    wine, 108–113; and inspiration, 109; linked with other metaphors,
        110–112, 146
    woman, 25–31; as archetypal beauty, 26; as muse, 29–30; and music,
        29–30
Metaphors for the poet: charioteer, 82, 193; elf, 79, 187; epic hero, 133;
        gardener, 165, 211; horseman, 81–83, 196; knight-at-arms, 193–194;
        lover, 25, 29; mariner, 87–88; monk, 142–143, 175; priest, 207, 209;
        prince and king, 193, 200–201; sage and humanist, 155; santon, or
        dervish, 145; sower, 35; spider, 162, 164; swimmer and fish, 89–90;
        troubadour, 193; weaver, 162, 197; *see also* Apollo
Milton, John, 143, 155, 159, 179; "Comus," 80; *Paradise Lost*, 25, 27–28,
        58, 59n, 68, 72n, 123, 180
Mind, in creative process, 24
Morpheus, 59n, 63–64, 124

Narcissus, 139, 168

Odyssey, The, 49, 163n
Organicism, 8–9, 161, 198, 209n, 211, 216
Orpheus, 53, 180
Ovid, 63–64, 179, 200–201

Peckham, Morse, 8n
Perkins, David, 108n
Petrarch, 27
Pettet, E. C., x
Plato, 9, 92, 96n, 122, 212n
Pope, Alexander, 5
Poetry and knowledge, 155, 159–160
Potter, John, 104, 106
Poussin, Nicolas, 82
Primary creation, realm of, 35–36, 72n
Pythia, 104

Religious imagery, 143
Reynolds, John Hamilton, 15–16, 22, 47, 75–76, 100, 117–118, 190
Reynolds, Sir Joshua, 7
Rice, James, 81, 93n
Romanticism, 217–218